T3-BNI-254

Bank Holding Companies and the Public Interest

Bank Holding Companies and the Public Interest

An Economic Analysis

Michael A. Jessee
Federal Home Loan Bank of
San Francisco

Steven A. Seelig
Fordham University

Lexington Books
D.C. Heath and Company
Lexington, Massachusetts
Toronto

Library of Congress Cataloging in Publication Data

Jessee, Michael A.
Bank holding companies and the public interest.

Bibliography: p.
Includes index.
1. Bank holding companies—United States I. Seelig, Steven A., joint author. II. Title
HG2481.J48 332.1'6 76-8744
ISBN 0-669-00689-0

Published simultaneously in Canada.

Printed in the United States of America.

International Standard Book Number: 0-669-00689-0

Library of Congress Catalog Card Number: 76-8744

To Our Parents and Wives

Contents

List of Tables

Preface

The expansion of bank holding companies has been one of the most significant developments in banking during the first half of this decade. As a result, this development has received increasing attention from bankers, regulators, scholars, and the press. This book examines some of the public interest implications of the bank holding company movement.

We have directed the book at those interested in the phenomenal growth of bank holding companies, regulation of that growth, and its impact on the public welfare—including bankers, regulators, and members of the academic community. We believe that the book will also serve well as a supplement to required texts in college courses dealing with the institutional and regulatory aspects of commercial banking and financial institutions, at both the undergraduate and graduate levels.

This book evolved in part from research on the bank holding company movement conducted while the authors were economists in the Banking Studies Department of the Federal Reserve Bank of New York. The review and evaluation of the orders of the Board of Governors of the Federal Reserve System concerning applications by bank holding companies to acquire or form banks and nonbanking firms, which is contained in Chapters 5 and 6, is an extension of earlier work by the authors reported in the June 1974 *Monthly Review* of the Federal Reserve Bank of New York. The analysis of the impact of bank holding company affiliation on bank soundness, which is discussed in Chapters 7 and 8, is based primarily on Dr. Jessee's doctoral research.

The authors wish to acknowledge the contribution and help of several associates in the preparation of this study. A great debt is owed to the Federal Reserve Bank of New York for providing the environment in which to conduct the type of research embodied in this book. We wish to thank several present and former members of the Banking Studies Department whose suggestions and constructive criticism aided the development of earlier drafts of some parts of the text. In particular, Leon Korobow, Richard Nelson, David Holdsworth, and George Juncker. Raymond Wallin and Robert Gibbs, also of that department, provided valuable research assistance for parts of the study. Nannette Ingrao and Stephen Turrise, graduate students at Fordham University, also provided assistance in the preparation of the manuscript. Dr. Jessee also expresses his appreciation to Jack Guttentag, Almarin Phillips, John Mason, and David Hildebrand—members of the faculty of The Wharton School who guided his research on risk taking in bank holding companies. Dr. Seelig wishes to acknowledge a debt of gratitude to Donald Savage and Howard Nicholson, his former professors, who stimulated and encouraged his early interest in bank structure. Of course all errors in the book are those of the authors. Moreover, the views expressed are those of the authors and are not necessarily those of the Federal Reserve System, the Federal Reserve Bank of New York, the Federal Home Loan Bank of San Francisco, or the Federal Home Loan Bank System.

Finally, the authors wish to express their debt of gratitude to the secretarial staff of the Banking Studies Department for their assistance in the typing of the manuscript. In particular, Janet Bisogni and Marie Dynes were largely responsible for the typing of the final manuscript.

Part I
The Bank Holding Company Movement

1 Introduction

The movement to form holding companies within the banking industry in the United States has been rapid in recent years and has had a significant impact on both the financial system and consumers of financial services. The holding company form of organization in banking has been around since the 1800s but did not gain significance until 1970 when federal legislation widened the scope of bank holding company activity. This legislation, the 1970 Amendments to the Bank Holding Company Act of 1956, gave impetus to a conglomerate movement in banking, whereby banks could expand and finance such expansion in ways not permitted before. And, as one would expect, the banking industry quickly took advantage of its new opportunities to expand and diversify to the point that two out of every three dollars of bank deposits are in banks affiliated with holding companies.

The near wholesale entrance of the banking industry into holding company arrangements is a priori an indication that banks expect gains from such involvement. To some extent these gains have apparently been realized, and we shall give them notice. However, the main thrust of this book is to examine the effects of holding company banking from another point of view: that of the public welfare. As former Federal Reserve Board Governors Robertson and Brimmer have aptly pointed out: ". . . it is the public's interest–not Applicant's–that is paramount."[1] Public welfare is an important concept in economic theory and must be analyzed within the context of microeconomic principles. The remaining chapters of this book attempt such an analysis.

The authors examine both the competitive implications of the bank holding company movement and the implications for soundness and stability of the banking system and the efficiency of bank operations. A great deal of research by others has been conducted in these fields, and this book attempts to integrate this rather diffuse information to give a complete picture of the effects of the holding company movement to date. In addition, the authors have investigated the effects of Federal Reserve System supervision and regulation on bank holding companies and the consequences for the public interest, the impact of the industry's expansion on the concentration of economic resources, and the impact of that expansion on bank financial soundness. This new research is reported here as well.

The remainder of Part I is devoted to a brief history of the institutional development and regulation of bank holding companies. Chapter 2 is a discussion of the expansion of bank holding companies since the nineteenth century, with particular emphasis on the period 1950–1970. The chapter addresses the development of legislation and federal regulation as well as the motivations for holding company formations. Chapter 3 addresses the 1970 Amendments to the Bank Holding Company Act of 1956 and the congressional intent and debate leading to the passage of this important legislation. Chapter 4 discusses the institutional growth of bank holding companies since 1970 and the impact of regulatory interpretations of the 1970 legislation on that growth.

Part II, "The Public Interest: An Economic Analysis," is a study of the consequences of past bank holding company growth for the public interest. It presents an in-depth economic analysis of the impact of decisions of the bank regulatory agencies on the bank holding company movement and also the effect this movement has had on the safety of our nation's banking system. Chapters 5 and 6 analyze the benefits to the public resulting from bank holding company expansion in banking markets and entry into nonbanking industries, respectively, during the period 1971–1976. This analysis is based primarily on our analysis of the decisions of the Board of Governors of the Federal Reserve System regarding applications by holding companies to acquire or form banks and nonbanking firms. Chapter 7 is a theoretical investigation into the risk-taking behavior of bank holding companies and the consequences of such behavior for the soundness of affiliated banks. Chapter 8 provides empirical tests of the theories developed in Chapter 7.

Part III, "Public Policy Implications," addresses the significant public policy issues arising from the bank holding company movement. Chapter 9 analyzes the impact of holding company growth on competition in financial markets, the aggregate concentration of economic resources, financial flexibility and soundness in banking, and the regulation of financial institutions in the United States. This chapter integrates previous research in these areas with the authors' own findings. Chapter 10 summarizes the principal conclusions of our study.

2 Early Development of the Bank Holding Company Movement

Commercial banking in the United States has been characterized by a diversity of organizational forms, each evolving out of a desire to meet a new financial need. At present, the holding company form of organization appears to dominate the banking industry. Year-end 1975 data show bank holding companies controlling more than one-half trillion dollars in bank deposits—two thirds of all bank deposits. But, as the history described below indicates, holding companies have grown by fits and starts and have suffered important setbacks. The dominant role that the holding company organizational form currently enjoys in banking is relatively new; however, the ideas and practices behind it were developed as early as the nineteenth century. Thus, we should view the holding company movement today as part of an evolutionary process, with no one form of group banking being a "revolution" in the banking industry.

The Early Years Prior to Federal Regulation

During the first third of the nineteenth century, branch banking flourished. Multioffice banking was more or less a common-law right. At that time, however, banks more closely resembled bank holding companies than branch banks. For example, branches of the First Bank of the United States not only had their own directors and presidents but also functioned autonomously. Several large state banks also had many of the characteristics of holding companies. However, as a result of the Civil War and the National Bank Act, which incorporated many of the principles of the free banking laws of the 1830s, few branch banks remained in operation after the 1860s. Unit banks almost completely dominated the American banking structure as the twentieth century began.

A new form of multiunit banking appeared in the 1880s. With branching prohibited for national banks and severely restricted for banks chartered by many of the states, bankers were faced with a serious problem of servicing customers located in dispersed areas without the use of branch offices. Some turned to chain banking, which consisted of a number of small institutions managed separately and owned by a common group of individuals rather than corporations or trusts. This new form arose mainly in the north central states where investors were interested in selling mortgages in the East. However, this movement had little impact on the overall structure of the nation's banking system.

It was not until a little before 1900 that corporate bank holding companies became popular. As in the past, opponents of this organizational form claimed sanctity for the unit bank concept. Several states passed statutes disallowing ownership of bank stock by corporations. Most states, however, simply prohibited the purchase of shares of a state bank's stock by another state-chartered bank. Federal law was silent: The holding company was not considered a bank per se and was therefore outside the existing regulatory system.

By the 1920s the bank groups exhibited a new form of organization. They evolved from the small, closely held groups into corporate giants holding great financial power. The corporations' stockholders were widely dispersed, their management professional, and they typically included at least one metropolitan bank. Two characteristics set them apart from chain groups: a metropolitan lead bank and a form of centralized management.

The latter part of the 1920s represented the period of greatest growth for holding companies. Federal Reserve data (which combine figures for both corporate holding companies and chain banks) show that groups controlled 2,103 banks at year-end 1929. These banks constituted 8 percent of the nation's total number of banks and operated more than 12 percent of all banking offices. Loans and investments for this group amounted to $11 billion, or 19 percent of the $58 billion held by all U.S. banks. More precise data for this date, which exclude figures for bank chains, are reported by Eccles. There were 28 large holding companies controlling 511 banks with resources of $7.6 billion. Representing only 2 percent of the nation's total commercial banks, they controlled almost 10 percent of total bank assets. Of the 28 holding companies, 15 were located in the Midwest and Pacific states.[1]

This rapid expansion during the pre-Depression decade resulted primarily from two stimulants. First, bankers anticipated more liberal branching laws and wanted to acquire banks that could ultimately become branches. One such indication of government liberalization was the McFadden Act of 1927, which allowed member banks to retain existing branches and to open new intracity branches. Moreover, the Comptroller of the Currency stated in his 1929 *Annual Report* that new legislation should be passed to allow branching by large, adequately capitalized city banks. The second stimulant was the fact that many independent bankers feared the loss of their correspondent banking business to expanding holding companies. Therefore they sought to lock in their correspondent customers by forming their own holding companies with these banks as their affiliates.[2]

In addition to these factors, Gerald Fischer has noted two important causes of holding company growth during this period: the desperate condition of thousands of banks in this country and the speculative bull market in common stocks.[3] The weakness of banks made many of them anxious to join holding companies. The booming stock market enabled holding companies to obtain funds for acquisitions easily or made their shares attractively priced for exchange.

The uncontrolled growth of bank holding companies did not escape criticism of the regulatory authorities of both state and federal governments. In its 1927 *Annual Report* the Federal Reserve Board expressed its concern over the rapidly growing network of bank holding companies. This concern was directed toward the branching aspects of holding companies, as seen by the following statement in the *Report*:

Bank holding companies have been organized in increasing numbers to operate extensively in the field of banking, not simply as investment agencies, but specifically in individual instances to acquire control of corporately independent banking institutions through stock ownership and to exercise this centralized control in effecting bank mergers; in extending identical or virtually single corporate control over companies operating as subsidiaries in special fields of banking; in building up branch systems in states which permit branch banking; and in building up chain systems embracing in individual instances banking institutions operating under national and state charters in several states.[4]

After the stock market crash in 1929, public attention shifted to the nonbanking acquisitions of bank holding companies, particularly the securities business. Banks had acquired interests in insurance companies, real estate companies, investment companies, title companies, restaurants, safe deposit businesses, and many others. In January 1931, a subcommittee of the Senate Banking and Currency Committee began an investigation into stock market loans made by various types of banks prior to the 1929 collapse and concluded that such activities had a significant part in the speculative excesses of the 1920s. A House committee made similar investigations. Four bills designed to restrict holding companies were introduced into Congress in 1930 but with no final action taken on them. This was to be the familiar legislation pattern—except for minor successes—for the next quarter-century.

An interesting note is that during the Depression the survival record of holding companies topped that of independent banks. Federal Reserve data show 200 banks belonging to 39 groups suspended operation during the period 1930–1933, or 20 percent of the holding company population. In comparison, 35 percent of all independent banks failed during the same period. Some historians have stated that affiliation with a holding company lent an image of stability to a bank during this crisis.[5] A number of incidents reflected the public's confidence in the group device. One such event occurred in October 1933, when the governor of Nevada appealed to Transamerica Corporation to assist the state by organizing a new bank to replace its closed ones. The company subsequently purchased a major interest in the First National Bank of Reno.[6]

The Genesis of Federal Regulation

Immediately following the banking crisis of the early 1930s, government attention turned more to restructuring the general banking industry than to regulating the activities of bank holding companies. The Banking Act of 1933 (Glass-Steagall Act) contained only a few sections pertaining to group banking, and these were to have very little impact on the movement. However, the 1933 act did represent an important first attempt by the federal government to regulate bank holding companies. This act required holding companies to subscribe to certain conditions before they could obtain from the Federal Reserve Board a permit to vote in the selection of directors of affiliated banks. The more important conditions may be summarized as follows:

1. Agreement to examination by federal examiners of the holding company subsidiary banks;
2. agreement to complete divorcement of the holding company affiliates from investment business within five years from the date of its application;
3. agreement to hold a certain percentage of marketable assets other than bank stock; and
4. agreement to submit financial reports and to declare dividends only out of actual net earnings.[7]

The act was significant in that it took banks out of the securities business, but it did little to restrict bank holding company investment in other nonbanking ventures. Moreover, it granted a blanket exclusion to companies owning only one bank—a move that the Federal Reserve Board would regret in later years. Two other limitations of the act should also be mentioned. One is that holding companies were not required to register with the Federal Reserve Board if their systems contained only state banks. Thus holding companies could continue to acquire more banks within and beyond state borders without prior approval of the Board. Secondly, the act did not require that consideration be given to the effect on competition of holding companies' expansion.

For the next fifteen or so years after the Depression, growth of bank holding companies was virtually nonexistent;[a] however, public concern continued to rise over group activities of banks. As a matter of record, one or more bills designed in some way to restrict bank holding companies were introduced at every session of Congress between 1933 and 1955. Their substance ranged from the 1938 Roosevelt proposal to eliminate all holding companies through proposals involving a freeze on group activity to proposals for more control of the holding companies. Because virtually all of these bills were constructed in terms of "potential" abuses of holding companies rather than actual evils, sufficient support was never collected for passage. A major question as to the definition of holding company also arose. In particular, what percentage of ownership established control in the holding company arrangement and should it mean owner-

[a]In fact, a marked decline occurred in the ranks of bank holding companies from 1931 to 1936. The Federal Reserve Board reported that 97 bank groups with 978 banks were in operation in 1931 and only 52 groups with 479 banks were in existence in 1936 (39 *FRB* 99). By 1948, the number of holding companies reached a low of twenty.

ship of a single bank or two or more banks? Also, since many nonbanking corporations—both profit and nonprofit—owned banks, there was the question of what types of organizations would be exempt.[8]

Between 1949 and 1955, fifteen bank holding company bills were introduced in Congress. The view that holding company expansion should be regulated and that there should be divestiture of many of the nonbanking interests of group banks was gaining acceptance in Congress. The Federal Reserve Board, too, was concerned over the unfettered growth of bank holding companies.[b] Just prior to 1949, the Board instituted an administrative proceeding against Transamerica Corporation, the largest bank holding company, charging that as a result of its bank acquisitions Transamerica had violated Section 7 of the Clayton Act (restraint of trade). The Board of Governors charged that Transamerica Corporation controlled 41 percent of all commercial bank offices, 50 percent of commercial bank loans, and 39 percent of bank deposits in the states of Arizona, California, Nevada, Oregon, and Washington. While the U.S. Court of Appeals failed to sustain the Board's findings when Transamerica sought judicial review, the court's ruling in 1953 recognized the applicability of antitrust legislation to banking, although in this particular case the court found the Board's evidence was not conclusive. As a result of this ruling, congressional pressure to regulate bank holding companies gathered momentum.

The 1956 Legislation

As in the decade prior to the Depression and government investigation into group banking, bank holding companies expanded rapidly from 1949 to 1956. Anticipation of repressive legislation was the main stimulant. Many small banks eagerly joined groups while the way remained clear, and existing groups expanded for the same reason. Moreover, because of various economic factors to be discussed later, retail banking grew rapidly, thus adding to the expansion of bank holding companies.

---

[b]In 1952 the Board advised the House Committee on Banking and Currency as follows: "... the Board believed that the principal problems in the bank holding company field arise from two circumstances: (1) The unrestricted ability of a bank holding company group to add to the number of its banking units, thus making possible the concentration of a large portion of the commercial banking facilities in a particular area under single control and management; and (2) the combination under single control of both banks and nonbanking enterprises, thus permitting departure from the principle that banking institutions should not engage in business wholly unrelated to banking because of the incompatibility between the business of banking which involves the lending of other people's money and other types of business enterprises" (U.S. Congress, House, Committee on Banking and Currency, *Control and Regulation of Bank Holding Companies: Hearings on H.R. 6504,* 82nd Cong., 2nd sess., 1952, pp. 9–10).

During this period of frequently drafted legislation, the Federal Reserve Board popularized the one-bank definition of bank holding companies—that is, any corporation that controlled *one* or more banks was to be considered a bank holding company. In 1955 and 1956, hearings were held on a House bill containing the two-bank definition and on a Senate bill containing the one-bank definition. The Federal Reserve Board and the Comptroller of the Currency testified in favor of the one-bank definition and claimed that the potential for abuse arising from the combination under single control of both banking and nonbanking interests would just as easily exist in the case of a holding company with only one bank subsidiary as in multibank holding companies.

The final product of all this legislative activity was the Bank Holding Company Act of 1956. This act, however, did not conform to the position of the Federal Reserve Board, but rather defined a bank holding company as a corporation that controls two or more banks.

The Bank Holding Company Act of 1956 was the first piece of legislation aimed solely at the group banking movement. It defined in Section 2(a) a bank holding company as ". . . any company (1) which directly or indirectly owns, controls, or holds with power to vote, 25 per centum or more of the voting shares of each of two or more banks or of a company that is or becomes a bank holding company by virtue of this Act, or (2) which controls in any manner the election of a majority of the directors of each of two or more banks. . . ." It require in Section 5(a) each such company to register with the Federal Reserve Board of Governors and, in Section 3(a), to obtain the Board's approval before acquiring more than 5 percent of the voting shares of any bank. Board permission was also required for the formation of a new holding company, for the acquisition by a company (other than a bank) of all or substantially all of the assets of a bank, and for the merger of any two bank holding companies.[9]

The act empowered the Board to grant or deny applications, while directing the Board to obtain the views of the Comptroller of the Currency or the state supervisory authority, depending on the type of bank under consideration. In making its decision the Board was directed to consider the following factors listed in Section 3(c):

1. Financial and managerial resources;
2. Future prospects of the company and banks concerned;
3. The convenience and needs of the community to be served;
4. Whether the effect of any acquisition or merger or consolidation would be ". . . to expand the size or extent of the bank holding company system involved beyond limits consistent with adequate and sound banking, the public interest, and the preservation of competition in the field of banking."

Section 3(d) prohibited multiunit expansion across state lines. Sections 4(a) and 4(b) required that the registered bank holding companies divest themselves of ownership of any voting shares of any corporation engaged in activities not related to banking per se. A two-year divestiture time limit was set, with some special exemptions allowed. Also "cross-stream" lending by holding company affiliates was prohibited in Section 6(a).

In summary, the major purposes of the 1956 act were:

1. To maintain the separation of banking and commerce;
2. To preserve competition in banking markets;
3. To prevent undue concentration of economic power;
4. To protect the right of states to determine the type of banking structure within their borders.

The passage of the 1956 act resulted in a distinct dichotomy in the bank holding company movement. We shall examine the expansion of the two organizational forms—multiunit bank holding companies and one-bank holding companies—separately.

1956–1970: Split in Holding Company Organizational Structure

Multibank Holding Companies

The 1956 act satisfied neither the expansive desire of multiunit bankers nor the restrictive hopes of opponents of the group banking movement. Some felt the legislation was a victory for group banks. But most bankers were not so optimistic. Some provisions, such as the prohibition of interstate banking, were clearly punitive. Others hindered normal credit and investment operations. Compliance would entail much, heretofore unincurred, expense. And the wide discretionary power vested in the Federal Reserve Board would raise a great deal of dispute and many problems for all parties involved.

Sixty-nine bank holding companies registered with the Board of Governors during the first two years following passage of the act. By May 1958, the figure had declined to forty-four due to mergers and reorganizations. Deposits for this group totaled over $15 billion, or 7 percent of the national total. The Federal Reserve Board interpreted the act rather strictly, apparently in the belief that if any inequities existed, they should be removed by legislative action alone. By 1958, the Board had received two applications for new holding companies but had not acted upon them. Of seventeen applications for approval of bank acquisitions, nine had been approved, two denied, and the rest pending. In no case had state banking authorities or the Comptroller of the Currency recommended that an application be denied.

In the Federal Reserve Board's report to Congress in which it reviewed its first two years' experience under the act and in each of its *Annual Reports* thereafter, the Board made a plea for various revisions of the statute. Their suggestions for changes generally covered the following: to subject a holding company to the provisions of the 1956 act if it owned 25 percent or more of the stock of a single bank; to include not only corporations, business trusts, and the like but also long-term trusts; and to include a variety of types of organization (such as firms operated for religious, charitable, or educational purposes) that had been granted specific exemptions. Except for the inclusion of the ownership of one-bank in the definition of a bank holding company, all these suggestions were included in the 1966 Amendments to the Bank Holding Company Act (80 Stat. 236 [1966]).

In addition to these changes, Section 3(c) was made more specific as regards competitive effects, and Section 6 of the 1956 act was repealed. This latter section had provided restrictions on the sale of loan paper between banking subsidiaries of the same holding company and on loan participations within a holding company. However, at the same time, Section 23A of the Federal Reserve Act was amended so that its restrictions on banking affiliates were applied also to the subsidiaries of bank holding companies. These restrictions state, in effect, that a banking affiliate may extend credit to another affiliate only up to 10 percent of the lending affiliate's capital and surplus (20 percent to all affiliates). (Since the purchase of loan paper without recourse is not considered an extension of credit, no significant restrictions existed after 1966 on loan participations and the sale of loan paper within a holding company.)

After 1956 group banking experienced an irregular pattern of growth (refer to Table 2-1). The data show that except for total deposits and the proportion

Table 2-1
The Growth of Registered Bank Holding Companies, 1956-1970

	1956	*1960*	*1965*	*1968*	*1970*
Number of companies	53	47	53	80	121
Banks	428	426	468	629	895
Branches	783	1,037	1,486	2,262	3,260
Total offices	1,211	1,463	1,954	2,891	4,155
Offices as a percentage of all bank offices	5.7	6.1	6.7	8.9	11.8
Deposits (in billions of dollars)	$14.8	$18.2	$27.5	$57.6	$78.0
Deposits as a percentage of all bank deposits	7.5	7.9	8.3	13.2	16.2

Source: *FRB*, various years as shown.

Note: Only multibank holding companies were required to register prior to 1971; data do not include one-bank companies during period 1956-1970.

of total deposits, holding companies declined in importance for the first four years after passage of the act. The explanation, in part, for this decline is that many small holding companies reorganized, and so forth, to avoid regulation because they did not find abiding by the 1956 act's provisions to be feasible. Also prospective new holding companies held back until the policies of the Federal Reserve Board were clearly defined as to implementation.

During the 1960s holding company growth accelerated. By 1965, group banking had recovered most of the decline experienced during the period immediately following the passage of the legislation. However, the share of total deposits rose only slightly from 7.5 percent in 1956 to 8.3 percent in 1965. The surge of growth came during the five-year period ending in 1970. The number of affiliated banks more than doubled to 895. Even more significantly, group banking's share of total deposits went from 8.3 percent in 1965 to 16.2 percent in 1970.

Many interrelated factors accounted for this accelerated growth during the latter part of the 1960s: a growing national economy with a resultant need for efficient and adequate financing; the weakening of prejudices against multiunit banking from several old opponents; court rulings disputing several of the anti-expansion provisions of the 1956 act; and an easing of a restrictive federal regulatory stance. All of these had a major impact on holding company growth. Perhaps the last factor was the most significant, for until 1968, the Federal Reserve Board had maintained its tight rein on holding company growth. During the first twelve years after the 1956 act's passage, the agency approved 111 acquisition applications and denied 19. It approved the formation of 32 new groups and blocked 9. But the record is deceptive on two counts: (1) many banks that contemplated formation of registered holding companies were deterred by the Federal Reserve System's restrictive enforcement policies; and (2) the lengthy process of hearings, correspondence, and legal maneuvering also dissuaded many banks.

However, by 1968 the Federal Reserve Board's attitude began to change to one of less restriction and more liberal interpretation of the statutes.[c] On February 1, 1968, the Board approved a holding company's application for the establishment of two subsidiaries to issue insurance for its affiliate banks and their customers. Applications for acquisition or formation of firms engaged in leasing passenger cars or other equipment, and to own a mortgage servicing firm to originate, sell, and service real estate mortgage loans, were approved. Moreover, acquisition of new affiliate banks and the formation of new holding companies accelerated (see Table 2-2). Data in Table 2-2 show that in 1968 and 1969 combined, 99 of 104 acquisitions were approved, and 30 new holding

---

[c]Regulation Y was amended in 1968, eliminating several of the barriers to the application process and giving a more lenient definition to the nonbanking interests in which holding companies might invest. (Refer to Regulation Y [12 *CFR* 222], effective March 15, 1968.)

Table 2-2
Decisions of the Federal Reserve System on Applications for Bank Acquisitions and the Formation of New Holding Companies

	Bank Acquisitions: Section 3(a)(3) cases		*New Companies: Section 3(a)(1) cases*	
	Approved	*Denied*	*Approved*	*Denied*
1956	1	–	–	–
1957	7	2	–	–
1958	4	1	1	1
1959	7	–	–	–
1960	13	1	–	–
1961	9	3	2	–
1962	16	3	5	2
1963	5	3	2	1
1964	6	–	3	1
1965	12	2	2	1
1966	15	2	6	2
1967	16	2	10	1
1968	33	2	9	–
1969	66	3	21	1
1970	113	9	31	–
1971	143	15	65	2
1972	278	18	112	11
1973	379	18	146	1
1974	307	14	138	16
1975	137	17	141	15
Totals	1,567	115	695	55

Source: Federal Reserve System Board of Governors, *Annual Report,* Washington, D.C., various years as shown.

companies were formed (representing almost half of the new formations approved during the period 1956–1969).

The One-Bank Holding Company

In 1969 John Bunting, Jr., wrote: "The one-bank holding company movement is one of banking's few authentic revolutions."[10] Many others made similar statements, but a few recognized this new organizational form as an evolution—not a revolution.[11]

There were many causative elements in this evolution, and we should first consider the economic events occurring shortly after World War II. According to Harry Keefe, commercial banking has undergone two distinct periods of evolutionary change. The first period began at the early part of the postwar era with a greater orientation toward retail banking and a resulting increase in branch facilities. Banks aimed their activity at the individual consumer rather than the commercial customer. Installment loans grew rapidly, and banks boosted their share of this market from 24 percent in 1939 to 42 percent by 1968. The second period of change began in 1960 with the introduction of the negotiable certificate of deposit (CD), and this resulted in a reshaping of the liability side of bank balance sheets.[12]

Beginning in the latter part of the 1940s and continuing into the early 1960s, banks steadily lost their share of the savings market. Restricted by unrealistic ceilings on time deposit interest rates (under Regulation Q) and by similar restrictions on mortgage lending, banks were unable to compete with savings and loan associations (S&Ls), which experienced rapid expansion. Table 2-3 shows that during the period 1949-1959, time deposits at commercial banks grew at a 6.2 percent annual rate as contrasted with the 15.9 percent annual growth for S&Ls. Moreover, banks' share of the market declined from 54 percent to 43 percent whereas S&Ls' share rose from 18 percent to 35 percent.

During the 1950s banks regarded time deposits as a necessary but unprofitable evil. But as corporate customers began to draw demand balances to minimum levels and invest in marketable securities and as savers transferred funds to S&Ls, banks began to view this interest-costing source of funds in a different light. In the latter part of the decade, the low ceiling levels on time deposit interest rates were raised, and several banks were successful in attracting significant savings inflows. Gradually, most major banks began actively to seek time money, and by 1965 time deposits accounted for almost 50 percent of the total deposits of all insured banks. Also, in the first half of the 1960s, use of negotiable certificates of deposit grew rapidly. The federal funds market reached a high level of sophistication, and in 1966, domestic commercial banks began to purchase large sums of Eurodollars. Thus, as the last half of the 1960s ap-

Table 2-3
Year-end Savings Deposits at Financial Institutions ($ millions)

	1968	*Market Share*	*1959*	*Market Share*	*1949*	*Market Share*
Commercial banks	$203,154	51.0%	$ 67,473	43.0%	$36,900	54.1%
Savings & loan associations	131,620	33.0%	54,677	34.8%	12,471	18.2%
Mutual savings banks	64,507	16.0%	34,983	22.2%	18,949	27.7%
	$399,281		$157,133		$68,321	

Source: *FRB,* various years as shown.

proached, commercial banks were experiencing a significant inflow of funds into their institutions.

Many bankers still looked upon the inflow of time deposits as an unprofitable source of funds. Not until after the 1966 credit squeeze did they begin to appreciate the fact that this new money was here to stay. This prompted the search for new investment opportunities that would utilize the more costly time money at profitable rates of return. Liquidity was no longer a pressing problem. If a bank needed funds to meet short-term liquidity drains, it simply bought them—CDs, federal funds, Eurodollars, or even capital notes.

As commercial banks began to "buy" money they found that they could do so more effectively and with less cost than any other type of financial institution. As Keefe has pointed out, this inflow of new funds brought about a change in the appearance of the asset structure of banks. With the level of funds more or less assured, banks could be more aggressive in their asset mix and funds allocation.[13] Credit card operations, factoring subsidiaries, mortgage banking firms, and other financially related concerns became affiliated with banks. But, as noted above, registered bank holding companies, as well as independent banks in general, were kept in tight rein by the bank regulatory authorities in regard to financially related and nonfinancially related activities. The prime question for bankers became, more and more, how to invest profitably their increasing, but costly, sources of funds.

With the inflow of time deposits, banks were confronted with sharply rising interest costs. In a 1968 study of 25 major banks across the nation, M.A. Schapiro & Co., Inc., found that interest expense in 1967 was more than five times as great as in 1960. Because of rising interest payments alone, the average break-even point of the banks in the survey tripled in less than eight years.[14] Competition for funds in the deposit and money markets raised advertising and other general expense levels as well. The effect of all this was a reduction in profit margins. The Schapiro study revealed two factors relating to profitability:

1. The percentage of payout on common stock dividends remained fairly constant since 1960.
2. Pretax profits per $1,000 of loans and investments declined from $24.20 to $17 between 1960 and 1967.

Although the increased expense resulting from the inflow of time deposits had the effect of reducing banks' profit margins, bank earnings grew at accelerated rates in the latter part of the 1960s. For the twenty-year period ending in 1967, deposits increased at an annual rate of 5.15 percent while earnings rose at a rate of 6.6 percent annually. During the last part of this period (five years ending in 1968), deposits increased 9.4 percent annually versus a 10.2 percent annual increase in earnings.[15] Thus despite bankers' fears over declining profit margins, the industry was able to increase the rate of its earnings growth over the rate of growth of its funds.

Implicit in this brief sketch of banking's evolutionary history is the fact that organizational forms in banking have arisen not solely as responses to positive stimuli. The restrictive regulatory framework within which commercial banking must operate certainly may be considered a motivating force for change. This was one of the major factors contributing to the rise of one-bank holding companies. Unable to use their sizable inflows of funds in normal corporate expansion, the big banks sought new investment outlets. The one-bank holding company became a new vehicle for obtaining such outlets, for as long as the corporation owned no more than 25 percent of the voting stock of more than one bank, it was free of the regulations and prohibitions of the Bank Holding Company Act of 1956.

Although several small one-bank holding companies came into existence after the passage of the Bank Holding Company Act of 1956, not until 1967 did major banks begin to participate in the establishment of this form of group banking. A giant wave of announcements appeared in the latter half of 1968, when a significant number of the one hundred largest banks formed one-bank holding companies. By the end of 1968 one-bank companies held more than 25 percent of total insured commercial bank deposits.

In the late 1960s, banks using the one-bank holding company device were generally medium- to large-sized institutions. Of the 61 banks known to be originators of these holding companies as of November 30, 1968, 26 had deposits ranging between $100 to $500 million, 12 had deposits exceeding $1 billion, and 2 were over $15 billion in deposit size. These figures do not include one-bank holding companies that were formed by nonbank corporations. As of year-end 1968, there were reported to be more than 710 such companies involving total deposits of $22.4 billion.

Apparently, one of the most important influences leading to the formation of one-bank holding companies was that under existing regulation, banks could not find sufficiently profitable outlets for their investable funds. Twenty years ago a good banker was judged by his liquidity position and the conservative nature of his asset structure. The emphasis was on size. Banks were "depositor dominated" in that large depositors and corporate borrowers had a major voice in bank policy. Little emphasis was placed on growth in earnings per share, and bank stocks, traded mostly over-the-counter, were purchased mostly for dividend yield. But as new sources of bank funds developed in the latter half of the 1960s and stock market activitiy increased generally, a new generation of bank management that had not experienced the Depression became more interested in the bottom line. Bankers, led by the large New York banks, became profit-oriented entrepreneurs who were responsive to investment analysts' opinions. The registered bank holding companies contributed much to the development of this attitude, because a high price-earnings multiple for their stock made their terms of trade more attractive for a potential acquisition. This attitude applied to the one-bank companies as well since their nonbank acquisitions depended upon the attractiveness of their stock exchange offers (in most cases, affiliates were acquired by exchange of stock rather than cash).

The potentially higher aggregate return on the investment of funds was considered, perhaps, the major advantage of the one-bank form of holding company. However, this claim to better profitability was never substantiated satisfactorily. During the height of the one-bank holding company movement, several theoreticians tried to demonstrate, by means of a "portfolio approach," how one-bank groups could become highly profitable conglomerates.[16] (This approach was also applied to multibank holding companies.) The concept was that congeneric bankers should examine all financial and nonfinancial industries and acquire or establish subsidiaries in those areas that yield the highest relative return. Theoretically, those bankers organizing one-bank holding companies would have flexibility in their choice of expansion paths, with the determining factor being the relative rates of return, whereas bankers who manage conventionally organized banks would not have this flexibility. Entry into nonbanking fields was partially justified by the fact that a large bank already has a certain expertise in various financially related areas (e.g., through commercial loan and credit departments).[17]

Despite the rosy picture painted by the vision of higher earnings and unlimited opportunities for expansion, much concern arose over the rapid expansion of one-bank holding companies. In response to this concern, Congress ultimately amended the Bank Holding Company Act of 1956. And by New Year's Day, 1971, there was, in effect, no such thing as a "one-bank holding company" as distinct from any other type of bank holding company form of organization.

3 The 1970 Amendments to the Bank Holding Company Act

The rose-colored vision of higher earnings notwithstanding, a great deal of concern arose over the proliferation of one-bank holding companies. The Federal Reserve Board's failure to obtain inclusion of a provision for regulating one-bank holding companies in the 1966 Amendments to the Bank Holding Company Act simply prompted it to pressure Congress for such an amendment. Perhaps the most vigorous opponent, however, of the one-bank holding company was found in the House of Representatives in the person of the Chairman of the Committee on Banking and Currency, Wright Patman. Congressman Patman introduced legislation to bring one-bank holding companies under the Bank Holding Company Act on February 17, 1969. President Nixon, on March 24, 1969, offered a milder proposal than that introduced by Patman. In addition various other bills were introduced in both Houses of Congress.

The House passed a revised version of the 1970 amendments on November 5, 1969, and the Senate passed a milder version of the bill on September 6, 1970. A House–Senate conference committee filed its report on December 15, 1970, and the compromise bill was cleared by Congress on December 18. On December 31, 1970, culminating a two-year legislative effort, President Nixon signed the 1970 Amendments to the Bank Holding Company Act of 1956 into law (PL 91-607).

The following two sections of this chapter briefly summarize the 1970 amendments and trace their legislative history.

The 1970 Amendments

The 1970 amendments to the Bank Holding Company Act served to: (1) broaden the definition of a bank holding company; (2) establish a new standard for the determination of which nonbank activities would be permissible to a bank holding company; and (3) give the Board of Governors of the Federal Reserve System authority to determine whether a bank holding company with subsidiaries engaged in impermissible activities on or before June 30, 1968, may continue to engage in these activities.

Definition of a Bank Holding Company

As a result of the 1970 amendments, a bank holding company is presently defined as any corporation, partnership, business trust association, or similar organization that has control over any bank. This definition brings one-bank holding companies under the Bank Holding Company Act as well as eliminates the exemption previously enjoyed by partnerships. Control over a bank may be established on the basis of any one of three tests:

1. Controlling, directly or indirectly, 25 percent or more of any class of voting stock of a bank;
2. Controlling, in any manner, the election of a majority of the directors or trustees of a bank;
3. Exercising, directly or indirectly, a controlling influence over the management or policies of a bank. (Section 2(a)(3) of the Bank Holding Company Act states that there is a presumption that ownership of less than 5 percent of the voting stock does not constitute control.)

Nonbank Activities

In addition to bringing one-bank holding companies under the regulatory purview of the Board of Governors, the act for the first time explicitly offered bank holding companies the opportunity to expand into fields related to banking. Under the standard contained in Section 4(c)(8), the Board must determine whether an activity is "... so closely related to banking or managing or controlling banks as to be a proper incident thereto." In determining whether a bank holding company may engage in a particular activity, the Board must not only determine that the activity is closely related to banking, but must also determine that the performance of the activity by the proposed affiliate is expected to produce benefits to the public that outweigh possible adverse effects.

Grandfather Clause

Bank holding companies that came under regulation for the first time as a result of passage of the 1970 amendments were permitted to continue to engage in nonbank activities that would otherwise be prohibited, provided they were engaged in these activities continuously since June 30, 1968. The Board was given the authority to terminate this authority if it determines "... that such action is necessary to prevent undue concentration of resources, decreased or unfair competition, conflicts on interest, or unsound banking practices. . . ." Moreover, the Board was required to make such a determination by year-end 1972 for those newly registered holding companies with banking assets in excess of $60 million. Under the amendments a company is given ten years to divest itself of any activity that the Board has determined to be detrimental to the public interest.

Legislative History

On February 17, 1969, Congressman Wright Patman introduced a bill, H.R. 6778, to amend the Bank Holding Company Act. This bill was referred to the House Committee on Banking and Currency. In addition to the Patman bill, several other bills were introduced at about the same time. Senator Proxmire introduced a bill (S. 1052), on February 18, 1969, which would have created a National Commission on Banking to study the banking industry. Senator Sparkman introduced S. 1211, a bill designed to limit the acquisition of banks by nonbanking firms, on February 29, 1969, and Senator Brooke, on May 11, 1970, introduced a bill (S. 3823) designed primarily to prohibit tie-ins between banking and nonbanking activities. Additional bills were introduced in the House of Representatives by Congressman Bennett (H.R. 946) and Congressman Matsunga (H.R. 271 and H.R. 272).

On March 24, 1969, a Treasury Department-sponsored bill was introduced in the House of Representatives by Congressman Widnall (H.R. 9385) and in the Senate by Senators Sparkman and Bennett (S. 1664). This administration bill was referred to the respective Committee on Banking and Currency in each branch of Congress and, along with the bill introduced previously by Congressman Patman (H.R. 6778), became the primary concern of the committee hearings in both.

Comparison of the Patman and Treasury Department Bills

Both of these bills proposed to subject one-bank holding companies to regulation under the Bank Holding Company Act and to bar or limit the affiliation of banks and industrial firms. One-bank and multibank holding companies would receive equal treatment with respect to entry into nonbanking activities. The key areas of disagreement between these bills related to which agency would exercise regulatory authority, the degree of permitted diversification of nonbanking subsidiaries, and the degree of divestiture by one-bank holding companies of acquisitions previously completed (grandfather clause).

Dispersion of Regulatory Authority. Under the Patman bill (H.R. 6778), the Board of Governors of the Federal Reserve System would continue to have exclusive jurisdiction to approve or deny the acquisition by bank holding companies of banks and nonbanking firms.

The administration bill (H.R. 9385) would have divided regulatory jurisdiction between the Board of Governors, the Comptroller of the Currency, and the Federal Deposit Insurance Corporation. With respect to the formation of a holding company, the administration proposed that a company could, with the Comptroller's approval, become a holding company owning a national bank or, with the FDIC's approval, become a holding company owning an insured bank that was not a member of the Federal Reserve System. The Federal Reserve Board would have jurisdiction to approve the formation of bank holding companies only with respect to state-chartered member banks.

The Treasury Department proposal would have continued the Board's exclusive jurisdiction to approve acquisition of banks by both one-bank and multibank holding companies; however, the authority to approve acquisitions of nonbanking organizations by bank holding companies would have been divided between the Controller, the Board, and the FDIC. Jurisdiction over a proposed acquisition would have been determined by whether the preponderance of a holding company's banking assets were held by national banks, state member banks, or insured banks that were not members of the Federal Reserve System.

Nonbanking Activities. The Patman bill continued the separation of banking and nonbanking activities by not making any substantive changes in Section 4(c)(8) of the Bank Holding Company Act of 1956. Under that clause nonbanking subsidiaries were restricted to activities that the Board had determined to be a "proper incident" to banking or managing a bank, or were financial, fiduciary, or insurance in nature.

The administration bill would have amended Section 4(c)(8) to permit holding companies to acquire shares in companies engaged exclusively in activities that had been determined ". . . (1) to be financial or related to finance in nature or of a fiduciary or insurance nature, and (2) to be in the public interest when offered by a bank holding company or its subsidiaries." The authority over these nonbank acquisitions would be administered by the three bank regulatory agencies under guidelines unanimously agreed upon by the agencies. It should be noted that the separation of commercial and investment banking contained in the Banking Act of 1933 would be maintained.

Grandfather Clauses. The Treasury Department bill permitted one-bank holding companies to retain nonbanking subsidiaries engaged in activities not permitted to bank holding companies, provided these subsidiaries were acquired prior to June 30, 1968. The Treasury Department bill also would permit a firm that became a bank holding company by virtue of the bill to retain its interests in other companies provided it ". . . ceases to be a bank holding company no later than June 30, 1971." Such a firm could only achieve such status by divesting its bank by the date specified. The Patman bill contained no grandfather clause and would have required all one-bank holding companies to divest themselves of nonbanking affiliates engaged in impermissible activities, regardless of when these firms had been acquired.

The House Bill

As mentioned above, H.R. 6778 was introduced on February 17, 1969. Hearings were held by the House Banking and Currency Committee on April 15-18 and April 21-25, 1969, and the bill was reported on favorably by the committee on July 23, 1969.[1] On November 5, 1969, this bill was passed by the House of Representatives, with amendments adopted on the floor. While the ultimate bill considered by both branches of Congress was officially designated H.R. 6778 it should be noted that the various bills bearing this designation bore little resemblance to the bill introduced by Congressman Patman.

The House Committee Bill. A majority of the members of the House Banking and Currency Committee rebelled against Chairman Patman's restrictive bill and substituted a compromise piece of legislation that completely replaced the original H.R. 6778. The version of H.R. 6778 as reported by the committee was similar to the original Patman bill in that it: (1) subjected one-bank holding companies to the Bank Holding Company Act of 1956; (2) maintained the Board of Governors' regulatory authority over bank holding company formations and acquisitions, both bank and nonbank; and (3) did not require notification of the Justice Department for all proposed acquisitions as requested by the administration.

The bill differed from the one originally introduced by Patman with respect to the following issues. First, the Patman bill would have eliminated the exemption enjoyed by partnerships under the Bank Holding Company Act of 1956 while the committee bill retained this exemption. Second, the Patman bill required divestiture of all impermissible activities while the committee bill grandfathered the activities of subsidiaries of bank holding companies that the company legally engaged in on February 17, 1969. Third, the Bank Holding Company Act of 1956 defined a bank holding company as any company that directly or indirectly owns, controls, or holds power to vote 25 percent or more of the voting stock of two or more banks. The Patman bill would have broadened the definition of bank control while the committee bill retained this definition. Fourth, the committee bill amended Section 4(c)(8) of the Bank Holding Company Act to require the Board to grant or deny any nonbank application within ninety days or the application would be automatically approved; this amendment was not contained in the Patman version.

A notable change in the bill reported by the House committee relates to the nonbanking activities permitted bank holding companies. The bill significantly amended Section 4(c)(8) of the Bank Holding Company Act to permit holding companies to acquire shares

> . . . with the approval of the Board in any company performing any activity that the Board has determined . . . is functionally related to banking in such a

way that its performance by an affiliate of a bank holding company can reasonably be expected to produce benefits to the public that outweigh possible adverse effects.

The revision represented a clear liberalization of the language contained in the act. In granting this additional freedom the House committee bill specifically excluded two activities: acting as an insurance agent and "engaging in the underwriting, public sale, or distribution of mutual funds." Moreover, the committee bill would have required the Board to establish regulations, including guidelines, that incorporated the standards specified above. The Board would then follow the regulations in approving any proposed acquisitions. The guidelines were to be developed by the Board after consultation with the Comptroller of the Currency and the FDIC. The proposed amendment also explicitly permitted the Board to differentiate between entry by acquisition of an existing firm and de novo entry.

The House Banking and Currency Committee in its report accompanying the version of H.R. 6778 indicated its reasons for revising the original Patman bill.[2] In particular, the committee indicated that it recognized that many one-bank holding companies were insurance oriented, as were some multibank holding companies, and consequently it included the grandfather clause to allow the retention of these insurance activities.[3] With respect to the Section 4(c)(8) of the amended act, the committee indicated it had opted for its proposal rather than a laundry list of permissible, or impermissible, activities because it

> . . . felt that establishing a rigid standard or attempting to specify in detail what activities are bank-related, is far too inflexible an approach which would tend to put bank holding companies in an economic straitjacket in an economy that is changing very rapidly.[4]

While the bill reported by the committee was voted favorably upon by twenty-nine members, twelve members indicated some dissatisfactions, although only five members voted against reporting the bill out of committee. Among the most vociferous of the critics was Chairman Patman who indicated that the key deficiencies of the bill were the grandfather clause, the need to tighten the definition of what constitutes control of a bank, and the proper test for determining nonbank activities of bank holding companies.[5]

This opposition manifested itself in the amendments that were offered to the committee bill when it reached the floor of the House of Representatives.

Debate in the House of Representatives. On November 4 and 5, 1969, the entire House of Representatives debated the version of H.R. 6778 reported out by the Committee on Banking and Currency. During the course of the debate a number of key amendments to the bill were approved. These amendments involved changing the grandfather clause, tightening the definition of a holding company, and incorporating a laundry list of impermissible activities.[6]

An amendment was offered by Representative Bevill to change the grandfather date to January 1, 1965; this amendment was subsequently revised as a result of an amendment by Congressman Wylie who proposed permitting bank holding companies to retain subsidiaries engaged in impermissible activities provided these subsidiaries were acquired prior to May 9, 1956 (the date the original Bank Holding Company Act was passed). Congressman Bennett subsequently was successful in his attempt to revise this section of the bill to exempt from the divestiture requirements bank holding companies with bank assets of less than $30 million and nonbank assets of less than $10 million, if the holding company engaged in nonbank activities prior to May 9, 1956.

Amendments were passed that also included partnerships in the definition of bank holding companies and that defined control to cover situations where a firm owning less than 25 percent of the voting stock of a bank nevertheless exercises control. Foreign bank holding companies and U.S. firms owning banks in foreign countries were exempted from the act.

Probably the most significant amendments were those offered by Representatives Blackburn and Morehead. The Blackburn amendment, which was hotly debated before being passed by a vote of 50-25, incorporated in the bill a laundry list of prohibited activities. Under the revised bill bank holding companies would be prohibited from having nonbank subsidiaries engaging in:

1. The securities business;
2. Providing insurance as principal or agent, except for credit life and disability insurance;
3. Acting as a travel agency;
4. Accounting and auditing;
5. Data processing services, except (a) those that are incidental to banking such as the preparation of payrolls and (b) to the extent necessary to make economical use of equipment used by the bank or bank holding company;
6. Leasing, except where the lease is full payout and the lessee gets ownership of the property at the end of the lease term.

The Moorehead amendment defined the criteria to be used by the Federal Reserve Board in determining that an acquisition resulted in "benefits to the public" and the "adverse effects" that were to be outweighed. This amendment reflected the sentiments of many members of the Banking and Currency Committee. The amended Section 4(c)(8) that passed the House read as follows:

> . . . will be functionally related to banking and can reasonably be expected to provide benefits to the public, such as greater convenience, increased competition, or gains in efficiency, that outweigh possible adverse effects such as undue concentration of resources, decreased or unfair competition, conflicts of interest, or unsound banking practices.

The bill that passed the House of Representatives by a vote of 352–24 contained these amendments and was sent to the Senate for its consideration.

The Senate Bill

The Committee on Banking and Currency of the Senate held hearings on H.R. 6778 (as passed by the House), as well as the other bills introduced by various senators, between May 12 and 28, 1970. On August 10, 1970, the committee reported an amended version of H.R. 6778 to the Senate.

The Senate Committee Bill.[8] The committee amended H.R. 6778 rather than offer a substitute bill. The key differences between the House bill and the bill reported out of the Senate Committee on Banking and Currency are discussed below.

The Senate committee bill adopted a provision that established a grandfather date of March 24, 1969, for a company to retain subsidiaries engaged in activities deemed impermissible. The bill required divestiture of nonbanking activities acquired or begun after that date, except if the activities resulted from an acquisition ". . . pursuant to a binding written contract entered into on or before March 24, 1969, of another company engaged in such activities at the time of that acquisition."[9] The Senate committee adopted a provision to allow a five-year period for divestitures with an additional five-year extension on approval of the Federal Reserve Board, because of the following concerns: (1) the committee was concerned with the uncertainties holding companies would face relative to their tax structure if required to divest subsidiaries; (2) economic conditions might result in less than ideal market conditions for the sale of a firm; and (3) the committee was aware that a large number of firms would be divesting subsidiaries at the same time, thereby creating a buyer's market that would result in prices below the fair market value for the assets to be divested.

The bill also exempted from the prohibitions on acquisitions of going concerns engaged in nonbanking activities those holding companies intending to divest their bank subsidiaries. In the case of a company making nonbanking divestitures, the Senate committee bill included a provision to permit these organizations to expand their holdings or activities during the divestiture period in order to improve their position in divestiture: "In order to insure that there is no evasion of the general intent of this provision, the committee provided that companies utilizing this authority must comply with such conditions as the Board may by regulation or order prescribe."[10]

As was true of the House bill, the Senate committee bill removed the exemption one-bank holding companies enjoyed under the Bank Holding Company Act of 1956. However, the Senate committee added provisions that would have exempted two types of one-bank holding companies in addition to the exemptions covered by the grandfather provision. First the committee proposed exempting from the prohibitions regarding nonbanking activities all one-bank holding companies whose bank's net worth was $3 million or less on the date of enactment of the proposed legislation. The second type of one-bank holding company exempted from the prohibitions on nonbanking activities would be those conglomerates where the bank subsidiary had a net worth equal to ". . . 25 percent of the combined net worth of the holding company and all of its subsidiaries, or $50 million, whichever is the lesser." The bill also gave the Federal Reserve Board limited authority to modify or terminate this exemption. In addition, exemptions were granted for family-held companies and certain trust companies organized under Missouri state law.[11]

The Senate committee adopted the "functionally related" criteria contained in the House bill and also incorporated the public benefits criteria contained in the House bill. The major difference between the House and Senate committee versions of Section 4(c)(8) was that the Senate committee rejected including a laundry list of impermissible activities.

The last major area of departure between the Senate committee version of H.R. 9778 and the House bill was the inclusion of a provision that prohibited any condition for the granting of credit that required a customer of the bank to use any other service of the bank, the bank holding company, or its subsidiaries.

In the supplementary views to the Senate committee report, Senators Bennett, Tower, Percy, and Packwood objected to the provision prohibiting banks from tying the granting of credit to other banking services.[12] The senators claimed that this provision, if adopted, would disrupt the operations of banks and change the "whole structure of the U.S. banking system." They also noted that as written the prohibition would apply to all banks regardless of whether or not they are federally chartered, federally insured, or federally supervised.

Senators Proxmire and Goodell objected to the exemption granted conglomerate firms because it exempts "the vast majority of one-bank holding companies; it gives these companies an unfair competitive advantage over their competitors; it provides an incentive for nonbanking acquisitions contrary to the purposes of the act; and it presents the Federal Reserve Board with an impossible administrative task."[13]

The Senate Bill. The Senate, on September 16, 1970, by a vote of 77-1, passed H.R. 6778.[14] The bill passed by the Senate was identical to the bill reported by its Committee on Banking and Currency except for three amendments that were passed on the floor of the Senate. These amendments are discussed briefly below.

Senator William Proxmire, who was the only senator to vote against the bill, offered an amendment to change the date contained in the grandfather clause from March 24, 1969, to June 30, 1968. This amendment was adopted by a vote of 42-31.[15] Senator Proxmire also offered an amendment to delete the exemption offered small banks and conglomerate holding companies; this amendment was defeated 34-37.[16] He subsequently tried to amend the bill to apply the June 30, 1968, grandfather date to diversified holding companies and those one-bank holding companies owning a small bank. This amendment also was defeated.[17]

Senator Pastore of Rhode Island was able to win approval for an amendment to extend the exemption provided for Missouri trust companies in the bill to mutual savings banks in Rhode Island.[18] The Senate also accepted by a vote of 62-14 an amendment offered by Senator Bennett to exempt bank services in connection with loans, deposits, discounts, and trust services from the prohibition against the tying of credit to other banking services.[19]

The Conference Report

Inasmuch as the versions of H.R. 6778 passed by the House and Senate were not in agreement with respect to certain issues, a committee of conference made up of members from both houses met and reached a compromise version of the Bank Holding Company Act Amendments of 1970. The *Conference Report*[20] issued by this committee on December 15, 1970, recommended passage of the compromise bill; however, there was disagreement between the Republican and Democratic members as to the interpretation of certain sections. Nevertheless, the House adopted the *Conference Report* on December 16, 1970, by a vote of 366-4, and the Senate cleared the bill by a voice vote on December 18. The following discussion covers the key compromises contained in the *Conference Report.*

Exemptions. The Senate Version of H.R. 6778 would have exempted from the provisions of Section 4 of the Bank Holding Company Act very small one-bank holding companies and conglomerate firms. No similar provision was contained in the House bill. The conference substituted a provision that authorized the Federal Reserve Board to ". . . grant exemptions for one-bank holding companies formed before July 1, 1968, if such action would not substantially be at variance with the purpose of the Act, and it is determined that the exemption is justified in any one of three kinds of situations."[21] These exemptions would be given to: (1) avoid disrupting long-standing business relationships; (2) avoid the forced sale of small, locally owned banks to purchasers not similarly representative of the community interests; and (3) allow retention if the banking activities are so small in relation to the holding company and to the banking market as to minimize the influence of the holding company's other interests on the bank's credit-granting power.

Grandfather Clause. The bill passed by the House of Representatives required divestiture of nonbanking activities engaged in subsequent to the passage of the 1956 act. The Senate version authorized retention and continuation of activities begun prior to June 30, 1968. The conference version accepted the Senate's date, but brought under the potential coverage of the act all bank holding companies regardless of size or date of creation. However, both to protect the "traditional small town holding company" and to guard against detrimental effects resulting from the clause, the conference version requires the Board to determine whether a holding company may retain activities begun prior to that date by using the same public benefits test it applies to nonbanking activities acquired after June 30, 1968. In addition, the Board was required to make a determination as to the grandfather benefits within two years for banks with assets in excess of $60 million. The Board also was charged with maintaining continuing surveillance over the exemptions given to some bank holding companies to conduct activities that were grandfathered and not otherwise permissible under the act.

Tie-In Provision. The House bill as originally introduced by Representative Patman contained an anti-tie-in provision. However, the bill ultimately passed by the House did not contain such a provision. The conference bill adopted the Senate provision that prohibited a bank from providing any credit or service for a customer on the condition that he obtain from the bank, bank holding company, or any of its subsidiaries some additional credit, property, or service. Exempted from this provision are transactions involving certain traditional banking services. The Senate conferees indicated that even with the exemptions in the anti-tie-in provision, nothing in the provision exempted banks or bank holding companies from the anti-tie-in provisions of the antitrust laws.

Nonbanking Activities. The language of Section 4(c)(8) represents the most significant compromise reached by the conference committee. As discussed previously, the House bill took a restrictive approach in defining those activities permissible to bank holding companies. The House adopted language that required the activities of the nonbank subsidiaries of bank holding companies to be "functionally related to banking," with the public benefits outweighing adverse effects. The House also tacked on a laundry list of activities that were to be prohibited. The Senate bill was less restrictive in that it accepted the "functionally related" language and the public benefits test, but it did not include a list of prohibited activities.

The conference bill adopted language similar to that contained in the Bank Holding Company Act of 1956 to define permissible activities, but added the public benefits test contained in the earlier versions of the bill. In particular, the language agreed to by the conferees for amending Section 4(c)(8) reads:

(8) shares of any company the activities of which the Board after due notice and opportunity for hearing has determined to be so closely related to banking or managing or controlling banks as to be a proper incident thereto. In determining whether a particular activity is a proper incident to banking or managing or controlling banks, the Board shall consider whether its performance by an affiliate of a holding company can reasonably be expected to produce benefits to the public, . . . that outweigh possible adverse effects, . . .[22]

The compromise language contained in the legislation lies somewhere between the divergent views of the House and Senate bills. However, the legislative history fails to identify clearly the "intent of Congress." For example, the majority of the House conferees (who prepared and signed the *Conference Report*) argued that the new section retained the 1956 standard for determining those nonbank-related activities a holding company may engage in.

According to the *Report,*

. . . the Congress intends that those activities which the Board and other witnesses claim would have been permitted under the "functionally related test," are not authorized by our decision to retain the "so closely related" test, which is considerably less expansive than the rejected "functionally related test."[23]

Senator Sparkman, who headed the Senate conference, took a different position when he reported on the floor of the Senate that the language of the conference bill ". . . conforms in all major respects to the objectives and even the language of the Senate-passed bill."[24]

Inasmuch as the views expressed by the conferees and various other senators and representatives differed greatly regarding the congressional intent of the "closely related" clause, the decision as to what is closely related to banking has for all practical purposes been decided by the Board of Governors of the Federal Reserve System. In the following chapters the Board's rulings are examined closely. However, it is doubtful that a final determination of congressional intent will be made until a Board ruling on the permissibility of an activity is challenged in court.

Public Benefits Test

While the two branches of Congress may have disagreed on the criteria for determining the permissibility of an activity, they were in complete agreement on the requirement that bank holding company entry into nonbank activities must result in public benefits.

The role of the public benefits test in protecting the public from possible adverse competitive effects was made very clear in the Senate committee report, which quoted the testimony of the assistant attorney general (Antitrust Division) who concluded that:

. . . the "public interest" standard makes absolutely clear that expansion into a particular nonbanking activity should be authorized only where affirmative advantages to the public can reasonably be established.

We regard the public interest standard as being particularly important. As the Supreme Court has said, the public interest is not a concept without ascertainable criteria and the public interest standard makes allowance for competitive needs as the Supreme Court has recognized on a number of occasions.[25]

In addition, both the Senate committee report and the *Conference Report* made it very explicit that a bank holding company making an application under Section 4(c)(8) of the act must bear the burden of proof in showing that its carrying on a particular nonbank activity would produce benefits to the public that outweigh any adverse effects.

Congress in passing the 1970 Amendments to the Bank Holding Company Act clearly felt that the combination of banking and nonbanking business had a clear potential for adverse consequences to the public interest. These potential adverse consequences, which are listed in Section 4(c)(8) of the act, were discussed in some detail in the *Conference Report.*[26] In particular, the dangers of undue concentration of resources, decreased or unfair competition, conflicts of interest, and unsound banking practices are included.

According to the majority of House conferees ". . . the danger of undue concentration of economic resources and power is one of the factors which led to the enactment of this legislation. . . ." The *Conference Report* goes on to indicate that the probability of undue concentration of resources and power occurring is ". . . enhanced when concentrations of power are centered about money, credit and other financial areas. . . ."[27]

In situations where a holding company is already engaged in providing the products or services in a market, the elimination of an independent competitive alternative should weigh heavily against approval according to the conferees. However, the conferees considered the "adverse competitive effects which may result from a bank holding company's acquisition of a going concern with which it may not presently compete" to be equally important.[28] The *Conference Report* made special mention of the inclusion of "unfair competition" as a factor in the public benefits test. The conferees stated that unfair competition

. . . is an important factor for the Board to consider in its broadest context, especially in light of the testimony concerning the potential for unfair competition to be carried on by bank holding companies against small independent businesses.[29]

The *Conference Report* continued with an enumeration of the kinds of potential practices that might arise. These include the potential for: (1) intimidation of customers that causes them to refrain from purchasing a competitor's products; (2) commercial espionage to gain confidential information that could be used to compete unfairly with a nonbank competitor (this is applicable to banks that deal with confidential information gained from customers); (3) induced breach of contract; (4) hiring away competitor's employees; (5) price discrimination; (6) selling a service below cost or offering a service at no charge in order to obtain business for another subsidiary; and (7) intimidating customers and/or competitors.[30]

4 The Bank Holding Company Movement Since 1970

The major accomplishment of the 1970 federal legislation was to bring the formerly "untouchable" one-bank holding companies into the sphere of the Federal Reserve System's control. By April 1, 1970, one-bank holding companies had grown in number to more than 1,100, or almost ten times the number of multibank units. On January 29, 1971, there were 1,195 one-bank groups, all of which had to register with the Federal Reserve Board by June 29, 1971, to comply with the Bank Holding Company Act.[a]

Moreover, early indications were that the formerly one-bank groups would take advantage of their new registered status by acquiring or establishing new banks as affiliates within their states. For example, immediately after passage of the new legislation, three major New York City one-bank firms—First National City, Chase Manhattan, and Chemical New York—announced intended acquisitions with several banks within their state. In the four-year period immediately following the 1970 amendments, the percentage of all bank holding companies consisting of one-bank firms declined from 89 percent to 83 percent. The number of multibank holding companies increased from 161 at the end of 1970 to 272 at the end of 1974—an increase of almost 69 percent. Even more striking is the change in the control of deposits between one-bank and multibank firms during this period. At year-end 1970 subsidiary banks of all types of holding companies held 52 percent of all U.S. bank deposits, with multibank firms controlling 18 percent and one-bank groups holding 34 percent. By the end of 1974, however, the percentage of total U.S. bank deposits controlled by holding companies had reached more than 68 percent, with 39 percent accounted for by multibank groups and a little less than 30 percent held by the single-bank organizations.[1]

Contrary to the wishes of many legislators (Congressman Patman, in particular) and special interest groups, there was no "laundry list" of nonbanking activities prohibited to bank holding company investment. As noted in the previous chapter, the Board of Governors was given wide discretionary powers in determining which nonbanking activities are ". . . so closely related to banking or managing or controlling banks as to be a proper incident thereto" (Section 4[c] [8]). On January 25, 1971, the Board published a proposed list of ten

[a]However, under special conditions allowed by the Board with respect to Section 4(c)(12), a holding company that filed an irrevocable declaration that it will cease to be a bank holding company by January 1, 1981, would normally be allowed to expand without regard to the limitations imposed by Section 4(c)(8).

activities "closely related to banking." A period of thirty days was granted to interested parties to comment on the various activities, and, where deemed worthwhile, hearings were conducted on the controversial ones. Approved activities are listed as amendments to Regulation Y (the Federal Reserve System's regulation on bank holding companies).[2] As of year-end 1976 all of the original ten proposed activities with some modifications have been incorporated in Regulation Y, and five new activities have been added. Also, thirteen activities have been declared impermissible by the Board, and there are four activities on which the Board has not ruled definitely on permissibility. These three categories of nonbank activities are listed on Table 4-1.

Implementation of the 1970 Legislation

The legislation, which seemed initially to be a harsh rein on the bank holding company movement, became a boon and appeared to lead to an expectation by federal bank regulators that there were significant benefits to be gained by the public from the holding company format. A headline in *The Wall Street Journal,* January 1972, exemplifies the early regulatory stance: "Banking Backfire–Holding Firm Law Designed to Limit Banks Instead Opens New Finance Service Vistas."[3] The article noted that while prior to the Federal Reserve Board's implementation of the legislation, there was a presumption that the statute would serve as a barrier between commercial banking and other types of business, in fact the law was having the opposite impact in terms of opening new profitable outlets for bank investments.

The Federal Reserve Board began administering the law in what might be considered a very positive fashion. It acted speedily on individual applications: A bank group could establish a new subsidiary permitted under Section 4(c) of the act, unless the Board issued a denial, within forty-five days after receiving notice. The Board appeared to believe that bank expansion into nonbanking lines of business would well serve the public and promote greater efficiency in the supply of financial services. Former Board member William W. Sherrill, for example, predicted that the nonbanking services of group banks will become "much more profitable" than bank lending.[4]

In mid-1974, the Board of Governors' "positive" attitude appeared to wane somewhat, and it implemented a "go-slow" policy toward bank holding company external expansion. (Reasons for this apparent change of policy orientation are discussed below.) However, during the 1970-1974 period, expansion of these firms was phenomenal, both along bank lines and in nonbank activities.

Holding Company Growth

As noted in Table 4-2, the Federal Reserve System processed 4,512 applications of all types under the amended Bank Holding Company Act during the period

Table 4-1
Activities Ruled on by the Board of Governors under Section 4(c)(8) of the Bank Holding Company Act, as of December 31, 1976

Permitted by regulation

1. Extensions of credit
   a. Mortgage banking
   b. Finance companies: consumer, sales, and commercial
   c. Credit cards
   d. Factoring
2. Industrial bank, Morris Plan bank, industrial loan company
3. Servicing loans and other extensions of credit
4. Trust company
5. Investment or financial advising
6. Full-payout leasing of personal and real property
7. Investments in community welfare projects
8. Providing bookkeeping or data processing services
9. Acting as insurance agent or broker—primarily in connection with credit extensions
10. Underwriting credit life, accident, and health insurance
11. Providing courier services
12. Management consulting for unaffiliated banks

Permitted by order

1. Issuance and sale of travelers checks
2. Buying and selling gold and silver bullion and silver coin
3. Land escrow services

Activities denied by the Board

1. Insurance premium funding (combined sales of mutual funds and insurance)
2. Underwriting life insurance not related to credit extension
3. Real estate brokerage
4. Land development
5. Real estate syndication
6. General management consulting
7. Property management
8. Nonfull-payout leasing
9. Trading in commodities
10. Issuance and sale of short-term debt obligations ("thrift notes")
11. Underwriting mortgage guaranty insurance[a]
12. Operating a savings and loan association[a]
13. Operating a travel agency

Activities under consideration

1. Underwriting and dealing in obligations of the United States and certain municipal securities
2. Underwriting the deductible part of bankers blanket bond insurance (withdrawn, apparently because of unfavorable IRS tax ruling)
3. Issuing money orders and variable denominated payment instruments
4. Management consulting to nonaffiliated, depository type, financial institutions

[a]Board orders found these activities closely related to banking but denied proposed acquisitions as part of its "go-slow" policy.

1971-1975 and approved about 93 percent of these. Furthermore, there was an approximately fifteenfold increase in the number of registered bank holding companies over the period, with the total rising from 121 (excluding one-bank companies) in 1970 to 1,821 by the end of 1975 (see Table 4-3). If one-bank holding companies are included in the 1970 data, the five-year percentage change was 29 percent.

The commercial banking activities of holding companies have shown a similar record of expansion. Table 4-3 indicates that banks affiliated with registered bank holding companies increased in number from 895 (2,241 if banks of all holding companies are included) in 1970 to 3,674 by year-end 1975. The percentage of total U.S. deposits controlled by these banks rose from 16 percent (52 percent if all banks are included) to 67.1 percent during the same period. Thus, in this short span of five years the deposit market share of bank holding company banks increased by 15 percentage points. Additional evidence of the

Table 4-2
Holding Company Applications Processed by the Federal Reserve System, 1971-1975

Applications by Type	*Number Approved*	*Number Denied*	*Total*	*Percentage Approved*
Bank and Holding Company (Section 3)				
Board decided	1250	131	1381	90.5
3(a)(1)	298	45	343	86.9
3(a)(3)	927	82	1009	91.9
3(a)(5)	25	4	29	86.2
Delegated cases	583	–	583	100.0
Total Section 3	1833	131	1964	
Nonbank (Section 4(c)(8))[a]				
Board decided	748	187	935	80.0
Mortgage banking	92	10	102	90.2
Finance	432	160	592	73.0
Factoring	9	0	9	100.0
Insurance agencies	105	6	111	94.6
Insurance underwriting	39	0	39	100.0
Trust activities	10	0	10	100.0
Leasing	17	2	19	89.5
Community development	0	1	1	0.0
Financial advice	17	3	20	85.0
Data processing	17	1	18	94.4
Others	10	4	14	71.4
Delegated cases	1371	0	1371	100.0
Total Section 4(c)(8)[a]	2119	187	2306	
Foreign (Section 4(c)(9))				
Board decided	2	2	4	50.0

Table 4–2 *cont.*

Applications by Type	*Number Approved*	*Number Denied*	*Total*	*Percentage Approved*
Cessation of BHC Status (Section 4(c)(12))				
Board decided	2	0	2	100.0
Delegated cases	221	0	221	100.0
Hardship Exemption (Section 4(d))				
Board decided	11	4	15	73.3
Total	4188	324	4512	92.8

Source: Data used in the compilation of the above summary was obtained in the weekly Federal Reserve System Release H.2, "Applications and Reports Received or Acted on and All Other Actions of the Board," Washington, D.C., various issues for the years shown.
[a]The data for section 4(c)(8) decisions, particularly those related to finance company acquisitions, do not give an accurate representation of holding company expansion, and the approval rate is therefore downward biased. Oftentimes, the offices of an acquired finance company are separate corporate entities, and each must be treated by the Board as a separate case, which thus results in multiple approvals and denials. (For example, in the BankAmerica–GAC application decision, September 5, 1973, 107 offices were approved and 133 were denied.) If these inflated figures are excluded, the approval rate for finance company decisions as well as for all Section 4(c)(8) applications is greater than 90 percent for the period.

popularity of the holding company form of organization as a means of bank expansion is found in the rise in bank holding company acquisitions relative to bank mergers in recent years. Table 4–4 shows that in 1960 slightly more than 12 percent of all bank consolidations were accounted for by bank holding companies. This proportion rose to almost 51 percent in 1970 and 74 percent by year-end 1973 (the latest date for readily available data).

Expansion into nonbanking activities by bank holding companies has been equally as rapid during the period 1970–1975. Table 4–2 indicates the extent of such expansion into the primary permissible categories of nonbank industries by the end of the period. Clearly, mortgage banking, consumer and commercial finance companies, and insurance activities have been the most attractive fields for bank holding company entry. Table 4–5 gives a breakdown of such entry for each year of the period. These data indicate that holding companies aggressively pursued diversification into nonbank activities with increasing intensity as the Federal Reserve Board's implementation policies became more firmly defined. The decline in the number of acquisitions between 1973 and 1974 reflects the genesis of the Board's "go-slow" policy, which is discussed below. Finally, data from the Board of Governors show that the number of bank holding companies owning nonbank subsidiaries increased from 531 to 721 between 1970 and 1973 (the latest date for precise data). During these three years the number of non-

Table 4-3
The Growth of Registered Bank Holding Companies, 1970–1975

	1970	*1971*	*1972*	*1973*	*1974*	*1975*
Number of companies	121	1,567	1,607	1,677	1,752	1,821
Banks	895	2,420	2,720	3,097	3,462	3,674
Branches	3,260	10,832	13,441	15,374	17,131	18,382
Total offices	4,155	13,252	16,161	18,471	20,593	22,056
Offices as a percentage of all bank offices	11.8	36.1	42.1	45.7	48.2	49.4
Deposits (In billions of dollars)	$78.0	$297.0	$379.4	$446.6	$509.7	$527.5
Deposits as a percentage of all bank deposits	16.2	55.1	61.5	65.4	68.1	67.1

Source: *FRB,* various years as shown.
Note: Only multibank holding companies were required to register prior to 1971; data do not include one-bank companies in 1970.

bank subsidiaries rose from 3,632 to 4,812, and today there are estimated to be more than 6,000 such subsidiaries. Nonbank assets experienced a decline from $46.4 billion in 1970 to $45.6 billion in 1973, but recent data indicate a sizable increase since 1973.[b]

Board of Governors' Policies

As mentioned earlier, the Federal Reserve Board initially appeared to be rather permissive in ruling on holding company expansion under the amended Bank Holding Company Act. The record of bank holding company expansion between 1970 and 1974 seems to verify this attitude. The Board's policies, evidenced in its orders and statements in the *Federal Reserve Bulletin* and the *Federal Register,* focused primarily in these early years on the effect of holding company expansion on competition, convenience and needs of the public, improved efficiency, and concentration of resources. The first three are generally identified as "public benefits," and the majority of the Board's policies regarding holding company expansion dealt with fulfillment by bank holding companies of the public benefits requirements of the act. The public benefits requirements and the Board's implementation of these requirements are discussed in detail in Chapters 5 and 6.

[b]This decline actually is due to a technical adjustment of the data for 1973 that eliminates several holding companies with large nonbank assets that have obtained Section 4(d) exemptions or have filed Section 4(c)(12) declarations to cease to be bank holding companies by 1981. The assets for such firms are included in the 1970 nonbank asset data.

Table 4-4
Number of Mergers and Acquisitions Approved by Banking Authorities, by Year, 1960-1973

	Number of Bank Acquisition and Merger Approvals		
Year	*Bank Holding Companies*	*Banks*	*Percent of All Mergers and Acquisitions Accounted for by Bank Holding Companies*
1960	11	78	12.3
1961	7	95	6.9
1962	33	181	15.4
1963	8	133	5.7
1964	6	135	4.3
1965	8	150	5.1
1966	29	124	19.0
1967	25	130	16.1
1968	33	127	20.6
1969	102	145	41.3
1970	146	143	50.5
1971	154	104	59.7
1972	229	115	66.6
1973	341	120	74.0

Source: *FRB,* various years as shown.

During the period 1971 to mid-1974, financial factors ordinarily were not emphasized in Board orders evaluating the merits of proposed holding company expansion. This is not to say that the Board was not concerned with the financial condition of banks and their holding companies. Indeed, in several cases the Board either approved or denied the applications on financial grounds.[5] But this period was one of essentially strong economic activity, and banks were generally in sound condition.

From approximately mid-year 1974, banks and their holding companies began to experience financial difficulties. The increasing severity of the economic downturn in 1974 coincided with the financial failure of several large banks in the United States and abroad (i.e., Franklin National Bank, Security National Bank, and Herstatt Bank). The adverse impact of the recession on many banks was evidenced by the deteriorating asset quality, especially in real estate-related investments. Moreover, the rapid expansion experienced by most banks in the United States over the preceding few years was taking its toll in declining capital ratios, excessively risky lending policies, decreasing liquidity, and increased use of volatile, short-term debt.

The Federal Reserve Board became concerned at this time that the accelerating diversification of bank holding companies into nonbanking areas would increase the risk exposure of affiliated banks, particularly in two re-

Table 4-5
Acquisitions of Nonbank Firms by Bank Holding Companies, by Activity and Year, 1971-1975

	Number of Approved Acquisitions					*Total*
Activity	*1971*	*1972*	*1973*	*1974*	*1975*	*1971-75*
Mortgage banking	2	11	34	33	12	92
Finance companies[a]	2	26	231	160	21	440
Factoring	–	4	3	2	–	9
Insurance agencies	–	13	25	34	33	105
Insurance underwriting	–	–	13	13	13	39
Trust activities	1	1	4	1	3	10
Leasing	1	1	8	4	3	17
Community development	–	–	–	–	–	0
Financial advice	–	–	5	11	1	17
Data processing	–	1	6	6	4	17
Others	–	2	3	–	5	10
Total	6	59	332	264	95	756
Number of de novo entries into all activities[b]	77	251	495	542	285	1,650

Source: Federal Reserve System Board of Governors, *Annual Report,* Washington, D.C., various years as shown.

[a]The large numbers for finance companies are, in part, due to the fact that some of the acquired companies' individual offices were separate corporate entities. In these cases, each corporation was reviewed by the Board as a separate acquisition application.

[b]These figures do not necessarily reflect the initial entry of a holding company into a nonbank activity through formation of a new company. A substantial proportion of those entries simply involve setting up an additional office (e.g., consumer finance or mortgage banking) by an existing company. The data include a small number of small acquisitions.

spects: First, resources of the holding company, if used to finance nonbank growth, would not be available to support a financially troubled subsidiary bank; and second, investments in enterprises that are of an overly risky nature and/or whose business is cyclically sensitive might weaken the resources of the holding company through losses. Therefore, the Board instituted a "go-slow" policy toward holding company expansion in mid-1974.

Manifestations of the Board's "go-slow" intentions first appeared in June 1974. Applications by BankAmerica Corporation and Citicorp to engage in foreign joint ventures were denied on June 19, and on June 27 a similar application by First Chicago Corporation was denied.[6] The following statement in the denial order regarding BankAmerica Corporation indicates the Board's general concern for increasing expansion and diversification by bank holding companies at a time when their subsidiary banks were experiencing deteriorating financial positions:

The Board also noted its general concern with the tendency of many U.S. banking organizations to pursue a policy of rapid expansion in domestic and foreign markets. Such expansion can expose the organization to potential liabilities and risk disproportionate to the stated size of their investment in any particular venture. Such expansion should therefore be premised on a strong capital base. While the Board recognizes the quality and experience of the Applicant's management, the present capital position of the Applicant is somewhat lower than what the Board would consider appropriate in light of its recent growth. In such circumstances, the Board would prefer to see funds first used to enlarge the capital position of such organizations.[7]

Later in 1974, two proposed new nonbanking activities were denied under the "go-slow" policy. These new activities were underwriting mortgage guaranty insurance and operating savings and loan associations.[8] In the order denying the latter proposed activity, the Board explicitly expressed its desire to slow holding company expansion, as noted by the following language:

The Board has previously expressed the view that at this time bank holding companies generally should slow their rate of expansion into new activities and should direct their energies toward strengthening existing operations, particularly where such expansion may be into new activities in which bank holding companies have not previously engaged. That view is especially applicable to bank holding companies applying to acquire companies which are highly leveraged and which would require continuing infusions of capital. The Board has frequently reiterated its view that the primary role of a bank holding company should be to serve as a source of financial strength and support for its subsidiaries. The financial and managerial resources of a bank holding company should not be unduly diverted from that role. Applicant has in the past two years consummated four significant nonbanking acquisitions. The acquisition of Southwest, even absent any commitment by Applicant to inject capital into Southwest, would further divert its resources away from Bank's possible future needs and would require a significant increase in Applicant's debt. Such diversion and increase in debt constitute significant adverse effects of the proposed affiliation which are not outweighed, at this time and under these circumstances, in the Board's judgment, by any benefits to the public that can reasonably be expected to be produced by the affiliation.[9]

Subsequently, on December 12, 1974, a member of the Board announced in testimony before the House Committee on Banking and Currency the Federal Reserve System's formal adoption of a "slow-down" policy for all bank holding companies. Governor Holland stated:

Beginning last June, we introduced a "go-slow" policy regarding bank holding company expansion. This policy remains in effect today; its future will have to be determined by the Board in the light of emerging economic and financial conditions. The policy is evident in cases in which we felt that either an organization's capital or its liquidity positions have been stretched. We have denied, in such cases, applications for acquisitions of other firms in permissible lines of activity, except when we felt the public benefits of a particular acquisition were exceedingly strong. We have also refused, for the time being, to add new lines of activity to the permissible list for bank holding companies.[10]

The vigor of the Board's "go-slow" policy is evidenced by its applications processing activity in early 1975. In the first half of 1975 the total number of holding company applications processed by the Board was 375, which represents a 46 percent drop from the 697 applications completed during the first six months of 1974. Moreover, the completed de novo nonbank applications evidenced a 57 percent decline from 339 in the first half of 1974 to 145 in the same period in 1975. The de novo bank applications processed fell by only 10 percent from 118 in the 1974 period to 107 in 1975. There were no entries into new nonbank activities ruled on by the Board in the first half of 1975, whereas four such cases were decided in the first six months of 1974.[11]

In addition, acquisition approvals dropped sharply during the second half of 1974 and in 1975. During 1974 and 1975 the Federal Reserve Board denied 85 applications to form new bank holding companies or to expand nonbanking activities and 31 proposals to acquire banks. Of the 85 denials, 43 were on the grounds that the proposals would have a potentially adverse effect on the soundness of affiliated banks. During 1975, there were only 285 de novo entries into nonbanking activities by holding companies compared to 542 in 1974. There was also a decline in the number of bank acquisitions approved in 1975 to 137 from 307 in the previous year, but the number of new holding companies approved in 1975 rose slightly to 141 from 138 in 1974. (Data include delegated cases; see Table 2-2 of Chapter 2.)

Data available for applications processed by the Federal Reserve System during the first nine months of 1976 show that of the 210 Section 3 (bank) applications received, 189 or 90 percent were approved. Of this total, 35 out of 45 holding company formations and 55 out of 65 bank acquisitions were approved. Ninety-six of the 189 approved applications of all types were delegated cases, representing mostly de novo bank formations. Data on Section 4 applications processed during this period show that 351 out of 353 nonbank applications were approved—a near 100 percent approval rate. Of these approvals, 234 were delegated cases, representing mostly de novo office or firm formations.

The 1976 data does not yet make clear whether the "go-slow" policy has been significantly relaxed. The Board of Governors in 1976 considered several new nonbanking areas (e.g., mortgage guaranty insurance, underwriting and dealing in government securities, management consulting to thrift institutions) for holding company entry. No new activities were permitted, however, during that year. In any case, the Board has made explicitly clear that it will continue to monitor holding company expansion on an individual basis and will not grant in the foreseeable future a blanket liberalization of its "go-slow" policy. That the impact of expansion and diversification on financial condition will continue to weigh heavily in the Board's policies was argued pointedly in the 1976 denial of Bankers Trust's proposed acquisition of the First National Bank of Mexico, Mexico, New York. The Board's order read as follows:

> With regard to the financial and managerial resources and future prospects of Applicant, information in the record . . . indicates that Applicant has been experiencing financial difficulties that have detracted from its overall financial condition and lessened its ability to serve as a source of strength for its subsidiaries. The subject application by its very nature would to some extent impose an additional burden on Applicant's operations. In these circumstances, it is the Board's view that Applicant's resources should be directed toward developing and maintaining strong and efficient operations within its existing structure.[12]

As can be seen from the above historical sketch, although the bank holding company has evolved into a dominant role in the banking industry, it has brought with it problems associated with increased risk exposure for subsidiary banks. The "go-slow" policy of the Federal Reserve Board is evidence of the realization by regulators of potential problems—mostly of a financial nature—that are inherent in this form of organization.

Some of these problems may be the result of the general downturn in the economy or the result of trends in commercial banking not associated with holding companies. However, several of the problems that have been manifested in the mid-1970s may be identified as unique to the holding company form of organization. In Chapter 7, the reasons for such problems are hypothesized, and their potential manifestations are studied.

Part II
The Public Interest: An Economic Analysis

Introduction to Part II

The Board of Governors of the Federal Reserve System, in considering proposals of bank holding companies to acquire banks, is required by Section 3 of the Bank Holding Company Act, as amended, to deny a proposal if its

> . . . effect in any section of the country may be substantially to lessen competition, or to tend to create a monopoly, or which in any other manner would be in restraint of trade, unless it finds that the anticompetitive effects of the proposed transaction are clearly outweighed in the public interest by the probable effect of the transaction in meeting the convenience and needs of the community to be served.

In addition, the Board is required to consider the financial and managerial aspects of the proposal. Apparently, the Board could thus approve the acquisition of a bank where the proposal would yield relatively modest, or even insignificant, benefits for the public's "convenience and needs," provided any anticompetitive effects were not substantial and no adverse financial or managerial factors militated against approval.

The requirements relating to the public interest are stated more explicitly regarding proposed acquisitions of nonbank firms by bank holding companies. Section 4(c)(8) of the Bank Holding Company Act requires the Board to determine whether a proposed nonbanking activity is

> . . . so closely related to banking or managing or controlling banks as to be a proper incident thereto. In determining whether a particular activity is a proper incident to banking or managing or controlling banks the Board shall consider whether its performance by an affiliate of a holding company can reasonably be expected to produce benefits to the public, such as greater convenience, increased competition, or gains in efficiency, that *outweigh* possible adverse effects, such as undue concentration of resources, decreased or unfair competition, conflicts of interests, or unsound banking practices [emphasis added].

In essence, the public interest requirement contained in Section 4(c)(8) suggests that every nonbank acquisition must yield net benefits to the public for it to be approved.

This emphasis on requiring that the public must benefit as a result of an acquisition is unique to bank holding company regulation. While presumably regulators of public utilities require that the actions of those regulated firms are in the public interest, most regulation relating to mergers and acquisitions only requires that the public not be harmed. The antitrust laws, for instance, do not require that the public be better off as a result of the acquisition of one firm by another. For this reason, as well as others, we might ask why bank holding companies deserve such special treatment. To answer this question, we must again return to the intent of Congress when it passed the 1970 Amendments to the Bank Holding Company Act.

Congressional Intent

As was shown in Chapter 3, the compromise language contained in Section 4(c)(8) of the 1970 amendments was a product of nearly two years of congressional debate. One of the major topics of debate was the relevant criteria for determining permissible activities. The House bill took a restrictive approach and contained a so-called laundry list of prohibited nonbank activities. The Senate, on the other hand, took a more liberal approach and allowed the Federal Reserve Board power to determine which activities were "functionally related to banking." However, while the two branches of Congress may have disagreed on the criteria for determining the permissibility of an activity, they were in complete agreement on the requirement that bank holding company entry into nonbank activities must result in public benefits and that a bank holding company making an application under Section 4(c)(8) of the act must bear the burden of proof in showing that its carrying on of a particular nonbank activity would produce benefits to the public that outweigh any adverse effects.

Rationale for Public Benefits Test

Most policy aimed at regulating merger activity is solely concerned with assuring that there are no social costs associated with the acquisition of a firm by another institution. Typically, any decline in the welfare of the public from a merger or acquisition arises from any anticompetitive effects attendant to the transaction. In the case of bank holding company acquisitions, however, there is a presumption that an acquisition will result in certain future social costs, and therefore these must be offset by a showing of net public benefits.

The requirement that an acquisition by a bank holding company can only be approved when there is a showing of net public benefits is a sound and nondiscriminatory policy if a future decrease in public welfare is possible. A reading of the previously cited congressional reports makes clear that Congress believed that regulation of the expansion of one-bank holding companies was necessary to protect against "the possible perpetration of abuses" that might arise from the combining of banking and "business." Presumably, the combination of bank and nonbank businesses under a single management structure will implicitly yield social costs in the future, and these costs are not apparent or measurable in the present. In fact, the social costs associated with adverse effects such as may arise from concentration of resources can be cumulative. Given this assumption, sound regulatory policy should be aimed at assuring that these potential future costs are offset by public benefits.

The approach specified in the Bank Holding Company Act is to require that public benefits be associated with the entry into a nonbank activity by every bank holding company. These benefits must offset any explicit social costs (i.e., lessening of actual or potential competition) and implicit costs that may arise in the future. Pursuing such a policy, the Federal Reserve Board, in effect, attempts to ensure that future social costs of an acquisition are at least neutralized by the net public benefits derived in the present. The Board has chosen to implement this policy on a case-by-case basis.

Chapters 5 and 6 present analyses of the impact of the expansion of bank holding companies' bank subsidiaries and nonbank subsidiaries, respectively, on competition, concentration of resources, allocational efficiency, convenience and needs of the public, and other public interest factors. The analyses are based on an examination of the rulings by the Board of Governors of the Federal Reserve System on applications by bank holding companies wishing to expand their operations.

Chapters 7 and 8, "Impact of Holding Company Affiliation on Bank Soundness: Theory" and "Tests of the Impact of Affiliation on the Soundness of Bank Subsidiaries," address the effects of the bank holding company form of organization on the behavior of bank and nonbank subsidiaries, particularly as regards their proclivity toward risk taking. In light of the failures of several large banks in recent years and the Board's fairly recent focus on the financial position of a holding company as a relevant public interest consideration, risk characteristics of holding companies appear particularly relevant to the public interest.

5 Analysis of Public Benefits: Bank Expansion

This chapter examines the nature of the public benefits required by the Board of Governors of the Federal Reserve System in connection with the applications of bank holding companies to acquire banks. The findings are based primarily on a review of the Board orders published in the *Federal Reserve Bulletin* (*FRB*), between January 1971 and June 1976, and in the *Federal Register* (*FR*). To learn how the Board has interpreted the public interest requirements of Section 3 of the Bank Holding Company Act, we examined orders where the Board approved acquisitions of banks. Bank cases in which the Board denied the proposed acquisition were studied as the control group.

Our analysis of the Board's decisions revealed six major types of benefits that the Board anticipated would result from the bank expansion of bank holding companies. These benefits, which are discussed below, encompassed: (1) improvements relating to the convenience and needs of the community to be served, (2) increased competition, (3) improved operational efficiency, (4) expanded financial resources for the bank to be acquired, (5) improved management for the acquired bank, and (6) assorted other benefits.

While holding company expansion frequently implied positive economic consequences, the Board's decisions to deny proposed acquisitions also indicated that had the proposal been approved, adverse consequences would have resulted. The principal adverse effects cited by the Board when it denied proposals comprised: (1) significantly reduced existing competition within a particular banking market; (2) probable elimination of significant future or potential competition in a particular market where alternative forms of entry were feasible; (3) the tendency toward an undue concentration of resources within a state; and (4) a possible weakening of the holding company's ability to support its existing banking subsidiaries.

By examining the above mentioned benefits and adverse consequences associated with a proposed acquisition, we can ascertain the degree of benefits the Board has required for a finding that a particular acquisition by a bank holding company is in the public interest. We are also able to focus on the severe adverse effects that may outweigh potential benefits by examining cases that have been denied.

Role of Public Benefits in Board Orders of Approval

The following discussion of the role of specific public benefits is organized by the type of benefit most frequently cited by the Board. A listing of these benefits by type is presented in Table 5-1. In general, these cases all involved applications that presaged neither severely adverse consequences from the loss of existing, future, or potential competition nor significant danger to the public interest from unsound banking practices. Neither did these acquisitions involve the weakening—financially or managerially—of the banks concerned.

Convenience and Needs

Improvements affecting the convenience and needs of the community are the benefits that have been most often accepted by the Board in its approval of bank acquisitions and bank holding company formations. Such improvements have often taken the form of new services or the expansion of new services or facilities, thereby facilitating the economic growth of the area in which the acquired bank is located. The Board has been especially responsive to the introduction of new services not yet offered in the area. However, it has also recognized benefits in the provision of an alternative source of services that are already provided in

Table 5-1
Types of Benefits Cited by the Board of Governors of the Federal Reserve System in Orders of Approval of Bank Holding Company Acquisitions of Banks

Type of Benefits	*Bank*
Convenience and needs:	
Providing an alternative source of services to a market	Missouri Bancshares, Inc. (71 *FRB* 143)
Increased lending capacity to support strong economic growth in an area	Texas Commerce Bancshares, Inc. (74 *FRB* 595)
Increased lending capacity to stimulate growth in economically depressed areas	First Union Inc. (71 *FRB* 531)
Expansion of specialized credit services	(see Table 5-2)
Increased competition:	
Increased competition through de novo entry	Atlantic Bancorporation (71 *FRB* 689)
Reduction of rates charged on loans or other services	First National City Corp. (71 *FRB* 944)
Strengthening the competitive position of a small firm through affiliation with a larger bank holding company	First Florida Bancorporation (71 *FRB* 256)
Increasing competition by changing a limited service institution into a full-service firm	Barclays Bank DCO (71 *FRB* 45)
Changing a conservative firm into a more aggressive competitor	Barnett Banks of Florida, Inc. (71 *FRB* 529)

Table 5-1 *cont.*

Type of Benefits	*Bank*
Improved efficiency:	
Economies of scale	First Security National Corp. (71 *FRB* 1005)
Complementary skills	First American Bancshares, Inc. (72 *FRB* 730)
Improved financial resources:	
Acquiring a financially weak firm	Landmark Banking Corp. (76 *FRB* 375)
Improving the debt-to-equity ratio of the acquired firm	Continental Bancor, Inc. (71 *FRB* 676)
Injecting a specific amount of equity capital into the acquired firm	Great Lakes Holding Co. (71 *FRB* 545)
Providing "access to the greater financial resources" of the holding company	First Alabama Bankshares, Inc. (71 *FRB* 404)
Injecting a specific amount of equity capital into existing bank subsidiary	First Bankshares of Florida, Inc. (76 *FRB* 53)
Improved managerial resources:	
Alleviating management succession problems	Depositors Corporation (71 *FRB* 36)
Providing management depth	First National Charter Corp. (71 *FRB* 37)
Access to managerial resources of holding company	CleveTrust Corp. (76 *FRB* 261)
Other benefits:	
Lowering management fees for subsidiary banks	Bank Securities Inc. (72 *FRB* 280)

an area and has frequently stated that an alternative source of services would stimulate competition. (See, for example, Missouri Bancshares, 71 *FRB* 143, and First Florida Bancorporation, 73 *FRB* 183; the former is an alternative source for retail services and the latter a source of wholesale banking services.) Table 5-2 lists a sampling of the new services that bank holding companies have proposed to introduce if their bank acquisitions were approved.

The introduction of more active lending and business development policies by banks has been held by the Federal Reserve Board to be beneficial in those areas that have been economically depressed.[1] The Board has also considered beneficial the expansion of bank lending and the introduction of new credit services necessary to sustain the rate of economic expansion in those areas experiencing strong economic growth. San Antonio, Texas, is an example of an area that fits this description. Following the reasoning noted above, the Board approved a bank acquisition in San Antonio by Texas Commerce Bancshares, Inc.[2]

Increased Competition

De novo bank entry into a market by a bank holding company has usually been regarded by the Board as an enhancement of competition, on the grounds that such an entry adds "a new decisionmaker" to the market.[3] Likewise, rate reductions on banking services are regarded as an important direct benefit to the public and conducive to an improvement in the quality of competition in the markets for the services involved. In a number of proposed acquisitions of

Table 5-2
New Services Proposed in Bank Acquisition Cases

Services	*Bank Case*
Trust Services	Society Corp. (71 *FRB* 52)
Increased commercial lending	Commerce Bankshares, Inc. (71 *FRB* 133)
Electronic data processing	Security N.Y. State Corp. (74 *FRB* 133)
Bond portfolio management (internal)	Florida National Banks of Florida, Inc. (71 *FRB* 939)
New physical facilities	Boatmens Bancshares, Inc. (71 *FRB* 39)
Remodeling and modernization of facilities	CleveTrust Corp. (76 *FRB* 540)
Increased parking facilities	Northeast United Bancorp., Inc. (76 *FRB* 154)
Drive-in facility	Landmark Banking Corp. of Florida (74 *FRB* 591)
Leasing	First National Charter Corp. (71 *FRB* 754)
Internal auditing	Florida National Banks of Florida, Inc. (71 *FRB* 939)
International services	Huntington Bancshares Inc. (71 *FRB* 940)
Venture capital	Central and State National Corporation of Alabama (71 *FRB* 939)
Urban and business development	First Virginia Bankshares Corp. (71 *FRB* 1022)
FHA and VA loans	BancOhio Corp. (71 *FRB* 1035)
Overdraft checking	First Virginia Bankshares Corp. (72 *FRB* 288)

Table 5-2 *cont.*

Services	*Bank Case*
Salary deposit plans	Security New York State Corp. (74 *FRB* 372)
Long-term certificate of deposit	Wyoming Bancorporation (75 *FRB* 37)
Credit cards	State Street Boston Financial Corp. (73 *FRB* 526)
Accounts receivable financing	Shorebank Inc. (72 *FRB* 914)
Investment management services for small investors	First National Boston Corp. (73 *FRB* 759)
Municipal bond financing	Security New York State Corp. (71 *FRB* 133)
New branches	Merrill Bancshares Co. (71 *FRB* 262)
Longer banking hours	First Bankshares of Florida, Inc. (76 *FRB* 52)
Saturday banking hours	Michigan National Corp. (76 *FRB* 53)
Wholesale banking services	First Florida Bancorporation (73 *FRB* 183)
International banking services	DETROITBANK Corp. (75 *FRB* 313)
Consumer financing and financial counselling	First Florida National Banks of Florida (74 *FRB* 46)
Lock boxes	DETROITBANK Corp. (75 *FRB* 313)
Expand student loan services	Southern Bancorporation (76 *FRB* 158)

banks, applicants promised to reduce interest rate charges on loans below those charged by other banks in the market (e.g., First National City Corporation, 71 *FRB* 944), or to eliminate fees or service charges on demand deposits (e.g., First Holding Company, 71 *FRB* 139), or to pay more competitive rates on time and savings accounts (e.g., First National State Bancorporation, 38 *FR* 6236, and Chemical New York Corporation, 38 *FR* 31472).

In its application to acquire Second New Haven Bank, Colonial Bancorp, Inc., proposed to decrease service charges on checking accounts, increase interest rates on time and savings deposits, and lower interest rates on consumer installment loans.[4] The Board noted that the bank would be able to offer expanded services to the state's largest banking customers and "generally be able to compete more effectively with larger banking organizations" operating in its market. The Board therefore concluded that these considerations lend weight toward approval and ". . . outweigh any slight anticompetitive effects on existing competition that may result from the proposed transaction."

The affiliation with a large bank holding company of a small bank that competes ineffectively with much larger banks in its market area has been recognized by the Board as strengthening the competitive position of the smaller bank.[5] Also, the formation of regional bank holding companies within a state has been viewed by the Board as a competitive stimulant to the larger statewide holding companies (e.g., First American Bancshares, 72 *FRB* 730).

Other examples of proposed actions the Board has regarded as beneficial to the public through the enhancement of competition include the following: (1) changing a foreign banking agency into a full-service bank;[6] (2) acquiring a conservative bank and reorienting its operating policies to make it aggressively compete for funds and expand its lending activities;[7] and (3) severing of chain banking ties, thus reducing concentration of resources.[8]

Improved Efficiency

Both bank acquisitions and holding company formations may give rise to operating efficiencies or economies of scale. (See Chapter 7 for a discussion of the statistical evidence on scale economies.) On several occasions, the Federal Reserve Board has taken the view that the organizational form of the bank holding company is conducive to such economies. In a case involving the "corporate reorganization of established interests and relationships" into a multibank holding company (First Security National Corporation, 71 *FRB* 1005), the Board noted:

> Although Applicant proposes no signficant changes in services to the public as a result of the proposed acquisitions, the convenience and needs of the communities involved should benefit from the improved economies and efficiencies of operation expected to result from the proposed restructuring of Applicant into a coordinated multibank holding company organization.

Furthermore, in a concurring statement to the order approving The First National Bancorporation's acquisition of The Exchange National Bank of Colorado Springs, Governor Mitchell cited various studies that indicate significant economies of scale exist in banking—economies that tend to be passed on to the public through additional convenience in offices and facilities—and noted that ". . . banking competition can only exist in a meaningful sense if at least some banking units have the capacity to broaden their services and make them more conveniently available. Their capacity to do so is a matter of realizing economies of scale."[9]

Other references to such efficiencies are frequently found in Board orders, which often also refer to the "pooling of resources and complementary skills" that allow the holding company to utilize the expertise of one affiliate to expand the services of the other affiliates.[10] Recently, in its approval of the acquisition of First National Bank and Trust Company of Naples by Southwest Florida Banks, Inc., the Board noted that the affiliation would enable the acquired bank "... to offer expanded and improved services by drawing on Applicant's expertise and resources."[11]

Improved Financial Resources

The infusion of capital funds to a newly acquired bank is an often-cited indirect benefit to the public. There have been several cases where the applicant holding company has promised a specific amount of capital contribution to the proposed bank affiliate.[12] More frequently, applicants have argued that affiliation of the proposed banks with bank holding companies would provide access to the financial resources of the applicant. The acquisition by DETROITBANK Corporation (76 *FRB* 313) is an example of such a case. The Board in analyzing the financial considerations of proposed acquisitions has also been concerned with the capital positions of existing bank subsidiaries of the applicant. In fact, the Board conditioned its approval of the acquisition of a bank by First Bancshares of Florida, Inc. (76 *FRB* 53) on the applicant's injection of $500,000 of additional equity capital into one of its subsidiary banks.

There are also examples in bank cases where holding company affiliation was expected to result in the strengthening of a financially weak bank. In several bank acquisitions, the acquired bank had been experiencing financial problems and eventually might have been declared insolvent. A vivid example of this situation was provided by the proposed acquisition of Security State Bank of Pompano Beach by Landmark Banking Corporation (76 *FRB* 375) where the Board concluded in its order that in the absence of the proposed acquisition, "the failure of the Security Bank would be probable."[13] In another instance, the Board ruled that it was beneficial for the debt-to-equity ratio to be lowered in the case of an otherwise strong bank through the establishment of a debt repayment program scheduled by the applicant holding company (Continental Bancor, Inc., 71 *FRB* 676).

Improved Managerial Resources

Another indirect benefit to the public is found in cases where the managerial resources of the acquired firm are to be substantially improved. Applications have been approved where it was found that the acquisitions would alleviate management succession problems[14] or provide needed management depth.[15] The Federal Reserve Board has also recently recognized (i.e., CleveTrust Corporation, 76 *FRB* 261) that the affiliation of a bank with a holding company will give it access to the holding company's managerial resources and thus "should permit banks to offer new and expanded services to their customers."

Other Public Benefits

Other significant benefits to the public that have been cited in the Federal Reserve Board's orders include: (1) agreement by the applicant holding company to lower its management fees charged to its subsidiary banks,[16] and (2) the correction of an unfair competitive situation.[17]

Treatment of Public Benefits in Board Denials of Applications

An important consideration regarding the Federal Reserve Board's public benefits test is the circumstances under which an applicant's claimed public benefits would outweigh or be outweighed by adverse effects expected to arise from the transaction. Some insight into this issue may be gained from an examination of the factors that resulted in the denial of bank holding company applications to acquire banks.

In the Board's denials of proposals by bank holding companies to acquire banks, the principal adverse factors have involved a lessening of existing or potential competition, a weakening of the financial and/or managerial condition of the bank, and unsound banking practices. When considering the proposed benefits embodied in these applications, the Board has not been willing to conclude that the gains from prospective new services would offset the adverse factors unless it was satisfied that the community involved had significant unmet needs that would be fulfilled. In this regard, the Board denied a number of cases where competition or financial factors were adverse and it had concluded that the community was already being served adequately.

In a case involving Cegrove Corporation (73 *FRB* 676), the Board determined that the applicant would be unable to service the debt incurred in financing the acquisition and suggested that the capital position of both the bank to be acquired and the existing subsidiary bank might consequently be impaired. As a benefit, the applicant proposed to offer services that were not being offered by the banks involved. However, the Board determined that the relevant markets were being adequately served and therefore concluded that ". . . considerations relating to the convenience and needs of the community to be served are regarded as consistent with, but lend no weight toward, approval."[18]

In the case of the First International Bancshares, Inc. (73 *FRB* 453), the Board determined that the acquisition not only would eliminate both existing competition and a foothold for another potential entrant to the market but would also increase deposit concentration among the largest organizations in the market. The Board concluded that the needs of the residents of the Dallas area were being adequately served by the existing facilities and that consummation of the proposed acquisition would have little impact. The Board determined, therefore, that the benefits would not outweigh the adverse competitive effects.

In other cases the Federal Reserve Board has denied acquisitions if there were significantly adverse competitive consequences even if the convenience and needs of the community would be enhanced by approval. One example of this regulatory posture is the case of Alabama Bancorporation (75 *FRB* 672) where the Board determined that "... approval of the application would eliminate meaningful existing competition between Applicant and Bank, as well as reduce the number of banking alternatives operating in the market." The Board considered the competitive consequences all the more serious because the market was not particularly attractive for de novo entry by banking organizations seeking entry into the market and because a potential foothold acquisition was being eliminated. Consequently, the Board concluded that "... the competitive factors lend substantial weight toward denial...." The financial and managerial factors were consistent with but lent no weight toward approval. In its application, Alabama Bancorporation proposed to assist the bank in establishing branch offices by providing the necessary capital and to provide the bank with managerial expertise in the areas of dealer, floor plan, and inventory loans, as well as leveraged leasing. While the Board determined that the considerations relating to the convenience and needs of the communities to be served "lend some weight toward approval," they did not, "in the Board's view, outweigh the substantially adverse competitive effects...."

Some cases have been denied when there was no existing competition between the holding company's subsidiary banks and the bank to be acquired. One such case (subsequently approved a year later) involved the proposed acquisition of Citizens National Bank, Englewood, New Jersey, by Midlantic Banks Inc., Newark (71 *FRB* 684). With five governors voting, the Board concluded that the acquisition would result in: (1) the foreclosure of a substantial amount of potential competition, (2) the elimination of a desirable foothold entry for holding companies located in other banking districts within the state, and (3) the possible development of a trend toward concentration within banking districts. The Board determined that the public benefits from the applicant becoming an additional competitive alternative for large customers in the market were not sufficient to outweigh the adverse effects. The Board further concluded that consummation of the acquisition would have an adverse effect on the convenience and needs of the community since it would preserve home office protection.[a]

In another denial (First International Bancshares, Inc., 74 *FRB* 43) in which existing competition was not an issue, the Board expressed its concern over the

---

[a]In 1972, as the holding company movement in New Jersey gathered momentum, the applicant reapplied and the Board in a four-to-three decision approved the acquisition after the applicant indicated that it would move the head office of the bank. This move would open its previous home community to branching by other banks.

size disparity among the holding companies in Texas and the likelihood that the concentration of deposits among the five largest holding companies might increase as a result of the acquisition. The Board stated that it

> . . . is not required to await the development of undue concentration among bank holding companies in Texas before it intervenes. Indeed, the underlying purpose of the Clayton Act, as incorporated in the Bank Holding Company Act, is to break the force of a trend toward undue concentration before it gathers momentum. . . . It is, therefore, the tendency toward undue concentration the Board must guard against when viewing the probable effect of an acquisition upon future competition in a banking market.

The Board further concluded that the entry into small markets by the state's largest holding companies through the acquisition of large independent banks would increase the levels of concentration in these markets.

In the cases discussed above, as well as others, the Board concluded that the financial and managerial conditions of the bank and the holding company and their future growth prospects were satisfactory. It therefore considered these factors as consistent with approval. However, in none of these cases did these factors lend any weight toward approval.

On March 1, 1974, in an order of denial involving another proposed acquisition by First International Bancshares, Inc., the Federal Reserve Board reaffirmed its position of guarding

> . . . against the tendency toward undue concentration not only in a local market but at the Statewide level as well when viewing the probable effect of an acquisition upon potential competition.[19]

The Board concluded that the acquisition would have significant adverse effects on potential competition in the local bank market and throughout Texas.

In discussing the applicant's proposal to inject equity capital into the bank to be acquired, the Board stated that affiliation with First International Bancshares was not the only means by which the bank's financial resources could be strengthened. The Board indicated that the acquisition of the bank by a smaller holding company could result in similar assistance without the anticompetitive effects attached to the proposal then under consideration. The Board recognized that its approval of the affiliation would result in the applicant's managerial resources and expertise being available to the bank and in new services being offered to the public. While both of these factors would lend weight toward approval, it nevertheless concluded that banking factors and convenience and needs considerations did not outweigh the substantially adverse effects the proposal would have on potential competition.

In at least two cases in which it denied the acquisition of de novo banks, the Board found that adverse competitive effects were likely because the applicants were already represented in the market. In one case, the Board concluded that further offices would raise barriers to entry by other organizations and increase concentration of banking resources in the market. It held that the proposed benefits (i.e., the addition of new services not readily available in the market) did not lend sufficient weight to offset the adverse effects.[20] In the second case, the Board concluded that a recently established bank would be hurt by the opening of yet another de novo bank in the same market and consequently that the proposed new bank would have an adverse effect on the development of future competition. In discussing the applicant's claim that the convenience of the community would be enhanced because the new bank would be closer to its potential customers than existing banks, the Board held that this factor lent very little weight toward approval.[21]

An interesting example of how management factors can impinge on the Federal Reserve Board's public interest determinations is provided by the denial of a proposed acquisition by NBC Company (74 *FRB* 782) of a minority interest in a bank. In this case the Board concluded that approval would not eliminate any significant existing or future competition between NBC Company and the bank it wished to acquire. The Board also determined that the financial and managerial resources of the applicant and its subsidiary were satisfactory. However, in assessing the public interest consequences of the proposal, the Board noted that NBC Company was seeking to acquire less than a majority interest in the bank and would not be in a position to control or significantly influence the bank's management. Moreover, the controlling shareholder was opposed to the acquisition, which the Board felt could lead to management dissention. On the basis of these factors the Board determined that no benefits to the public would result from the proposed acquisition since ". . . the convenience and needs consideration lent no weight toward approval."

Since approximately mid-year 1974 the Board has instituted a "go-slow" policy toward bank holding company expansion. As discussed in Chapter 4, this policy has manifested itself in the Federal Reserve Board's denying applications for acquisitions when it felt the holding company or its subsidiary banks' capital or liquidity positions have been strained. The Board has indicated on numerous occasions that it feels that the holding company should be a source of managerial and financial strength to its subsidiaries. Consequently, the Board has considered an acquisition that imposes any financial or managerial burden on a holding company (which in the Board's view should strengthen its subsidiary banks) as being one where the financial and/or managerial factors weigh against approval. In the case of Bankers Trust New York Corporation's proposed acquisition of First National Bank of Mexico (76 *FRB* 794), the Board did not accept the applicant's offer of additional services to the bank's customers, including trust and investment services, international banking, savings incentive plans, and underwriting and advisory services for municipalities as being sufficient to outweigh the adverse banking factors. There have been no instances where the

Board has accepted public benefits offered by an applicant as outweighing adverse banking factors under the "go-slow" policy.

Board Treatment of Public Benefits—An Overview

In proposals where the anticompetitive effects were either slight or nonexistent, published orders of the Federal Reserve Board have seldom dwelt on the public benefits of the case. Frequently, the Board has stated that "banking factors are regarded as consistent with approval" and that "considerations relating to the convenience and needs of the communities to be served are also consistent with approval." Consequently, a number of acquisitions of banks were approved where there were no significant direct benefits to the public. However, it should be noted that the Board approved a number of cases with only indirect benefits on the grounds that direct gains to the public would eventually be forthcoming.

In contrast to the Board's position in situations where there are no anticompetitive effects, we found that the Board required concrete benefits if an application was to be approved in the face of probable anticompetitive consequences. However, if the competitive consequences were significantly adverse, the Board generally did not consider any benefits offered by an applicant as sufficient to outweigh the anticompetitive effects.

Analysis of Public Benefits: Nonbank Expansion

This chapter presents the results of our investigation into the nature of the public benefits involved in applications by bank holding companies to acquire nonbank firms. The findings presented in this chapter, as in the preceding one, are based on an inspection of the Federal Reserve Board's orders published in the *Federal Reserve Bulletin* (*FRB*) between January 1971 and June 1976. In addition, approximately thirty nonbank orders published in the *Federal Register* (*FR*) were examined.

Our analysis of the Board's decisions revealed the same types of public benefits found in bank cases: improvements relating to convenience and needs, increased competition, improved operational efficiency, expanded financial and managerial resources for the firm to be acquired, and other benefits unique to a particular case. In nonbank cases denied under Section 4(c)(8) of the Bank Holding Company Act, the principal adverse effects cited by the Board comprised: (1) significantly reduced existing competition within a well-defined geographic market for a particular product(s); (2) probable elimination of significant amounts of future or potential competition in a particular market where alternative forms of entry (i.e., de novo or foothold entry) were feasible; (3) the accumulation of financial resources to such an extent as to lead to possible abuse of economic power; (4) a possible weakening of the holding company's ability to support the growth of its banking subsidiaries; and (5) covenants restricting competition.

As in the previous chapter, we examine the above-mentioned benefits and adverse effects to ascertain the magnitude of benefits required by the Board for a finding that a particular nonbank acquisition is in the public interest. By examining cases that have been denied we are able to identify those adverse effects that may outweigh potential benefits.

Role of Public Benefits in Board Orders of Approval

The following discussion of the specific public benefits is organized along the lines presented in Table 6-1. In general, these cases (as with bank applications) all involved applications that indicated neither severe adverse consequences resulting from the loss of existing, future, or potential competition nor significant danger to the public from an undue concentration of resources. Neither did they involve the weakening—financially or managerially—of the holding

Table 6-1
Types of Benefits Cited by the Board of Governors of the Federal Reserve System in Orders of Approval of Bank Holding Company Acquisitions

Type of Benefits	*Nonbank Case*
Convenience and needs:	
Providing an alternative source of services to a market	Tennessee National Corp. (75 *FRB* 251)
Increased lending capacity to stimulate growth in economically depressed areas	Marine Bancorporation (72 *FRB* 504)
Expansion of specialized credit service	Mortgage: First Chicago Corp. (72 *FRB* 175). Consumer: First Bank System, Inc. (72 *FRB* 172). Commercial: Bank of Virginia Co. (72 *FRB* 934). Agricultural: Western Kansas Investment Corporation, Inc. (72 *FRB* 737). Leasing: Provident National Corp. (72 *FRB* 933).
Geographic expansion of service	American Fletcher Corp. (72 *FRB* 741)
Improving allocational efficiency	First Union National Bancorporation, Inc. (72 *FRB* 72)
Increased competition:	
Increased competition through de novo entry	U.N. Bancshares, Inc. (73 *FRB* 204)
Reduction of rates charged on loans or other services	Manufacturers Hanover Corp. (75 *FRB* 42)
Strengthening the competitive position of a small firm through affiliation with a larger bank holding company	Chemical New York Corp. (76 *FRB* 388)
Increasing competition by changing a limited-service institution into a full-service firm	Bank of Virginia Co. (72 *FRB* 934)
Improved efficiency:	
Economies of scale	First National Holding Corp. (74 *FRB* 603)
Complementary skills	State Street Boston Financial Corp. (74 *FRB* 515)
More efficient pricing of services	The Citizens and Southern Corp. (74 *FRB* 226)
Improved financial resources:	
Acquiring a financially weak firm	BankAmerica Corp. (73 *FRB* 687)
Injecting a specific amount of equity capital into the acquired firm	Security Pacific Corp. (74 *FRB* 607)
Providing "access to the greater financial resources" of the holding company	Third National Corp. (38 *FR* 9686)
Improving capital position of affiliated banks	Bancshares of Indiana, Inc. (75 *FRB* 40)

Table 6-1 *cont.*

Type of Benefits	*Nonbank Case*
Improved managerial resources:	
Alleviating management succession problems	Northwest Bancorporation (73 *FRB* 701)
Providing management depth	Bank of Virginia Co. (74 *FRB* 512)
Other benefits:	
Correcting an unfair competitive situation	Newport Savings and Loan Association (72 *FRB* 313)
Preventing the termination of a financial service	American Fletcher Corp. (38 *FR* 14203)

company or its subsidiary banks. The Board's treatment of public benefits in cases where adverse factors predominated is discussed later in the chapter.

Convenience and Needs

In proposed nonbank acquisitions the introduction of new, or the extension of existing, services to a market has been cited by the Federal Reserve Board as a public benefit, particularly the provision of specialized credit services. For example, many of the approvals of acquisitions of mortgage banking firms by bank holding companies have been granted on the expectation that such affiliation would result in increased flows of funds into residential or low-income housing and urban renewal. In these instances, however, the applicant must indicate that the acquisition would not cause a reduction of credit to independent mortgage companies that may be customers of the bank affiliates of the bank holding company.[1] Even when the Board found slightly adverse competitive effects, as in the case involving the retention of a mortgage company by The Citizens and Southern Corporation (75 *FRB* 321), it ruled that the increase in the available funds to meet growing credit demands for housing and other construction offset the adverse factors.

Increases in the supply and availability as well as reductions in the cost of consumer credit to individuals have been cited frequently as significant public benefits in approvals of acquisitions involving consumer finance companies and firms that extend second mortgages.[2] In a recent case involving the acquisition of a consumer finance company by Southern Bancorporation, Inc. (76 *FRB* 273), the Federal Reserve Board determined that "... affiliation will enable Company to offer higher risk loans and, ... expand the insurance activities of Company by introducing credit-related property and casualty insurance."

Further, acquisitions of commercial finance firms and factoring concerns have been granted on the expectation of expanded flows of commercial credit.[3] In two such acquisitions the Board determined that the expanded flow of commercial credit would yield benefits for small businesses[4] and high-risk enterprises.[5] Also cited by the Board as beneficial to the public are the provision of personal property leasing services[6] and agricultural lending through the acquisition of agricultural credit companies.[7] In its approval of a joint venture between Fort Worth National Corporation and Shawmut Association, Inc. (74 *FRB* 382) to provide agricultural commodity financing and servicing, the Board noted that the financing needs of the Southwest, particularly that of feedlots, will be met. The Board further observed that these needs were not being met by local financial institutions.

The Federal Reserve Board has held as beneficial the geographic expansion and the offering of new products by bank holding companies in the fields of insurance and mortgage, consumer, and commercial credit. In at least one case involving the de novo expansion of insurance agency activities (First Tennessee National Corporation, 75 *FRB* 251), the Board concluded that the expansion would enable the company "... to provide its customers with convenient, alternative source for these additional types of insurance." Several applicants have specifically stated that their newly acquired affiliates would expand outside their respective current market areas.[8] In one order approving the acquisition of a mortgage banking firm, the Board noted that an improved flow of funds would take place from capital-surplus areas to those in deficit.[9] Moreover, in the BankAmerica–GAC Finance case (73 *FRB* 687), the Board on reconsideration of a revised application determined that one of the benefits inherent in the acquisition would be a more efficient allocation of consumer credit.[a]

Providing a stimulus to the economic growth of an area has been cited as an important public benefit in several nonbank cases where the applicant argued that approval would result in increased flows of mortgage credit to depressed areas and would aid municipal governments in obtaining long-term funds.[10]

Increased Competition

De novo entry into a market by a nonbank affiliate of a bank holding company has usually been regarded by the Federal Reserve Board as enhancing competition since entry of this type adds a new decision maker to the market.[11] These

[a]On July 27, 1973, the Board denied BankAmerica Corporation's application to acquire GAC Finance, Inc., on the grounds that the acquisition would result in reduced competition and an undue concentration of resources. On reapplying, the applicant proposed the divestiture of a significant amount of sales finance and commercial finance receivables and of all of GAC's offices that were competitive or potentially competitive with the applicant. The Board determined that such divestiture removed its initial objections to the acquisition on competitive grounds. Moreover, based on new information, the Board concluded "... that [GAC] Finance must be sold ... to a buyer of considerable financial strength to avoid the collapse of Finance and its parent, and possibly serious financial repercussions of a more serious nature."

instances involved such nonbank firms as factoring companies[12] or mortgage banking firms,[13] which formerly had been acquired under Section 4(c)(5) of the Bank Holding Company Act prior to 1970 and operated as loan production offices.[b] The acquisitions of de novo firms in mortgage banking and bank management consulting have also been viewed by the Board as being pro-competitive.[14]

Reductions in interest rates on loans also have been viewed by the Board as a significant public benefit in nonbank cases, particularly acquisitions of consumer finance companies.[15] Indeed, with regard to applications to acquire credit life insurance underwriters or reinsurers, Regulation Y explicitly requires an applicant to demonstrate

> . . . that approval will benefit the consumer or result in other benefits. Normally such a showing would be made by a projected reduction in rates or increase in policy benefits due to bank holding company performance of this service.

The Board has approved applications that have provided for rate reductions of 2 to 20 percent below existing average levels for each state in which consumer credit is extended by the bank holding company.[16] In response to states reducing their prima facie rates, the Board, in June 1976, issued an interpretation of that portion of Regulation Y dealing with the underwriting of credit life and credit accident and health insurance. The published interpretation imposes a ". . . continuing obligation upon all bank holding companies authorized to underwrite credit insurance . . . to maintain a public benefit such as was anticipated and considered by the Board at the time of the original approval. . . ."[17] Moreover, the Federal Reserve Board has held that credit life insurance subsidiaries of bank holding companies must refrain from underwriting level term insurance to cover installment loans—that is, coverage in excess of the outstanding loan balance.[c]

Other examples of proposed actions the Federal Reserve Board has regarded as beneficial to the public through the enhancement of competition resulted from the holding company strengthening the new affiliate. For example, in its approval of the acquisition of an investment advisory firm by Chemical New York Corporation (76 *FRB* 388), the Board noted that affiliation ". . . should enable Company to improve the quality and depth of its investment advisory services and thereby enable it to compete more effectively with the large organi-

---

[b]Subject to Board regulations and interpretations, limited purpose subsidiaries can be acquired by bank holding companies under Section 4(c)(5), which allows the ownership of shares in firms that a national bank could own under Section 5136 of the revised statutes.

[c]See, for example, Fidelity Corporation of Pennsylvania (73 *FRB* 472). However, the Board has determined that the issuance of level term credit life insurance is permissible in connection with single-payment loans (Winters National Corporation, Board Press Release, December 27, 1973).

zations in the market." In at least two other cases, the Board concluded that the expansion of financial resources available to the new nonbank affiliate would result in an increase in its competitive effectiveness.[18]

Improved Efficiency

In several cases the Federal Reserve Board has recognized that the nonbank acquisition may give rise to operating efficiencies for the firm to be acquired or may lead to a more efficient allocation of resources by customers of the nonbank firm. In its decision in the First National Holding Corporation (74 *FRB* 603) case, the Board determined that the acquisition would improve efficiency of existing consumer finance offices through centralized purchasing, advertising, and recordkeeping. Furthermore, in a case involving the acquisition by State Street Boston Financial Corporation (74 *FRB* 515) of a de novo joint venture to offer data processing services, the Board noted that the acquisition would increase efficiency in shareholder accounts services provided by the holding company's bank. In cases involving acquisitions of de novo bank management consulting firms, the Board has concluded that client banks will be better able to judge the value of the services on an explicit fee basis than if provided as part of a correspondent relationship.[19]

Improved Financial Resources

The infusion of capital funds to a newly acquired nonbank firm is an often-quoted benefit to the public. There have been several cases where the applicant holding company has committed itself to a specific capital contribution to the proposed nonbank affiliate.[20] More frequently, applicants have argued that affiliations of the proposed nonbank firms with bank holding companies would provide ". . . access to the greater financial resources of applicant."[21]

This argument regarding access to a holding company's resources implies that the affiliation of a small bank-related firm with a large bank holding company gives that small firm an "assured" source of working funds at probably lower cost than is obtainable as an independent firm.[22] Another argument is that this source of funds would be likely to be more "stable" than one obtainable independently.[23]

Finally, there are examples of nonbank cases where holding company affiliation was expected to result in the strengthening of a financially weak firm. In several nonbank acquisitions the acquired firm had been experiencing financial problems and eventually might have become insolvent.[24] In one case the acquisition resulted in the revitalization of a credit office that otherwise would have been closed.[25] In another instance the holding company provided equity capital and the proceeds of commercial paper sales to a mortgage banking firm that otherwise would have had to withdraw from its market.[26] There has been at least one instance where the resources of the nonbank firm were used to bolster the capital position of a bank. In its application to acquire Goodwin Brothers Leasing, Inc., Bancshares of Indiana, Inc. (75 *FRB* 40) stated that it intends to "run off" the assets of the firm and that ". . . it intends to use the assets of the Company for the purpose of increasing the capital position of the Bank."

Improved Managerial Resources

An indirect benefit to the public is also found in cases where the managerial resources of the acquired firm are to be significantly improved. Applications have been approved where the Federal Reserve Board found that the acquisitions would provide needed management depth[27] or alleviate management succession problems.[28] In at least one instance the Board has recognized the provision of experienced personnel and assistance in areas of financial planning, sales, and marketing to be beneficial to the acquisition of a consumer finance company.[29]

Other Public Benefits

Other benefits to the public cited in the Federal Reserve Board's orders have, typically, related to the continuation of a particular financial service being provided in an area.[30]

Treatment of Public Benefits in Board Denials of Applications

As of June 1976, thirty-eight orders of denial under Section 4(c)(8) were published in the *Federal Reserve Bulletin*. These cases represent a very small percentage of the total number of nonbank applications. Table 4–2 in Chapter 4 gives the distribution of applications by the type of activity and the Federal Reserve Board's record of denials and approvals of holding companies' proposed nonbank acquisitions through mid-year 1976. The table shows that about 92 percent of the applications were approved. Most applicants have recognized that the acquisition of close competitors or of major firms where smaller ones are available would encounter stiff Board opposition. Moreover, the Board's practice of formally determining permissible nonbank activities has precluded many opportunities for denial.[d] In addition, some bank holding companies consult their local Federal Reserve Bank to obtain an indication of the likelihood that a contemplated acquisition will be denied. This practice has increased as a result of the Board's "go-slow" policy inasmuch as banks wish to avoid the adverse publicity associated with a denial on financial grounds.

In fifteen of the denials, public benefits were not treated in detail—that is, the benefits the applicants claimed would result from the acquisition were not mentioned or received only brief mention in the order.[31] Apparently in these cases the Board believed the adverse effects from the reduction of existing and potential competition, the undue concentration of resources, or the adverse financial factors to be so obvious and overwhelming and/or the benefits to be so weak that no explicit treatment was deemed necessary.

In twenty-three cases in which the proposals were denied, the Board treated the public benefits explicitly. In these orders the Board not only discussed the expected adverse effects, but also presented each of the applicant's major arguments regarding public benefits and, in turn, commented on each argument.

The vast majority of the denials involved the proposed acquisition of a mortgage banking firm or a consumer finance company. In every one of these cases disapproval was based primarily on the reduction of existing and/or potential competition, which would result from the loss of competition between the firm to be acquired and either a bank or nonbank affiliate of the holding company. In a mortgage banking case involving Pittsburgh National Corporation (74 *FRB* 391), the Board noted that the holding company already owned the tenth largest mortgage banking firm in the country and that it seemed likely that this firm would continue to compete aggressively to maintain its position. Consequently, the Board concluded that approval of the acquisition of another mortgage company that lends in the same market is "likely to eliminate the prospect of increased potential competition in the market." In a denial of three applications by Citicorp (75 *FRB* 896) to acquire finance companies, the Board noted that approval of the proposals would eliminate some existing competition between Nationwide Financial Services Corporation (Citicorp's consumer finance subsidiary) and two of these companies and would result in the elimination of future and potential competition. The Board went on to state:

> Applicant has the financial and managerial resources to expand Nationwide on a de novo basis into many, if not most, of the other areas served by each of the Finance Companies. Furthermore, Nationwide's past expansion . . . demonstrates an inclination toward such expansion.

---

[d]There have been five proposed nonbank acquisitions that were denied on the grounds that the activities were not closely related to banking: R.I.H.T. Corporation (72 *FRB* 595); First Commerce Corporation (72 *FRB* 674); Marine Midland Banks, Inc. (72 *FRB* 676); and Union Bond and Mortgage Company (75 *FRB* 112); and BankAmerica's proposed formation of BAC Computer Corporation—a nonpayout computer leasing firm—which was denied by letter in 1972.

The Board also, for the first time, indicated that it felt that a holding company such as Citicorp could overcome regulatory barriers imposed by states and enter de novo. Recent research by Seelig indicates that convenience and advantage clauses in state small loan laws have not deterred bank holding companies from opening consumer finance offices.[32]

One benefit claimed by practically all of the applicants seeking to acquire mortgage banking firms or consumer finance companies was that affiliation would result in the affiliate's assured access to greater working capital at more competitive rates. The Board has typically responded to this argument with the following type of statement:

> While the acquisition of a mortgage company by a bank holding company could have the effect of strengthening the company in certain markets, it appears certain that such increased ability and service, if it came from a bank holding company not now competing or not likely to compete in the market, would have a substantially more desirable impact on the public interest.[33]

In some instances the Board considered such claims to be "essentially conjectural."[34] Governor Bucher explained, in his concurring statement in two cases involving acquisitions by Mellon National Corporation (73 *FRB* 910) and Manufacturers Hanover Corporation (73 *FRB* 908), that:

> Serious questions can arise as to whether the public benefits relating to operating efficiency, better services, and lower cost, which are frequently ascribed to proposed affiliations of mortgage banking firms with bank holding companies, exist to a significant degree, especially when larger firms are involved. The advocacy voiced by applicants may not reflect the actual probability of the occurrence of the asserted benefits. Bank holding companies bear the burden of demonstrating that their proposed nonbanking acquisition will have public benefits outweighing any adverse effects, inasmuch as the basic balancing test of Section 4(c)(8) requires a showing of public benefits.

Several other cases, denied because of anticompetitive effects, include proposed acquisitions of a sales finance firm (First Commercial Banks, Inc., 73 *FRB* 118), an industrial loan and thrift company (Tennessee National Bancorporation, 73 *FRB* 700), and consumer finance companies.[35]

There have been several denials where the principal objection related to possible adverse effects for the banking affiliates of the holding companies. At least two of these denials related to the acquisition of a savings and loan association by bank holding companies during the period when the Federal Reserve Board was implementing its "go-slow" policy.[36] Another denial related to a shortage of capital in a bank affiliate.[37]

One denial related to a leasing firm (Chemical New York Corporation, 73 *FRB* 698), where the principal difficulty involved possible adverse effects for the banking affiliates of the holding company. Chemical New York Corporation sought to acquire CNA Nuclear Leasing, Inc.—a firm that had a high debt-equity ratio and would have required heavy financing to meet its long-term growth objectives. Such affiliation would have required Chemical to increase its short-term borrowings substantially, thereby possibly sapping the financial strength of the company. In its order of denial, the Board stated that "... one of the primary purposes of a holding company is to serve as a source of financial strength for its subsidiary banks." It concluded that this acquisition would reduce Chemical's ability to supply capital to its banks in the future.

A widely publicized denial of the acquisition of a financial conglomerate engaging in commercial finance, factoring, consumer finance, and other activities related to the limited managerial and financial resources of the holding company. In denying Franklin New York Corporation's application to acquire Talcott National Corporation (74 *FRB* 458), the Board concluded that "... this proposal may constitute an undue claim on Applicant's managerial and financial resources and concludes that this represents an adverse effect to be considered under Section 4(C)(8)." In addition the Board noted that consummation of the proposal would eliminate some potential competition and that questions regarding concentration of resources also added marginal adverse weight. Franklin contended that the acquisition would lead to the provision of new services. However, the Board concluded that such services were available in the New York area and consequently the "... provision of such additional services would constitute only a minimal public benefit."

Three of the denial orders that involved explicit treatment of public benefits were denied on grounds that included undue concentration of resources. These involved BTNB Corporation (72 *FRB* 71), First National City Corporation (74 *FRB* 50),[38] and The Chase Manhattan Corporation (74 *FRB* 142). The latter two orders presented detailed discussions of the applicants' arguments relating to benefits to the public.

First National City Corporation named the following benefits: (1) the affiliation of applicant and Advance Mortgage Corporation (this was a retention application) had made available funds that allowed Advance to increase its volume of originations of construction loans; (2) the applicant allowed Advance to originate and warehouse $30 million of mortgages without investor takeout commitments (this, the applicant contended, had a countercyclical effect on the flow of funds into mortgage lending); and (3) the applicant would expand Advance's geographic operations.

The Federal Reserve Board, however, argued regarding the first benefit mentioned that the construction loans of the applicant's bank had increased by a greater margin during this period than did those of Advance. Moreover, the Board noted that originations of one-to-four family mortgage loans by Advance had increased by a lesser margin than the industry as a whole. In regard to the second benefit, the Board noted that both affiliated and independent mortgage banking firms appeared to warehouse an increased volume of mortgages during periods of tight money. With respect to the third benefit, the Board called attention to the applicant's resources that give it the capability to enter new markets de novo or through the acquisition of a smaller firm. In addition, the Board was evidently concerned with the possible adverse implications of the acquisition of the third largest mortgage banking firm in the nation by the second largest banking organization. The application was denied on the grounds of reduced existing and potential competition and an undue concentration of resources.

The Chase Manhattan Corporation's proposed acquisition of Dial Financial Corporation (74 *FRB* 142) was another application denied primarily on the grounds of undue concentration of credit-gaining resources and the elimination of potential competition. The applicant stated that the proposed affiliation would result in the diversification by Dial into such product lines as small business loans, farm loans, and first and second mortgage loans. The Federal Reserve Board noted that many consumer finance companies are diversifying into these areas and that Dial has the ability and resources to do so. The order also declared that Dial is capable of opening new offices and, indeed, appears to have planned to do so in the absence of the affiliation. The Board noted that while it recognized rate reductions on consumer loans constitute a significant public benefit, it considered Chase's proposal in this area similar to one that Dial had already instituted and had the resources to expand.

On the subject of increased availability of capital and credit to Dial, the Board noted that Dial was able to obtain funds in national markets and that its rate of return on equity significantly exceeded the industry average. The Board summarized its arguments in this case as follows:

> While the proposed acquisition would clearly lead to some public benefits, there is little indication that the above or other claimed benefits are not likely to be obtained in the absence of the acquisition.

Moreover, the Board's order noted the following in regard to the issue of concentration of resources:

> . . . the issue of concentration in credit-granting resources . . . was within the intent of Congress in enacting the 1970 Amendments. While the matter is not free of doubt and is one on which reasonable differences of judgment may occur, the Board has concluded that, at a minimum, this factor weighs against approval of the application.

Shortly after the denial, Chase filed a new application to acquire Dial Financial Corporation. In its order (74 *FRB* 874) denying this second application, the Board noted that the principal differences between the two applications was that Chase was offering to lower to 30 percent the maximum annual percentage rate charged by Dial for new loans. The Board observed, however, that such a rate reduction affects less than 7 percent of Dial's receivables and would benefit only certain customers of Dial. The Board concluded that although it regards rate reductions as constituting a public benefit it ". . . finds that the aggregate public benefits that may reasonably be expected from the affiliation . . . do not outweigh the possible adverse effects. . . ."

A significant adverse factor in certain nonbank cases has been the existence in employment contracts of covenants that, in effect, refrain certain executives from competing with the applicant for a stated period of time after employment has been terminated.[39] The Board expressed its views regarding such covenants most completely in its order denying Citizens and Southern National Bank's acquisition of Ison Financial Corporation (74 *FRB* 136). The acquisition agreement contained two employment agreements that included covenants ". . . to the effect that the respective executives would refrain from competing with Applicants for an additional seven years after termination of employment." The Board order noted:

> The record does not suggest that the executives who would enter into such covenants would be privy to information that could be characterized as trade or business secrets of Company; nor does it suggest that the duration of such covenants would be necessary to protect the good will of Company.

Moreover, the Board noted that the courts had refused to enforce such covenants entered into by employees of consumer finance companies when the length of time specified in the covenant is greater than necessary to protect the "legitimate" interests of the employer or, if in the absence of the management employee's knowledge of trade secrets, he does not deal with customers. Since the Board found that the covenants in this case were not necessary to protect a legitimate interest of the applicant either as employer or purchaser, the Board concluded that:

> . . . such covenants are in restraint of trade and therefore constitute a significant adverse factor in consideration of the applications.

In addition to the above-mentioned adverse factor, the Board order indicated that in one market where the two firms competed, the applicant is already dominant in a concentrated market and, therefore, the ". . . elimination of any independent competitive alternative is viewed as a significant adverse effect." The public benefits offered by applicant and recognized by the Board as likely to result from affiliation were (1) remove management limitations on the size of loans and increase them up to the legal limits permitted by state law; (2) provide mobile home, small appliance, and second mortgage loans in addition to the types of loans the company makes; and (3) increase the availability of financial resources and thereby lendable funds. Nevertheless the Board concluded that ". . . these expected benefits do not outweigh the adverse effects upon competition. . . ."

Concluding Comments–Public Benefits in Nonbank Cases

We conclude that the willingness of the Federal Reserve Board to attach significance to the public benefits cited by an applicant was heavily dependent on the severity, or lack thereof, of any adverse competitive, financial, or managerial factors the Board perceived to be inherent in the application. Where the Board determined a proposal involved no seriously adverse competitive or other effects, it generally accepted the applicant's claim of probable benfits to the public and approved the acquisition. We believe a particularly significant finding is, however, that the Board appears never to have found, so far as we can tell, proposed public benefits sufficient to outweigh the adverse effects of a substantial reduction of competition, unsound financial developments, or undue concentration of resources. Our review of the Board's orders in nonbank cases suggests that approval requires increasingly substantial evidence or demonstration from applicants that their proposals would yield net public benefits, particularly in cases where adverse effects were present.

Many public benefits, such as infusions of equity capital, access to lower cost funds, or economies of scale, are indirect and yield gains to the public only if the consumer realizes lower prices or better services. Governors Robertson and Brimmer have noted that ". . . it is the public's interest–not Applicant's–that is paramount."[40] In a majority of cases in which the Board has approved applications where the public benefits are indirect, it has done so on the grounds that direct gains to the public would eventually be forthcoming.[41]

Only recently has research been done to examine the claims of applicants against the ultimate outcome. In one such study Rhoades examined the claim that the acquisition of mortgage bankers by bank holding companies leads to an increased flow of funds to the mortgage market.[42] As discussed earlier in this chapter, this claim rests on the expectation that the mortgage company will have access to the greater financial resources of the holding company or to funds generated for the mortgage company in the commercial paper market. Rhoades' results indicate that mortgage banker affiliates of bank holding companies do not grow faster than independent mortgage firms and that affiliation does not affect the mortgage lending activities of affiliated banks. Rhoades concluded that his results ". . . suggest that bank-holding company acquisitions of mortgage bankers do not increase the flow of funds to the mortgage market and, therefore, should not generally be viewed as a public benefit."[43]

Perhaps significantly, the Federal Reserve Board's treatment of public benefits suggests only a narrow range within which the types of benefits discussed in this chapter would sway the Board when important adverse factors are present in a proposal. Our study indicates many instances where benefits that might ordinarily be considered significant were viewed as insufficient to outweigh substantially adverse effects. For example, the denial of First Commercial Bank's acquisition of Schenectady Discount Corporation (73 *FRB* 118) was based primarily on adverse competitive factors. However, one benefit (i.e., that the injection of capital would enhance loan expansion) claimed by the applicant—and recognized in other applications[44]—was discounted by the Board in this case. The Board noted that this benefit ". . . could be achieved by the investment by Applicant of capital funds into its own mobile sales finance operations."

7 Impact of Holding Company Affiliation on Bank Soundness: Theory

This chapter addresses a twofold question that has important theoretical and policy implications for the stable functioning of our financial system: Are there any characteristics inherent in the bank holding company form of organization that may augment the risk exposure of affiliated banks? And, if so, in what ways are these sources of increased risk manifested? We first examine from a purely theoretical point of view the nature of risk in banking and offer hypotheses of why holding company subsidiary banks may assume greater risk than independently owned banks. Second, consideration is given to factors that, on the other hand, may lead to risk reduction in bank holding companies. In Chapter 8, empirical models that test the impact of holding company affiliation on the risk exposure of subsidiary banks are developed and the results are discussed.

The Nature of Risk in Banking

The riskiness of banking organizations receives considerable attention in the operation and regulation of our banking system; yet the characteristics risk should entail often are not clearly defined. For the purposes of this study, ***risk*** refers to the uncertainty regarding a banking organization's ability to remain a going concern and to operate in such a way that any losses incurred will not lessen the bank's ability either to meet deposit withdrawals or to obtain new funds. This definition encompasses a spectrum of possible situations, including loss of public confidence as well as the more extreme case of bank failure.

Increased levels of risk in banks can be costly to society, especially in two respects. First, the soundness and safety of commercial banks has a major impact on the functioning of our financial system and in turn on the health of our economy. Traditionally, the safety of the deposits of individuals and of other entities held by a bank is the first area considered dependent on the degree of risk of a bank. Banks have a fiduciary responsibility in managing their operations such that the deposits of individual customers are not adversely affected. But certainly the more important aspect of this problem is the impact of one or more bank failures (especially large banks) on the stability and smooth functioning of the domestic and international financial systems.

A second and related consideration regarding the cost of increased levels of bank risk is the burden placed on the bank regulatory agencies. These groups perceive a somewhat vaguely defined schedule of costs associated with greater levels of risk. As a bank declines through increasingly deteriorating financial positions, the agencies involved become exposed to larger costs of examination, the expense of seeking potential merger partners, risky extensions of credit, and so forth. In extremis, a bank failure would result in a decline in the insurance fund of the Federal Deposit Insurance Corporation (FDIC). This latter result, if the failed bank were of substantial size, may in itself lead to a loss of public confidence in the ability of regulators to maintain a viable banking system in a crisis state of the world—a problem that regulators are acutely aware of and, perhaps, consider their primary function to prevent.

The bank holding company form of organization has become an important—if not dominant—factor in our contemporary commercial banking system. As noted in earlier chapters, bank holding company growth in terms of bank assets has been extraordinary since the mid-1960s, and after passage of the 1970 Amendments to the Bank Holding Company Act of 1956, these traditionally commercial banking organizations have moved aggressively into nonbanking fields, as well. This rapid expansion of holding companies and the reasons behind it lead one to suspect that banks operating within a holding company organization are affected by a somewhat different array of variables affecting risk from that faced by independently owned banks. Managerial and financing policies are frequently different and the legal environment in which bank holding companies operate is considerably different. The purpose of this chapter and the next is, therefore, to develop a theory of why bank affiliation with a bank holding company may lead to change in the risk exposure for that bank and to provide some evidence in the support of a hypothesis of greater postaffiliation risk.

Assumptions of Bank Holding Company Behavior

The theory of bank holding company behavior expressed below relies primarily on three assumptions. First, banks and bank holding companies are profit maximizers—that is, the objective of the banking firm is to maximize the value of the equity interests in the enterprise. Second, bank holding companies operate in an uncertain world. Third, the individual subsidiaries comprising a bank holding company form a "dependent system" in which the operations and soundness of the bank and nonbank subsidiaries are inextricably intertwined. The first two assumptions are clear and generally accepted; the third, however, requires further explanation.

The *assumption of dependence* implies that a bank holding company is organized as an unified (though multidivisional) profit-making entity, whereby each subsidiary acts in concert with all other subsidiaries to maximize a single objective function for the entire organization. This assumption may entail, among other things, the shifting of resources among subsidiaries to units where there is a comparative advantage and, if necessary, one subsidiary (or parent company) coming to the aid of a financially troubled sister affiliate. Moreover, groups outside the bank holding company system (especially, the capital market and bank regulators) perceive the risk of an affiliated bank to be a function both of variables endogenous to the bank's operations and of the risk exposure of the entire holding company.

The inverse of the dependence assumption—that is, independence—would imply that the level of risk of a bank is solely a function of variables peculiar to its banking operations and financial environment exclusive of any influence from the activities of affiliated holding company firms. This assumption implies a number of behavioral constraints regarding groups within and outside the organization. First, a bank subsidiary would not engage in various activities for the primary purpose of benefiting a sister subsidiary if it would, at the same time, increase its own risk exposure.[a] Second, the holding company would not rely on the resources of a bank subsidiary to aid the growth or financial condition of nonbank subsidiaries. Third, and most important, the capital market in performing its traditional policing function through the price mechanism would evaluate the riskiness of the entire holding company as if the resources of the bank subsidiaries are unapproachable. If, for example, the holding company or nonbank subsidiary should default on its debt obligations, investors would not approach the assets of the banks. Further, the market, in assessing holding company vulnerability, would not expect bank regulators to be concerned with any entity's safety but that of the bank.[b]

Another way of expressing the difference between the dependence assumption and its inverse is that under dependence, risks arising anywhere in the holding company system are borne by all affiliates, whereas under independence risks originating from a particular subsidiary are borne solely by that subsidiary. This is not to say, however, that in the case of dependence risks may not be borne by one subsidiary (or subset of subsidiaries) to a greater extent than others. Indeed, it is argued below that the bank subsidiaries may bear an inordinate amount of the risk of the conglomerate institution because of their regulated nature (i.e., there is incentive for the nonbank elements of the holding company to depend on bank regulators for support and also to shift risk to the subsidiary banks).

---

[a]For example, a bank would not purchase a block of excessively risky loans from an affiliate in order to provide needed liquidity to that firm.

[b]The assumption of dependence, on the other hand, does not necessarily imply that regulators will intervene to prevent an entire holding company's financial failure. It does mean, however, that regulators will expend resources in evaluating the overall operations of a bank holding company and attempt to correct conditions that would be adverse to the safety of affiliated banks. This regulatory intervention may result in the de facto insurance of holding company operations and is examined in more detail below.

Evidence appears to favor the dependence assumption as the most valid view of bank holding company behavior. First, however, let us consider the case for independent behavior. Bank holding company behavior under the assumption of independence is frequently expressed in the quasi-legal concept of separability of subsidiary firms—a perception of behavior that often has been subscribed to by bank regulators and some of the framers of the 1970 holding company legislation. The separability theory states that a bank's exposure to the, perhaps, riskier specialized activities of affiliated firms can be attenuated if each bank holding company subsidiary is maintained as a separate corporate entity. Under this umbrella of legal separateness, therefore, the practice considered preferable, for reasons of bank safety, is to place desired expansion into nonbank activities in separate subsidiaries of a holding company organization rather than incorporate such activities in direct subsidiaries or divisions of the bank.

However, as a practical matter, this theory of separability may not offer protection to banking affiliates of a bank holding company. The public may identify holding company banks with their nonbanking affiliates, and problems in the latter may lead the public to withdraw funds from the bank affiliates, even if reasonably sound as in the case of the former Beverly Hills National Bank. One possibility is, moreover, that the courts may decide to "pierce the corporate veil," although to our knowledge this has not occurred in the banking industry, or, as is more likely, a large bank holding company may decide not to let an important subsidiary fail, but to use its resources to rescue the troubled affiliate. There have been a number of instances of bank holding companies coming to the assistance of their subsidiaries to maintain their credit worthiness in the capital markets,[c] and thus we should not place much reliance on the "built-in" separability of the holding framework to insulate the banking affiliates.

The theorem of separability, moreover, is contrary to the position taken by the Board of Governors of the Federal Reserve System in its orders describing decisions on acquisition proposals submitted by bank holding companies. The Board views the holding company as a vehicle for providing financial strength to affiliated commercial banks—that is, an important function of the bank holding company is to provide financial and managerial assistance in times of individual bank weakness. The Board has often reiterated the position that ". . . one of the primary purposes of a holding company is to serve as a source of financial strength for its subsidiary banks."[1] Therefore, under this view, any activities undertaken by or under the direction of the parent company that weaken the financial soundness of the bank holding company inherently weaken the bank affiliates.

---

[c]For example, there are the well publicized cases of Hamilton Bancshares coming to the aid of its mortgage banking subsidiary in 1975 and 1st Wisconsin Corporation helping to prevent the bankruptcy of its advised REIT in 1974 and 1975.

The holding company serving as a source of strength to its banks is only one aspect of the dependence assumption. Dependence also means that the holding company relies on the bank subsidiaries as a source of financial (and other) strength, and the market, in turn, considers both directions of effect as valid interpretations of holding company behavior. A factor that should be recognized is that holding company dependence on the bank subsidiaries frequently may be beneficial to the welfare of those banks. In particular, loss of confidence in subsidiary banks might arise if a nonbank affiliate fails, and therefore the sister bank affiliates' providing sufficient financial aid to prevent the failure of that firm may be desirable.

The most convincing arguments in favor of dependence arise when we consider the various motivating forces behind the development of the holding company form of organization in banking. A frequently espoused stimulus has been employing the multibank holding company as a vehicle to elude restrictive state branching laws.[2] Although this reason for holding company formations considers only the commercial banking aspects of the bank holding company, such a stimulus implies that banks often were acquired by the holding company to extend the operations of the lead bank into new geographical markets. As some studies of holding company policy have shown, a majority of holding companies have centralized bank operating policies within their organizations.[3] In this case, it follows that the managements of parent holding companies and their affiliated banks recognize and desire a great degree of dependency within their systems.

Another well-known stimulus to holding company formation is the means to seek more profitable investment outlets for increasingly expensive sources of bank funds. This argument emphasizes the nonbanking aspect of the bank holding company. At the height of the one-bank holding company movement prior to the passage of the 1970 Amendments to the Bank Holding Company Act of 1956, the holding company was proclaimed to be a "revolutionary" vehicle that would lead banks out of their profit squeeze by affording investments in more profitable nonbanking areas.[4] Such a point of view certainly indicates that bank managers considered dependency a matter of implicit, if not formally explicit, policy.

We draw the conclusion, therefore, that bank holding company behavior may be best represented by the assumption of dependency. Internally, the validity of this assumption depends to a great extent on the degree of centralization or coordination of policies practiced by management and/or owners. Externally, however, dependency is the most likely rule of thumb since regulators and investors (and, to some degree, depositors in subsidiary banks) logically appear to evaluate risk in terms of the whole conglomerate firm. Although dependent behavior seems the overwhelming choice, each of the hypotheses concerning holding company risk presented below is analyzed both when dependence is assumed and when this assumption is relaxed.

Hypotheses of Increased Risk Exposure in Affiliated Banks

A theory explaining why affiliation with a bank holding company may lead to greater risk for a bank requires a formal set of hypotheses that offer reasons for such a change in riskiness vis-à-vis banks that remain independent. We might consider these hypotheses as general in nature because we are concerned here with an overall shift in the risk class of a bank as opposed, say, to a change to a more risky type of specific operating policy. From each general hypothesis can be traced operational implications as to how increased risk is manifested in the subsidiary banks and in the other parts of the holding company. The identification of each of these specific risk mechanisms and their possible measurement are discussed in subsequent sections.

Hypothesis I: Exploitation of Public Support

This hypothesis may be stated as follows:

A bank holding company can exploit the goal of the public to preserve the viability of the commercial banking system by implementing risky operating policies and undertaking risky nonbank ventures that have high expected returns, with the expectation that bank regulators will protect from financial failure any entity within the holding company in order to prevent loss of confidence in the subsidiary banks.

A corollary is that the capital market recognizes this "transference" of protection from the banks to other parts of the firm and allows the holding company to operate with a lower cost of capital than that commensurate with its risk class.

The hypothesis follows directly from the assumption of dependent behavior within the bank holding company and the likely recognition of such behavior by those outside the firm. A bank holding company's nonbank subsidiaries and parent company typically are identified with their bank affiliates and vice versa. Further, a reasonable expectation is that a holding company bank that is failing ultimately will be rescued by bank regulators in order to avoid loss of confidence in the banking system and/or a decrease in the insurance fund of the FDIC. (Of course, in all likelihood the probability of such intervention is dependent on the size of the subsidiary banks.[5]) This "insurance" against failure is part of a bank's "identity," and our hypothesis suggests that this characteristic is transferred to the nonbanking entities of the bank holding company to the extent that nonbank subsidiaries can trade on the presumed regulatory protection of the subsidiary banks.

An important implication of Hypothesis I is that the private capital market will not charge an appropriate risk premium on the debt and equity obligations of the bank holding company. While the authors believe that the market is efficient, there will always exist a potential downward bias in the market's pricing mechanism in the case of regulated industries such as banking.[d] Therefore, the traditional risk policing function of the market is not effective and bank holding companies are permitted to undertake additional risks without bearing the appropriate incremental cost.

Integral to the hypothesis is the dependence assumption: Holding company owners and management implicitly believe, rightly or wrongly, that the regulatory authorities will bail out the organization or one of its nonbank subsidiaries if bankruptcy is impending because they perceive that the regulators view the bank and nonbank firms as forming a dependent system, as defined above. However, if the assumption of dependence does not hold, this hypothesis would be incorrect. Obviously, there would be no transference of bank regulatory support to the holding company, and the market would evaluate the riskiness of the organization without the influence of regulatory protection. Regulators, management, and investors would believe that the holding company and/or one of its nonbank subsidiaries could fail without any adverse effect on the banking affiliates.

Hypothesis II: Widening of Investment Opportunities

A second hypothesis indicating greater risk exposure for a bank affiliated with a holding company may be more explicitly stated as follows:

The bank holding company serves as a vehicle for satisfying the greater risk preferences of owners (and/or managers) whose risk-seeking activities under conventional, independent commercial banking are constrained by statute or regulation through expanding the investment opportunity set to include riskier nonbanking activities, thereby increasing the risk exposure of the entire entity.

A corollary to this theory is that the holding company form of organization attracts decisionmakers whose utility functions exhibit less risk aversion than those of decisionmakers in independent banks.

---

[d]Evidence is given below indicating that bank holding company subsidiaries are more highly leveraged than comparable independent firms. At the same time, the capital market does not appear to be charging bank holding companies and their affiliates higher risk premiums on their increased level of debt obligations. (See, for example, R. Pettway, "Market Tests of Capital Adequacy of Large Commercial Banks," *The Journal of Finance* 31 (June 1976): 865-76, and D. Humphrey and S. Talley, "Market Regulation of Bank Leverage," Board of Governors of the Federal Reserve System, Washington, D.C., December 1975.) While this finding is consistent with the proposition that bank holding companies are more diversified and therefore less risky than independent firms, the more credible interpretation is that the market is not effectively regulating bank holding company leverage. The market may be relying on the willingness of bank holding companies to use their banking resources to prevent a default on any obligations of the parent or its affiliates.

Under this hypothesis, the bank holding company itself may be viewed by its decisionmakers as a vehicle for assuming greater risk than would be normally available through solely commercial banking activities. The major means by which greater risk is assumed are involvements in nonbank industries that entail a higher degree of risk (for example, through traditionally riskier extensions of credit, less conservative borrowing practices, and so forth). Such involvements for banks are only allowed, to a significant degree, via holding companies, not as independent banks.

The increased exposure to risk for the bank affiliates arise from two areas. First, as owners or managers of independent banks, the decisionmakers' risk seeking is constrained by law or regulation. There is only a narrow range in conventional commercial banking in which greater risk taking is permitted, and this range does not satisfy the risk preferences of many owners and/or managers. However, via the bank holding company these groups can undertake riskier operating policies in permissible nonbank subsidiary firms that are not examined, for the most part, by the bank regulators. Under Hypothesis I, we might expect these nonbank firms, therefore, to be riskier than comparable independent firms since these nonbank firms will not have to pay a market price on their obligations fully commensurate with their risk class.

Second, implicit in this theory is the fact that some or all nonbank activities permitted bank holding companies involve greater risk—and, most likely a greater expected return[e]—than commercial banking. As one Federal Reserve Board Governor stated: "Presumably it is an acceptable assertion that banks on average are less risky enterprises than their nonbank affiliates."[6] Therefore, holding companies involved in nonbank activities that are riskier than banking are unavoidably riskier than organizations not so involved.

The dependence assumption is required for both of these factors to lead to greater risk for the holding company's subsidiary banks. Under the assumption of dependent behavior, risks from holding company involvement in nonbank industries are shared by the bank subsidiaries. To the extent independence exists, on the other hand, riskier nonbank activities do not affect the banks.

Essential to this theory, moreover, is the argument that holding companies are formed and operated primarily by owners and/or managers who have preference for risk greater than that of owners or managers of independent banks.[f]

---

[e]Actual rates of return on bank holding company investment in several important nonbank activities have been poor relative to the return on bank capital or the average return on capital of the respective nonbanking industries. (See S. Talley, "Bank Holding Company Performance in Consumer Finance and Mortgage Banking," *The Magazine of Bank Administration,* July 1976.) Nevertheless, *expected* return more likely is high over the long run, especially in light of the high premia holding companies often pay for bank and nonbank firms. (See, for example, T. Piper, *The Economics of Bank Acquisitions by Bank Holding Companies* [Boston: Federal Reserve Bank of Boston, 1971].)

[f]Former Federal Reserve Board Governor Holland would appear to agree with this proposition. He states that subsequent to holding company formation by the lead bank(s), ". . . typically . . . banks acquired by bank holding companies had prior records of relatively conservative management, and their post-acquisition reports are more likely than not to

Their utility functions are not similar, in other words. More abstractly, if we assume that (1) owners are risk averse and (2) the traditional variables—risk and expected return—are the arguments of the utility function, then our hypothesis states that the partial derivative of the holding company owners' function with respect to risk is less than that for the utility function of the independent bank owners (since risk aversion requires that the partial derivative be negative).

However, we should recognize that even relatively riskier firms such as leasing or factoring may be operated conservatively if acquired by strongly risk-averse investors. Therefore, crucial to our theory is the fact that the decision-makers of bank holding companies are less risk averse than those of independent banks, as may be evidenced by the selective policies holding company managers pursue that represent their greater risk preference.

Thus far this discussion indicates that we should look to the nonbanking aspects of a bank holding company's operations for increased risk. However, the corollary to Hypothesis II leads to the conclusion that greater risk taking may be exhibited at the bank level as well. To the extent holding company managers are less risk averse than the managers of independent banks, in all likelihood the holding company management will pursue riskier operating policies within the banks that they acquire in addition to the pursuit of such policies in the non-banking subsidiaries. We are essentially addressing subsidiary banks other than the lead bank of the holding company, since these lead banks typically are the originators of bank holding companies and, under our hypothesis, would be just as risky before holding company formation as after.[g] Moreover, we should note that this direct increase in risk at the bank level would occur regardless of the assumption made about intersubsidiary behavior (i.e., dependent or independent). Although, if the assumption of dependent behavior is indeed valid, the degree of risk may be even greater since problems within nonbank firms might

show [for example] increased loans to their communities. Judged narrowly, such a change has to be scored as an increase in the potential instability of the particular subsidiary banks" (R. Holland, "Bank Holding Companies and Financial Stability," paper presented at the Conference of the Western Economic Association, San Diego, June 26, 1975, p. 7). Furthermore, Talley, in commenting on the statistical significance of portfolio shifts in banks acquired by holding companies, noted that ". . . the most plausible explanation is that managers of holding companies have a different risk-profit tradeoff. When the holding company acquires a bank, management of the holding company encourages the bank to sell some of its low-yield, low-risk governments and make loans or buy municipals with the proceeds" (S. Talley, "Developments in the Bank Holding Company Movement," *Proceedings of a Conference on Bank Structure and Competition* [Chicago: Federal Reserve Bank of Chicago, 1975], p. 5).

[g]See, for example, R. Lawrence, *The Performance of Bank Holding Companies* (Washington, D.C.: Board of Governors of the Federal Reserve System, 1976), for a discussion of post-acquisition shifts of banks to riskier operating policies. As Boczar notes, the assumption should be made that ". . . the changes in the operating policies of subsidiary banks reflect the existing practices of the lead banks which acquired them" (G. Boczar, "The Determinants of Multibank Holding Company Formations," *Southern Economic Journal* 42 [July 1975]: 123). Moreover, Mingo offers proof that banks, prior to joining a bank holding company, are no more risky than comparable independent banks. (See J. Mingo, "Capital Management and Profitability of Prospective Holding Company Banks," *Journal of Financial and Quantitative Analysis* 10 [June 1975]: 191-203.)

be transferred to the banks or the traditionally greater risk exposure of these nonbank firms might be identified and shared with the banks.

The hypothesis that greater risk taking occurs directly (i.e., without reliance on the dependence assumption) at the bank subsidiary level is reinforced by other considerations. First, there are two cost factors associated with affiliation that might lead a holding company bank to pursue higher risk-higher return activities in order to recoup its higher level of cost. Generally, holding companies pay very high premiums to acquire existing banks. Thus a holding company may believe in the necessity of operating an acquired bank in a relatively risky way—one that leads to higher profits—to justify the purchase cost.[h] Moreover, the extra layer of management introduced to a bank acquired by a holding company entails higher costs of operation as the parent company imposes management and service fees, higher dividend withdrawals, and so forth. Such new costs may induce the banks to initiate offsetting policies, such as relying less on expensive equity sources of funds, leveraging more, allocating less funds to nonearning (more liquid) assets, or seeking riskier outlets for investable funds that yield higher returns.

A second consideration is suggested by Mingo and involves the effect of the degree of separation between owners and managers in a firm on risk taking by management.[7] The greater separation between manager and owner in the holding company organization may lead to greater risk taking in affiliated banks relative to that in independent banks. The managers of an independent bank may not behave in the traditional wealth maximization fashion; rather they may be "earnings satisficers" who desire to maximize other arguments or minimize risk and thus treat earnings as a constraint imposed by shareholders. As Mingo notes, the likelihood of violating that constraint becomes less if the bank is managed in a conservative manner. On the other hand, the managers of an affiliated bank are immediately responsible only to the management of the parent company, not to the owners of the holding company, and we would expect the

[h]Implicit throughout the text of this chapter is the assumption that a firm can gain higher returns through various types of riskier operating policies. This assumption is probably valid, but it does not necessarily mean that the value of the firm will be higher. Market value is the present discounted value of the earnings stream and thus may be affected by changes in the flow of earnings, the discount rate, or the time horizon. If riskier policies lead to an increased earnings flow but also a rise in the discount factor (due to the market's perception of increased firm risk), the firm's value may increase, decline, or remain unchanged depending on the degree of the relative change in the two factors. Therefore, if we assume that the bank holding company follows the traditional theory of firm behavior, we must conclude that greater risk will not be undertaken unless the holding company expects the net effect on firm value of increased earnings to be greater than any changes in the discount rate. The firm's expectations may underestimate the market's perception of the potential increase in risk and, in turn, undertake greater risk. Or, alternatively, the market may not be able to evaluate fully the extent of risk taking at the subsidiary level because of inadequate disclosure of information. In any case, there is apparently sufficient leeway for a rational firm to undertake greater risks for the purpose of accruing higher profits.

parent simply to direct the subsidiary to maximize its earnings flows to the parent. The traditional wealth maximization process may lead the firm to assume greater risks in order to gain higher returns.

A final point that is tangential to the main issue is worth considering. This study assumes throughout all hypotheses that the objective of the firm is to maximize the value of the equity interests in the enterprise. Wealth maximization of owners constitutes a valid objective function for both an independent bank (except in the case of Mingo's theory) and a bank holding company. Under our present hypothesis the difference in risk between the two types of firms results primarily from the fact that the owners of the bank holding company do not have an opportunity set of production activities limited solely to commercial banking, as do independent banks' owners. The former are more interested in the profitability (i.e., present value of expected earnings flow) of the entire conglomerate—not just that of banks—and are motivated to seek out those investment alternatives with the highest expected return. Combining these potentially high-return firms with commercial banks in a holding company framework and optimizing the value of the entire organization necessarily involves the allocation of resources to the most profitable subsidiaries (to the extent permitted by law). The resulting risk-return tradeoff for each subsidiary may be such that the bank's position is relatively more risky than that of comparable independent banks.[i] There is evidence that indicates that holding companies tend to shift risk from nonbank affiliates and from the parent corporation to bank affiliates.[j] Since bank subsidiaries are the major component in most bank holding company systems, owners have an incentive to rely on them to support the system and its expansion. For example, this support might take the form of siphoning bank resources to foster aggressive growth in a specific nonbank area or of excessively risky credit extention policies that might favor an affiliate.

However, it is important to note that such intra-holding company shifts in risk, though they may imply greater risk exposure for a subsidiary bank at a point in time, do not necessarily indicate a net loss in the public's welfare at that moment nor for the long run. Within the context of our theory, as long as

---

[i]This argument is closely akin to viewing the bank holding company as a portfolio of assets or production activities, and the risk-return tradeoff can be approached in the framework of financial portfolio theory. Such an analysis is described below in a discussion of the effects of holding company diversification.

[j]See, for example, R. Nader and J. Brown, "Disclosure and Bank Soundness: Non-Bank Activities of Bank Holding Companies," Public Interest Research Group, Washington, D.C., June 30, 1976, and J. Guttentag, "Reflections on Bank Regulatory Structure and Large Bank Failures," *Proceedings of a Conference on Bank Structure and Competition* (Chicago: Federal Reserve Bank of Chicago, 1975), pp. 136–49. Guttentag states that a ". . . major supervisory dilemma may thus be emerging wherein the supervisory authorities will be forced either to create new and complex safeguards to prevent risk shifting to banks, or alternatively to control the risk exposure of the holding company as a total entity." The latter of these two alternatives is supported by the theory of this study.

the holding company is strengthened by these intrafirm policies to the point that it can support its banks in the event problems arise from such acts, there is no additional burden placed on the public. Only when the riskiness of the entire holding company is increased at the same time the upward shift in the risk of the bank occurs is there a loss in welfare.

Hypothesis III: Divergent Degrees of Ownership and Control

This hypothesis may be stated as follows:

In a case where a bank holding company owns a controlling interest in a bank but one that is a lesser percentage ownership than in its nonbank subsidiaries,[k] *the firm may find draining the resources of the bank to support the other subsidiaries advantageous, or it might require the bank to undertake excessive risks in order to benefit another affiliate.*

In such a situation, a holding company would only engage in such abusive practices if the value to be gained by the other subsidiaries was greater than its potential loss in equity investment in the bank. Under these circumstances the primary losers would be the minority stockholders, the depositors, and the general public.

The dependence assumption is not crucial to this theory. Dependence certainly implies greater risk under these outlined conditions because of the fact that the holding company is considered a total profit-making entity, with resources allocated to areas of the highest expected return (although the assumption of dependence does not necessarily imply that a bank subsidiary be intentionally weakened in order for a gain to arise elsewhere in the system). Nevertheless, independence of the bank subsidiaries does not preclude a policy whereby the controlling owners—though only partial owners—of a holding company desire to "milk" the resources of a subsidiary bank to further the other interests of the firm. At best, of course, such actions are contrary to the public good and bank regulatory desires and, in many cases, would be considered illegal and fraudulent, depending on the type and extent of actions.

Operational Implications of the Hypotheses

Hypotheses I through III have operational implications for increased risk to banks that are members of bank holding companies. Some of these risk mani-

---

[k]For example, it owns 51 percent of the outstanding shares of a bank but 100 percent of the shares of its other subsidiaries. (In many cases even less than a majority of shares would be sufficient to effect a controlling position.)

festations can be directly measured; some cannot, primarily because of lack of data. Moreover, the manifestations of one hypothesis may coincide with those expected to result from another hypothesis; they are not necessarily mutually exclusive. This section describes the types of risk that each of the three hypotheses implies.

Implications of Hypothesis I

The ability of the bank holding company to exploit public support through its identification with its subsidiary banks and thereby gain some degree of regulatory protection in the eyes of the capital market may lead the organization to institute financial policies at the nonbank level that normally would be considered excessively risky. In particular, the holding company might permit (or require) an inadequate level of capital, excessive debt leveraging, an illiquid financial position, and/or abnormally risky credit extension practices. All of these practices might take place without incurring a proportionate increase in the costs of raising funds in the market place.

This hypothesis, on the other hand, does not lead one to expect greater risk taking by the large bank subsidiaries of holding companies, since large independent banks have the same protection characteristics as holding company–affiliated banks. Differences in risk between the two groups of large banks would be just as probable before acquisition of the affiliated banks as after. However, we would expect small- to medium-sized bank subsidiaries to pursue riskier policies than comparable independent institutions if we impute much lower probabilities of intervention by bank regulators to save a bank from failure to smaller-sized, independent banks. Smaller holding company banks, in other words, benefit from their association with larger bank affiliates (if there are such sized firms in the holding company) in the same way that nonbank affiliates do—that is, bank regulators will not permit their failure for fear of an adverse impact on the large bank subsidiaries.

Implications of Hypothesis II

The widening of the investment opportunity set to include nonbank activities riskier than commercial banking and the attendant attraction to the firm of decisionmakers who exhibit less aversion to risk would imply greater risk taking in both the nonbank and bank subsidiaries of the holding company. At the nonbank subsidiary level, we might expect to find the same type of risky operating policies (i.e., less capital protection, more leveraging, less liquidity, and/or greater credit risk taking) anticipated to occur under the manifestations of Hypothesis I. The holding company might operate through these policies to such an extent that its nonbank subsidiaries are riskier than comparable independent firms. As explained above, the owners of a holding company, who are constrained as owners of an independent bank in their risk taking, may implement riskier policies in the nonbank subsidiaries. Under the dependence assumption, the risk of the affiliated banks would be increased if these nonbank firms operated in a riskier fashion than commercial banks (as well as independent firms in their respective industries).

The hypothesis also leads us to expect similar policies of greater risk assumption at the bank subsidiary level. As argued above, this behavior would most likely occur within the banks acquired after formation of the holding company by the lead bank. Nevertheless, there are factors that could imply greater risk taking at the lead banks, as well, after holding company formation. For example, the bank considered to be the pilot institution might originally have been acquired by a nonbanking organization that exhibits a greater preference for risk than that found in commercial banking. Also, and probably of more general application, a lead bank may change its attitude toward risk taking once it has become exposed to riskier operating policies—policies that may yield higher returns—in its nonbank affiliates. Thus, comparing the various risk-taking policies for all holding company-affiliated banks with those of independently owned banks is worthwhile.

Hypothesis II also implies that a bank holding company might institute operating policies that would intentionally weaken a bank subsidiary but would result in attendant benefits for other (nonbanking) parts of the conglomerate firm (or vice versa). Such policies are referred to as "abusive intracorporate practices" and would include any of the following: (1) excessive withdrawal fees, (2) bank and parent company guarantees of the obligations of nonbank subsidiaries, (3) risky extensions of credit to nonbank affiliates, (4) tie-in arrangements among subsidiaries, (5) participations of risky loans with affiliated firms, (6) shifts of risky assets from the holding company to its banks, (7) shifts of profitable bank assets to nonbank subsidiaries, and (8) policies that weaken the earning ability of the bank subsidiaries to gain tax advantages for the consolidated holding company.

Practices such as the above are difficult to identify and border on the untestable. The Federal Reserve System is provided data on most of these practices by the bank holding companies,[8] and it keeps close surveillance to detect situations that may be detrimental to subsidiary banks. The problem, however, is deciding when such transactions become abusive. Moreover, that practices of this type have occurred with any frequency in the industry seems unlikely. At present, nonbanking activities account for only a small portion of total bank holding company operations, on average, across the nation, and thus the magnitude of any such transaction, if it did occur, probably would not be significant. No attempt is made in this study to detect the existence of such policies.[9]

Implications of Hypothesis III

The withdrawal of resources from a subsidiary bank by a controlling stockholder in order to benefit that owner's welfare relative to another's is a practice that would be difficult to identify. Like the practice of fraudulent activities, it does not lend itself to statistical testing. Such transactions to withdraw or utilize bank resources to benefit another holding company subsidiary involves the "abusive intra-corporate practices" noted above. In addition to these practices, the controlling interest might find the bank's being highly leveraged desirable. In this case the owner's potential loss in equity value would be less than in a highly capitalized bank.

As indicated above, that practices of this type would occur with any frequency seems unlikely. In the majority of cases, holding company ownership interest in subsidiary banks approaches 100 percent, and banking is the main concern of the enterprise. Therefore, while the possibility exists that some of the practices mentioned here are realizable, they are unlikely to be currently prevalent in the industry.

Consideration of Factors Leading to Reduced Risk in Holding Companies

Before testing these manifestations of risk arising from the holding company form of organization in banking, digressing for a moment may be worthwhile in order to consider several factors unique to the holding company form of organization that may in fact lead to a reduction of risk for subsidiary banks. Such factors must be taken into account in any tests for increased risk to determine the net effect. Two factors are presented and appraised here.

Bank Holding Company Diversification

A potentially important benefit arising from bank holding company expansion into nonbanking activities is that such diversification will lead to reduced riskiness of the total banking organization via a stabilization of the flow of earnings. The diversification occurs both across product lines and across geographic areas. Moreover, to the extent that gains from diversification in bank holding companies are significant, they reduce firm risk and can be exploited by the holding company to undertake greater risk in other areas of operations (e.g., increased leverage).

Basically, the argument is that the variance of earnings of a conglomerate combination of firms is less than the weighted average of the variances of the earnings of the individual firms, if the earnings of the respective firms do not have a high positive correlation. Such gains increase the ability of the holding company to serve as a source of strength to its banks, particularly in times of financial weakness.

Moreover, as shown by Levy and Sarnat and Lewellen, increased stability of earnings strengthens the debt capacity of the combined firm, thereby reinforcing the parent company's ability to aid its banks.[10] These authors also demonstrated that conglomerate diversification reduces the probability of bankruptcy. Levy and Sarnat and Lewellen argue that the risk of bankruptcy is greater for two firms operating separately than if merged into one firm. Essentially, an investor in each firm cannot diversify away this risk of either one, but in a merged company (or holding company) one division (or subsidiary) can rescue another. In the case of bank holding companies, subsidiary banks are explicitly limited in the extent to which they can salvage an affiliate. However, through the various intra-corporate practices mentioned above, the holding company can subvert these limitations and use the banks to aid another subsidiary.

Heggestad has found that some of the presently permissible nonbanking activities (e.g., leasing, real estate financing, insurance agents, investment advisory companies) do exhibit returns that are negatively correlated with those in banking. However, Heggestad also found that some of the major industries into which bank holding companies have entered most extensively have earnings trends highly correlated (positively) with earnings trends in banking.[11] Jessee, moreover, has shown that there is no statistical difference between the variability of earnings of consolidated holding companies and that of independent banks. He also found that product diversification does not relate significantly to holding companies' earnings variability.[12]

In sum, the gains from bank holding company diversification do not seem to be significant. This finding is not surprising since the portion of holding company resources invested in nonbank activities currently is quite small relative to that in banking and because such activities are constrained by law to be "closely related to banking." Indeed, it is not likely that significant gains relating to risk exposure from product diversification will be forthcoming as long as the latter constraint is maintained.

Synergism and Other Financial Benefits

Factors that strengthen financially a bank holding company reduce the risk exposure of the subsidiary banks. This theme underlies much of the discussion of this chapter and rests on the argument that there is a public benefit associated with the holding company's ability to support its banks in periods of financial stress. Synergism encompasses these financial factors.

A synergistic merger or combination of firms is one in which more profits are generated than could be achieved by each of the firms operating separately. Or, more abstractly, synergism is cooperative action such that the total effect is greater than the sum of the separate effects taken independently. Synergy may arise from producing complementary services, achieving economies of scale, reducing the cost of capital, or spreading skilled management over a wide scope of operation.

All of these sources of synergy have been claimed by holding companies in their applications to acquire bank and nonbank firms, and in many cases they most likely exist to some degree. There are limitations, however. For example, the prohibitions on tie-in arrangements limit the synergistic benefits from producing complementary products. Also, on the one hand there is the difficulty of arguing that synergism in management skills is a public benefit when, on the other hand, a holding company claims that its banks and specialized financial nonbank firms operate in different markets (to avoid anticompetitive criticism), not to mention the claim that the holding company is ill equipped managerially to enter a particular nonbank field de novo.

Regarding scale economies, clearly the sharing of computer, auditing, marketing, personnel, and other services should produce such efficiencies, but the scant evidence available (which is often conflicting) appears to indicate that the economies are modest at best. For example, Schweitzer found evidence that suggests economies arise from affiliation for banks with less than $25 million in deposits.[13] Dugger found that affiliated banks regardless of size experienced gains in operational efficiency but that such gains disappeared approximately two years after affiliation.[14] In studies of unit and branch banks versus holding company banks, Kalish and Gilbert concluded that holding company banks exhibited greater technical efficiency than branch banks at small-bank size levels but less efficiency at larger sizes. Regardless of size, they found that unit banks were more efficient than affiliated banks.[15] Along these same lines, Longbrake and Haslem in examining the production of a specific product—demand deposits —found that unit and branch independent banks with small-account size and lower number of accounts per office have lower costs per dollar of demand deposits than affiliated unit and branch banks.[16] When the average account balance and the number of accounts per office are high, the reverse is true. Finally, a study by Mullineaux concluded that affiliation results in no statistically significant change in the efficiency of unit banks, while affiliation of branch banks actually reduced efficiency, primarily due to the extra expense associated with an additional layer of administration.[17]

In sum, there appears to be little compelling evidence indicating significant scale economies attributable to the bank holding company. This evidence is not entirely conclusive, however, since no systematic investigations have been made into the efficiency experience of the combined bank holding company or into the experience of nonbanking firms acquired by bank holding companies.

Finally, reduction of the cost of capital through affiliation with a bank holding company would appear most probable only in the case of small-sized banks and nonbanking firms. Economies in raising funds enjoyed by the parent company can be passed down to these firms, and these subsidiaries can also rely on the name of and identification with the holding company and its banks in marketing their own debt. Risk reduction through diversification of assets also would reduce the cost of raising funds for all sized firms, but the validity of this argument is subject to doubt, as discussed above. Robert Johnson, in his study of the reasons for bank holding company acquisitions of finance companies, concludes that these synergistic benefits appear "negligible, if not illusory."[18]

A more general criticism can be leveled at the concept of synergism and its role in the theory of the conglomerate firm. Mueller notes that synergistic effects are traditionally espoused as one of the significant motivating factors in mergers among firms whose objective function is the maximization of profits. However, he concludes that such effects are implausible when affiliation is between unrelated or loosely related enterprises, especially when a firm continues to operate following acquisition as an autonomous unit.[19] This criticism points to a basic conflict (or tradeoff) between risk reduction through diversification and synergistic benefits. For the former to be effective, firms acquired must be dissimilar in the sense that they have negatively correlated earnings flows. But dissimilarity in this sense makes benefits from synergism less probable.

8 Tests of the Impact of Affiliation on the Soundness of Bank Subsidiaries

The hypotheses presented in the preceding chapter are not directly testable; however, their operational implications are. As the theory developed above suggests, we would expect subsidiaries of bank holding companies to pursue riskier operating policies, ceteris paribus, than comparable independent firms. To determine whether bank affiliates of holding companies have actually assumed greater risk, we compared the capital levels, extent of debt leveraging, liquidity positions, and loan loss experience of holding company banks with those of independent banks by means of cross-section regression analysis.[1] Below are discussed the empirical models used in each of these four areas, the data and sample design, and the regression results.

The Models

Bank Capital Levels

As the earlier discussion of possible implications of Hypotheses I through III has shown, we might expect that banks affiliated with bank holding companies would maintain less capital than would independent banks. Holding companies that have openly maintained such a policy have often cited as a rationale certain unique advantages of this form of organization—that is, synergism, product and geographic diversification, and the capacity of the holding company to support its banks. Whether or not these claimed advantages exist, they may have induced many bank holding companies to maintain a level of capital in each subsidiary bank that is less than that of a comparable independent bank.

Furthermore, liberal dividend payouts by subsidiary banks and extensive debt leveraging can also result in relatively lower capital coverage in affiliated banks.[2] Although withdrawal of accumulated bank earnings through dividend payouts to the parent company is constrained by law, such regulations would still permit excessive payouts to the point where the bank's capital position could be weakened. Greater reliance on nondeposit debt to support asset growth retards the growth of equity capital necessary to protect (and, perhaps, attract) depositors. Bank holding companies and their subsidiaries have been heavy users of debt sources of funds in recent years. To the extent subsidiary banks have sought debt as a substitute for equity capital—perhaps by relying on the borrowing power of their holding companies to market this debt—their capital protection has been eroded vis-à-vis independent banks.

Early studies of the effect of bank affiliation with holding companies on various aspects of performance and balance sheet composition showed no significant change in the capital positions of banks after acquisition.[3] Lawrence states the conventional argument regarding capital tested in these studies:

> Among the most frequent arguments that are given in support of bank holding companies is the argument that holding companies are able to provide more capital to their subsidiary banks than independent banks are able to provide for themselves. The main thrust of this argument centers upon the greater ease of selling securities of holding companies . . . [whereas] independent banks must raise their capital in their local area. . . .[4]

Not only did these studies find no significant statistical change in capital ratios between pre- and postacquisition periods, but several authors detected negative trends—that is, a decline in capital positions of holding company banks. Such evidence is in line with the expectation of this study; however, little weight can be given to these past results because of methodological errors. In these previous studies the primary approach to examining the effect of holding company affiliation on banks was the simple before-and-after, paired sample analysis whereby differences between pre- and postacquisition characteristics of holding company banks and differences between holding company and nonholding company banks are examined by univariate differences-between-means hypothesis testing (t test). Such simple statistical tests fall far short of satisfying necessary ceteris paribus assumptions (i.e., the problem is multivariate in nature) and have been subject to much criticism.[a] The approaches used in the present study to test specifically for differences in risk between holding company and independent banks are designed to avoid the problems of the earlier investigations.

A more recent study by Johnson and Meinster of performance measures of banks acquired by holding companies did employ multivariate statistical techniques and found new (but conflicting) evidence of significant differences existing between affiliated banks and independent banks.[5] A stepwise multiple discriminant analysis procedure did not select the ratio of capital-to-deposits to be among the first five most significant characteristic variables of the discriminant function. However, in testing the impact of differences in postacquisition time intervals on the ability (as measured by an F test) of a prederived discriminant function to distinguish among holding company and independent banks, mixed results were obtained as regards capital adequacy. In some cases (two years after

[a] See, for example, R. Johnson and D. Meinster, "An Analysis of Bank Holding Company Acquisitions: Some Methodological Issues," *Journal of Bank Research* 4 (Spring 1973): 58–61. Furthermore, these studies have all examined data prior to 1971 and have thus omitted the recent period of rapid expansion by holding companies into nonbank areas. Such expansion may have had a major impact on bank performance and safety.

acquisition), the ratio—capital-deposits—of affiliated banks rose relative to that of nonacquired banks. Opposite results were obtained for an interval of four years after acquisition. Two other recent studies using multiple regression analysis found evidence that affiliation with bank holding companies leads to a statistically significant reduction in the capital-to-assets ratios of those banks.[6]

The Regression Model. A model is formulated to test the hypothesis that banks affiliated with holding companies have significantly less capital coverage (measured by capital-to-assets ratios, defined below, as the dependent variable) than do independent banks. Specifying the model properly in order to detect accurately the effect of holding company affiliation, ceteris paribus, is of course important. The study borrows from the previous literature on bank capital adequacy and investment.

Previous studies have found certain factors to be the main determinants of capital levels in banking.[7] As Peltzman and more recently Mingo have noted, capital serves as both an input into the production process and a means to attract deposit (and nondeposit) funds through its "protective" characteristics. In the present model, we abstract from the former function of capital, but as in Peltzman's model, the percentage growth in deposits is included as an independent variable in order to explain capital levels apart from direct responses to deposit changes.[b] The direction in which growth in deposits affects the capital-to-assets ratio of a bank a priori is not clear. Peltzman argues that a historically high rate of deposit growth should be associated with high rates of capital investment in the current period, since a bank needs capital to attract deposits.[8] However, capital investment is also a "lumpy" process (abstracting from the reinvestment of current period earnings), and thus the level of capital may lag behind deposit growth for several periods until the bank issues new equity, at which time the level of capital in relation to assets and deposits "jumps ahead." In the former case where capital investment lags deposit growth, the capital-to-assets ratio would be negatively related to deposit growth; in the latter case where capital stock is newly issued, there would be a positive relationship.

Also, regarding capital's response to deposit changes Peltzman noted that there is a tradeoff between FDIC deposit insurance and capital levels. The higher is the percentage of insured deposits, the less need there is for bank capital as

---

[b] As an input into the production process, capital should be responsive to its expected rate of return; the higher the expected return, the greater the capital levels. However, the Peltzman and Mingo models dealt with the investment (or flow) of capital in banks whereas the present model is intended to explain the *level* (or stock) of capital relative to assets. In this case, expected return is not appropriate. Moreover, the Peltzman model is a stock adjustment explanation of the supply of bank capital and represents the desired stock of capital as growing secularly with deposits. He posits that change in bank capital can be attributed to a discrepancy between the existing capital-to-deposits relationships and the long-run desired position—such an adjustment being represented by the one-period lagged capital-to-deposit ratio. Again, this variable is not appropriate to our model.

protection against failure. To capture the extent of insured deposits in a bank, the ratio of passbook savings deposits to total deposits is used.[c]

Another important determinant of bank capital levels is the return on assets, as measured by the ratio of net income to total assets (NI/TA). An expected positive relationship between capital levels and NI/TA is consonant with retained earnings being the primary source of increasing bank capital[9]—that is, the rate at which the firm can add to capital from internal sources depends on the level of current earnings.

In addition to the above factors that have been employed in previous research, this study's model explaining differences in the capital levels between holding company banks and independent banks must take account of four factors: size, benefits of holding company diversification, tradeoffs with other sources of risk, and holding company affiliation. This study uses data from banks of different sizes, and thus this influence must be held constant. Total assets represents this variable in our model and is expected to bear a negative relationship with capital-to-assets ratios.[10]

To the extent there are significant gains from product diversification in bank holding companies, these firms and their subsidiaries should be able to exploit such gains by undertaking greater risk in other areas of operation. Whatever benefits arise from bank holding company product diversification are approximated in their effect on bank capital adequacy by the ratio of nonbank assets of the holding company to total holding company assets (NBA).[d] We would expect NBA to be negatively related to a bank's capital position.

As mentioned earlier, tradeoffs can exist between various sources of risk such that an increase in one category of risk will be offset by decreases in one or more other categories. In the immediate context, for example, the effect of lower capital levels might be neutralized by less debt leverage, greater liquidity, and/or a conservative investment policy (i.e., low credit risks). These other measures of risk must be included in our model to isolate the sole effect of

---

[c]This ratio, of course, is only a crude proxy for the proportion of insured deposits. The ideal measure would include those demand accounts that are covered by insurance as well as all types of time deposit accounts so covered. However, the Consolidated Reports of Condition, which are a major source of data for this study (see detailed discussion below of data sources), do not break down the data in sufficient detail to construct such an ideal measure.

[d]Gorecki notes the use of this measure (variable D_3 in his study) to capture the effects of firm product diversification. (See P. Gorecki, "The Measurement of Enterprise Diversification," *The Review of Economics and Statistics* 56 (August 1974): pp. 399–401.) The variable, NBA, was constructed by summing the total assets of the nonbank subsidiaries, adding to this sum the total assets of the parent company net of its investments in subsidiaries, and dividing the total sum by holding company consolidated assets. We should note, moreover, that NBA is nonzero for most holding company banks and zero for independent banks. This type of construct is employed in all of the equations below. Normally, a singularity problem would arise because NBA and BHC would form a linear combination. However, NBA does have zero values for several of the holding company bank observations, and this eliminates the singularity problem.

holding company affiliation, apart from these potential tradeoffs. In this context, a negative sign would be expected on the coefficients of the other risk variables. On the other hand, these other risk variables may represent the desire of bank management to assume greater risk. In such a behavioral sense, a positive relationship would be expected between the dependent variable and the other measures of risk taking. Which course of action, if either, a bank will pursue cannot be determined a priori. Despite this inability to predict the direction of influence, in all the models in this study determining whether or not these variables have a systematic effect on bank capital levels (and the dependent variables of the other models) is important. The other risk measures are developed below and, for the present, will be represented by an ellipsis in the capital adequacy equation.

Finally, we hypothesize that affiliation with a bank holding company is a significant determinant of the level of bank capital—one that has a negative influence on capital. Since this factor is a qualitative one, the effect of affiliation is captured by the use of a dummy (binary) variable in the equation to be estimated, and we expect the sign on the coefficient of BHC to be negative.

The model is specified in the following functional form:

$$EC/RA = f_1\ [TA, NI/TA, \%GD, \%INS, NBA, BHC, \ldots], \tag{8.1}$$

where

EC/RA = equity capital to risk assets, a measure of bank capital adequacy (defined below),
TA = total assets of bank,
NI/TA = net income to total assets,
%GD = percentage change in deposits over preceding five-year period,
%INS = the proportion of deposits insured by the FDIC, as approximated by passbook savings deposits divided by total deposits,
NBA = total nonbank assets of the holding company as a percent of total holding company assets (zero value for independent banks),
BHC = 1 if bank is affiliated with a holding company and 0 if bank is independent,

and the ellipsis represents other risk variables that are developed in the following sections. All variables are as of the current period *t* unless otherwise noted.

Equation (8.1) is estimated for two different measures of capital adequacy: equity capital to risk assets (EC/RA)[e] and gross capital funds to risk assets

[e]Risk assets equal total assets minus the sum of cash and balances due from banks and U.S. Treasury securities. Also note the EC/RA is used as the dependent variable in equation (8.1) and GCF/RA is the dependent variable for equation (8.2), which is not presented in the text at this point. All equations are summarized in Table 8-1 below.

(GCF/RA), with the latter measure being used as the dependent variable of equation (8.2). These two dependent variables are simple, frequently used measures of the capital coverage of a bank's risk assets portfolio. The distinction between the two is that gross capital funds include long-term debt as well as equity capital (i.e., capital stock, surplus, undivided profits, and loan loss reserves); as discussed below, subordinated long-term debt offers a limited form of capital coverage upon liquidation.

Debt Leveraging Policies

The debt-to-equity relationship in the capital structure of a bank is an important factor in evaluating its liquidity and solvency. The issuance of debt creates additional fixed charges (i.e., interest payments) and, perhaps, sinking fund payments, neither of which can be deferred and both of which affect liquidity. Debt can also affect solvency in that the form of bank capital determines a bank's capacity to absorb losses without going into receivership.[f] A major function of bank capital is to act as a buffer against losses incurred in a bank's daily operations. Only equity funds except paid-in capital (i.e., surplus, undivided profits, and valuation reserves) can fulfill this function. Debt capital, on the other hand, adds nothing to this buffer role of capital, narrowly defined.

Nevertheless, debt can fulfill some of the functions of capital, but with important limitations. In order to absorb losses, debt must be unconditionally subordinated to depositors' claims. But even if this condition is satisfied, debt can only be used to redeem deposits in the case of liquidation, not to absorb losses from current operations in order to avoid liquidation. Also, debt is inferior to equity in its relative lack of permanency; debt funds must be serviced and eventually repaid at maturity.

To what extent debt should be employed to fulfill the functions of capital in bank holding companies, or what the appropriate level of capital is in holding companies and in their bank subsidiaries, is not clear. We do not pretend to have an answer to such questions. Nevertheless, we may conclude that, ceteris paribus, increasing proportions of debt in the capital structure of a bank raise the level of riskiness of that bank. This is due, first, to the burden of servicing and repaying the debt on the liquidity of the institution and, second, to the greater

---

[f]Broadly speaking, debt leveraging is embodied in the concept of "financial risk." As Van Horne notes, financial risk encompasses the risk of insolvency and the variability of earnings available to common stockholders. He states: "As the firm continues to lever itself the probability of cash insolvency . . . increases" as does the "relative dispersion of income available to common stockholders" (J. Van Horne, *Financial Management and Policy* [Englewood Cliffs, N.J.: Prentice-Hall, 1968], p. 145).

expected earnings variability associated with greater leverage and the attendant increase in the probability of insolvency.[g]

Whether affiliation with a holding company has led banks to become more highly leveraged than comparable independent banks is an empirical question. The implications of Hypotheses II and III lead us to suspect that holding company banks employ greater proportions of debt relative to equity. Furthermore, a comparison of individual firm data for holding company banks and independent banks supports such a suspicion. For example, Jacobs et. al. found that for their sample of bank holding companies the average debt leverage of these consolidated firms increased in each year between 1970 and 1974.[11] However, such univariate comparisons may be misleading, and factors other than bank holding company affiliation may have been the significant cause of changes in relative leverage positions of the two groups of banks. The statistical model below is designed to isolate the effect of affiliation from these other influences.

The Regression Model. We are interested in the extent to which banks affiliated with holding companies have leveraged their capital structure in comparison with a group of independent banks. As in the case of the model examining bank capital adequacy, the debt leverage model developed here borrows from the previous literature on debt-equity mix policies in the firm.

Weston and Brigham offer a descriptive model of the determinants of debt-equity relationships in the firm. They state that six factors account for the composition of a firm's financial structure: (1) growth rate of future sales, (2) stability of future sales and earnings, (3) competitive structure of the industry, (4) the maturity structure of assets, (5) management attitudes toward risk, and (6) attitudes toward the firm.[12]

The growth of total assets of a bank is analogous to the first factor. As the authors note, this future growth is a measure of the extent to which the firm's earnings are likely to be magnified by leverage. Moreover, rapidly growing firms typically have needs for funds to finance asset expansion that exceed the retained earnings available from high profit rates.[13] Thus, growth in bank assets should bear a positive relationship to the debt-equity position of the bank.

[g]No mention has yet been made regarding the maturity of debt. We may take issue as to whether a distinction should be made between long-term and short-term debt in leverage policies. Generally speaking, the cost of capital and capital structure literature has focused on long-term debt. Apart from the obvious difference in relative permanency (which may be ignored, in part, if we assume a steady "rolling over" policy), the major distinction between short-term and long-term debt as regards financial risk is the effect of the term structure of interest rates on the cost of such types of debt. Otherwise both categories of debt have a similar impact on the financial risk of the firm. The emphasis in the following discussion of bank leveraging will be on long-term debt, though in most cases the analysis can be applied to all maturities of debt, and our tests will include a separate model explaining the use of all maturities of (nondeposit) debt in addition to a model explaining long-term debt leverage.

The coefficient of variation of earnings is used to reflect sales and earnings stability. The greater the stability in earnings flow, the greater the bank's ability to incur the fixed charges of debt with less risk than when its earnings are subject to periodic declines. The coefficient of variation of earnings should, therefore, be negatively related to the ratio of debt to equity.

Since this study examines a cross-section of one industry and the sample firms involved operate in an area that is fairly homogeneous regarding entry, factor three can be ignored.[h] The fourth factor—asset maturity structure—is captured by a measure of the risk of illiquidity, which is described below. Weston and Brigham hypothesize that firms with long-lived fixed assets use long-term debt more extensively, whereas firms whose assets are of a short-term nature rely more on short-term debt. In this study the model explaining the relation of long-term debt to equity should show a positive relationship between debt-to-equity and the measure reflecting an illiquid asset position (i.e., longer-term assets). However, in the second model where short-term debt is added to long-term debt, the relationship between the dependent variable (i.e., total debt to capital) and the variable reflecting asset maturity is ambiguous.

The effect of management attitudes toward risk is captured by the various risk measures of capital adequacy, liquidity, and credit risk described above and in subsequent portions of this chapter. Except for capital adequacy,[i] the undescribed measures are denoted by an ellipsis as before. The expected relationships between these various measures and the leverage ratio of the present model is unclear, as explained above. To the extent inclusion of these independent variables allows us to account for tradeoffs with other forms of risk taking, they should bear an inverse relation with the dependent variable (i.e., greater capital levels, more liquidity, and/or less credit risk may offset higher debt leveraging). However, to the extent each risk measure reflects the overall risk-taking attitudes

---

[h]Nevertheless, in many cases the impact of the degree of competition in local banking markets on bank risk taking may be important. Several studies (e.g., J. Mingo, "Managerial Motives, Market Structure, and the Performance of Holding Company Banks," *Economic Inquiry* 4 (September 1976): pp. 411–24, and A. Frass, *The Performance of Individual Bank Holding Companies* [Washington, D.C.: Board of Governors of the Federal Reserve System, 1975]) have taken account of deposit concentration in models explaining differences in behavior among independent banks and holding company banks. But in order to account for the effects of competition on firm behavior properly, banking markets must be defined very specifically. The complexity of this task and the unavailability of data to satisfy the criteria of market definition make the inclusion of competition variables beyond the scope of the present study.

[i]We should note that there is oftentimes in banking firms an inverse relationship between the ratio of capital to risk assets and the ratio of debt to gross capital funds (the dependent variable of the debt leverage model)—that is, banks which have low EC/RA ratios will frequently have high ratios of long-term debt to gross capital as a result of regulatory pressure on bank capital adequacy (i.e., regulators will allow debt to substitute for equity to some extent). Theoretically, different risks result from inadequate capital levels and increased leverage; however, empirically the accounting tradeoff may dominate the relationship between the two variables in both models (equations [8.1] and [8.3]).

of management, a higher debt-equity position might be associated with greater proclivity for risk as measured by these other variables.

Finally, the sixth factor of the Weston and Brigham model—lender attitudes—is represented by a measure of debt service ability: the pretax profit margin (ratio of profits before taxes and extraordinary items to gross operating income). This measure has been determined by Fichthorn to be the most representative indicator of a bank's debt capacity.[14] A measure of debt service ability is, of course, only a proxy for lenders' attitudes, but to the extent financial analysts view this measure as a crucial factor in a bank's ability to market debt, it captures their attitudes toward a particular bank. We would expect, therefore, that a high profit margin would be associated with a benevolent attitude of lenders toward the bank and thus a higher level of debt-to-equity permitted by these lenders.

In addition to the six factors noted in the Weston–Brigham model, there are three other determinants that must be accounted for. As in the previous model, size and diversification into nonbanking fields must be included. Size is measured by total assets of the bank. Benefits from diversification are represented by the ratio of nonbank assets of the holding company to consolidated assets of the holding company (NBA). To the extent these benefits allow the firm to increase its leverage relative to an independent bank lacking such benefits, there should be a positive relationship between NBA and the debt–equity ratio.

The final argument of the function explaining bank leveraging is bank holding company affiliation. As explained previously, the hypothesized relationship (i.e., positive) between the dependent variable and the binary variable, BHC, representing holding company affiliation status, is tested using the intercept shift term defined above.

The model explaining the ratio of long-term debt to gross capital funds in banks is therefore specified in the following functional form:

$$\text{LTD/GCF} = f_3\ [\%\text{GTA}, \text{CV(NI)}, \text{NIBT/GI}, \text{TA}, \text{NBA}, \text{BHC}, \text{EC/RA}, \ldots\ ], \quad (8.3)$$

where

LTD/GCF = the ratio of long-term debt to long-term debt plus equity capital for the bank,
%GTA = percentage change in total assets over preceding five-year period,
CV(NI) = coefficient of variation of net income (i.e., standard deviation of net income divided by its mean) for a five-year period,
NIBT/GI = net income before taxes and securities gains and losses divided by gross income,
TA = total assets of bank,

NBA = total nonbank assets of the holding company as a percent of total holding company assets (zero value for independent banks),

BHC = 1 if bank is affiliated with holding company and 0 if bank is independent,

EC/RA = equity capital to risk assets,

and the ellipsis represents other risk variables that are defined below.

The same independent variables are hypothesized to explain a bank's total debt-to-equity position. This yields equation (8.4) below:

$$\text{TotD/GCF} = f_4 \; [\%\text{GTA}, \text{CV(NI)}, \text{NIBT/GI}, \text{TA}, \text{NBA}, \text{BHC}, \text{EC/RA}, \ldots], \qquad (8.4)$$

where TotD/GCF = the ratio of all maturity nondeposit debt to gross capital funds and the other terms are defined immediately above.

Liquidity Risks

The management of the liquidity position of a bank involves essentially two aspects of bank operations: managing the maturity structure of assets and the use of short-term borrowings to provide liquid funds, often referred to as liability management. Both types of operations and their impact on bank liquidity have been examined extensively elsewhere in the literature.[15] This section only briefly touches upon the theory of these liquidity factors.

The implications of liquidity asset management are fairly straightforward. The longer the average maturity of a bank's asset portfolio, the greater risk there is that funds may not be available to meet exigent cash requirements—such as those resulting from deposit withdrawals, fixed charges on debt obligations, and increased credit demands. Moreover, the necessary liquidation of assets that are of a long-term nature may result in significant losses if their sale occurs during unfavorable market conditions. By holding an adequate amount of liquid assets, most banks will be able to avoid sizable capital losses resulting from the forced sale of depreciated bonds and other investments.

Liability management has become in recent years a much publicized approach to providing bank liquidity and, in many cases, to financing asset expansion of banks and bank holding companies. Proponents of this approach maintain that depending only on liquid assets to meet probable liquidity needs is not necessary. Rather, as these needs arise, astute management of short-term obligations (e.g., negotiable certificates of deposit, purchased federal funds, Eurodollars, and loans from the Federal Reserve Bank discount window) can satisfy them. But as was witnessed during the 1970s, such use of short-term, often volatile sources of funds has resulted in negative profit margins and increased risk for many banks. Problems in the use of short-term debt by bank holding companies arise along various lines including: (1) short-term debt financing of long-term assets, (2) overextension of short-term debt, and (3) reliance on volatile sources of short-term debt that will disappear at the hint of internal trouble.

The financing by holding companies and their banks of expansion into long-term assets through short-term borrowings raises the possibility of liquidity problems if these sources of funds dry up and new sources are not available. Liquidating long-term assets in order to repay maturing short-term obligations may be difficult and costly, and, in turn, this difficulty may be exacerbated if the organization's financial problems become known and depositors make large withdrawals from the bank subsidiaries. Parent holding companies, in particular, have unique problems if liquidating assets becomes necessary in order to repay debt obligations, since most parent companies do not own significant tangible assets, aside from investments in subsidiaries, that can be liquidated for such purposes.[16]

As in the case of long-term debt, excessive use of short-term sources of debt funds taxes the solvency of the holding company or its banks through the increased level of fixed interest charges that must be borne. All other things the same, the probability that the firm will be unable to meet these fixed charges increases also. In addition, as the level of debt increases, so does the relative dispersion of net earnings after interest charges.[17]

Finally, reliances on volatile types of short-term debt to finance holding company or subsidiary operations may increase the risk of illiquidity because such sources have exhibited cyclical trends of unavailability. For example, during a period of monetary restraint, loan demands generally are rising but liability sources tend to become scarce and expensive, and their lack of availability may precipitate a liquidity crunch.

All of these problems can occur at either the parent company level or the bank or nonbank subsidiary level. For the moment, we are concerned primarily with the influence that a bank holding company exercises upon the management of asset maturity and the use of volatile, short-term funds by its subsidiary banks. Holding companies or their banks have been a major factor in the commercial paper and Eurodollar markets in recent years, not to mention their activity in negotiable CDs and federal funds. A model is developed below to test for differences in liquidity positions among holding company banks and independent banks.

The Regression Model. To capture the liquidity position of a bank, a composite dependent variable is constructed that reflects both the maturity composition of assets and the use of liability management. First, maturity composition is represented by the ratio of short-term assets to total sources of funds (STA/TSF), where short-term assets are defined as cash assets plus U.S. Treasury securities.

The denominator, TSF, is of course equal to total assets. Second, the extent of reliance on liability management to provide liquidity may be represented by the ratio of interest sensitive funds to total sources of funds (ISF/TSF), where the numerator is those sources of short-term funds that are volatile in nature (defined in greater detail below).

Combining these two measures of liquidity policy can be shown to yield the following composite variable: the ratio of interest sensitive funds to short-term assets (ISF/STA). This ratio is simply the ISF/TSF ratio weighted by the reciprocal of the STA/TSF ratio, or

$$ISF/STA = ISF/TSF \times (STA/TSF)^{-1}$$

We can see that the greater the value of ISF/STA, the greater the risk of illiquidity. We obtain this result because the larger the value of ISF and/or the lower the value of STA—both of which imply greater risk—the greater the value of the ratio of the two. Also, the greater is the relative percentage change of ISF to that of STA, the more risk that is implied, and this would also be represented by an increase in the ratio, ISF/STA. ISF/STA is the dependent variable of our model explaining liquidity differences between the two groups of banks.

Various models of bank liquidity preferences have been constructed by other authors who have devoted most of their analyses to the determinants of the demand for liquid assets. Hodgman developed a model in which the primary determinants are net changes in deposits and net changes in loans.[18] Morrison approached the problem somewhat differently: A bank's desired cash position is a function of (1) a penalty cost of borrowing to meet cash deficiencies (Federal Reserve Bank discount rate), (2) an opportunity cost of holding cash instead of other earning assets (represented by yields on securities of various maturities), (2) unexpected ("transitory") changes in deposits, and (4) an adjustment of actual to desired cash positions. Morrison specifically excluded bank size as a determinant.[19]

The model developed in the present study to explain ISF/STA makes use of the above models. To represent deposit changes, the coefficient of variation of total deposits is used. A greater degree of variability in deposit levels over previous periods is expected to be related to a more liquid position of a bank (i.e., there should be a negative relationship between the two variables CV(TD) and ISF/STA). In addition to volatility of deposits, the structure of deposits is considered in our model. The ratio of demand deposits to total deposits represents those sources of deposit funds that are potentially the most unstable. Thus, we would expect greater values of this variable to be inversely associated with the dependent variable.

As noted above, Hodgman posits that changes in loans and in investment in fixed assets as well as bank portfolio mix policies are important determinants of asset liquidity. These changes might be captured, for example, by the variable, percentage change in the ratio of long-term assets to total assets; the greater is this percentage growth, the less funds are being allocated to liquid assets. However, such a variable is, to a great degree, endogenous to a bank's decision making—that is, it reflects the managers' (or owners') decision to maintain certain types of operating policies that in turn affect bank liquidity. In our model, this type of decision making is what we hope to capture in the bank holding company affiliation variable, and therefore a specific endogenous variable representing changes in loans and investments is omitted from our function.

Contrary to Morrison's approach, our model must hold constant differences in size.[j] Total assets is used in this regard and is expected to be positively related to the dependent variable. Likewise, as in the above models, the ratio of nonbank assets to total holding company assets is used to account for the effects of bank holding company diversification, and various risk measures of other models are entered to account for specific risk tradeoffs (or risk-seeking behavior) as described above. The risk variables appear as an ellipsis, except for capital to asset and debt to equity ratios.

Finally, the bank holding company affiliation variable, BHC, is used to test for the hypothesized positive relationship between it and the dependent variable, ISF/STA. Using BHC in the intercept-dummy format yields the following functional relationship:

$$\text{ISF/STA} = f_5\ [\text{CV(TD), DD/TD, TA, NBA, BHC, EC/RA, LTD/GCF}, \ldots], \quad (8.5)$$

where

ISF/STA = interest sensitive funds to short-term assets is the sum of selected categories of purchased short-term funds such as net federal funds purchased and other liabilities for borrowed money including borrowings from the Federal Reserve Bank, divided by the sum of cash accounts and U.S. Treasury securities,[k]

---

[j]We should also note that our model differs from Morrison's in two other respects. The liquidity model of the present study is not an adjustment model and thus ignores bank liquidity as an adjustment response to actual versus desired liquidity positions. Moreover, the variables, penalty cost and alternative rates of return in Morrison's model, may be excluded from our function. They are necessary in a time-series study such as Morrison's; however, our model will be tested on cross-section data, and we may assume that all banks face the same penalty cost of cash deficiencies and the same alternative rates of return.

[k]The numerator of this ratio can be approximated because detailed breakdowns of these accounts are unavailable in the Consolidated Reports of Condition (F.R. 105). As a proxy for interest sensitive funds, the sum of the following variables is used: (1) net federal funds purchased (Item 23 minus Item 7) and (2) other liabilities for borrowed money (Item 24), which include borrowings from the Federal Reserve System, promissory notes, and term federal funds purchased. Eurodollars and negotiable CDs are not segregated into separate accounts, and for the majority of banks in our sample, these instruments are not used.

CV(TD) = the coefficient of variation of total deposits for the preceding five-year period,
DD/TD = total demand deposits divided by total deposits,
TA = total assets of bank,
NBA = total nonbank assets of the holding company as a percentage of total holding company assets (zero value for independent banks),
EC/RA = equity capital to risk assets,
LTD/GCF = long-term debt to gross capital funds,
BHC = 1 if bank is affiliated with a holding company and 0 if bank is independent,

and the ellipsis represents a risk variable presently undefined. All variables are as of the current period *t* unless otherwise noted.

Credit Risk Taking

A final category of measurable risk involves operating policies of the holding company that lead to unsound risk assumption in the extension of credit by the bank (and/or nonbank) subsidiaries. Such a practice may involve policy directives from the parent company for its banks to seek more profitable, but perhaps excessively risky, lending opportunities. This type of lending may represent a higher return on invested equity for the holding company but also may lead to an upward shift in the risk class of the bank.

Several of the previous studies of bank holding company performance cited above found that affiliated banks are more aggressive in their portfolio policies and invest more heavily in loans and obligations of municipalities and states. Lawrence, Talley, and Johnson and Meinster noted a significant shift out of U.S. governments into loans and municipals.[20] No significant differences existed in loan loss experience, however. Lawrence in his study of the operating policies of holding companies also found that relatively centralized companies (which made up the bulk of his sample) often do take an active role in the management of the total loan portfolio.[21] A model is developed below to test for differences between holding company and independent banks in their attitude toward credit risk taking.

The Regression Model. Generally speaking, when one analyzes attitudes toward risk assumption, ex ante factors are the actual consideration. When a bank faces a decision whether or not to extend credit, it forms (at least, implicitly) probability distributions of expected returns with expected dispersion properties. If the bank's general policy is one of greater risk assumption, its aggregate probability distribution for total period returns on the loan portfolio will have a relatively large variance and expected return compared to those of a bank with a more conservative (i.e., less risky) lending policy. Unfortunately, such ex ante measures of credit risk assumption attitudes are not available. In this study, therefore, an ex post representation of expected credit risk is used. The ratio of net loan losses (i.e., losses minus recoveries) to gross loans (NLL/GL) is assumed to approximate expected loan losses and is the dependent variable of our model.[1]

We hypothesize that the variable, NLL/GL, is a function of the following factors: (1) the maturity and purpose mix of the loan portfolio, (2) the state of the economy, (3) historical variability of earnings, (4) the size of the institution, (5) other measures of bank risk, and (6) holding company affiliation status. The first factor is represented by the ratio of commercial and industrial loans to gross loans (C&I/GL). This category of loans, while not necessarily the most risky of the loan portfolio, represents the greatest potential loss to the bank if a problem situation does arise (primarily because of the size of these credits). A positive relationship between C&I/GL and NLL/GL is expected. We should note that any measure of loan portfolio composition captures to some degree the bank's attitude toward risk, and this attitude is what we hope to detect through the holding company affiliation variable. However, we also want to be able to hold constant portfolio mix and to determine whether holding company banks are extending riskier credits based on the characteristics of their borrowers regardless of the classifications (i.e., industrial, consumer, mortgagor, broker-dealer, farmer) of those borrowers. C&I/GL serves another purpose as well. It accounts, in part, for the types of markets in which a bank operates and the economic influence of those markets on credit risk taking.

An additional variable is included in the model to capture more specifically the impact of the type of economic market in which a bank operates. This variable, SMSA, is a binary variable equal to one if a bank is headquartered in a standard metropolitan statistical area and zero if not. We hypothesize that an institution would be more risk seeking in a metropolitan area, due perhaps to greater competitive pressures, and thus experience greater credit losses. The influence of macroeconomic factors on the loan loss experience of a bank can be ignored since our study is cross-sectional and the assumption is that all banks in our sample face the same macroeconomic conditions at a point in time.

We assume that a bank reacts negatively to a historical trend of volatility in its earnings and would therefore increase its aversion to risk and make less risky

---

[1]The variable, NLL/GL, may not be an unbiased indicator of a bank's degree of credit risk taking. Banks differ in their policies as to when a credit should be restructured. Moreover, in many cases the level of loan losses depends upon when the bank was last examined by bank regulators and the policies of those examiners. There is no reason, however, to suspect banks to differ systematically on when loans are charged off.

extensions of credit. The coefficient of variation of net income, computed over the preceding five-year period, is used as a measure of this variability and is expected to be negatively related to NLL/GL.

Total assets, measuring size of the bank, enters the function but with a different interpretation than in the previous models. In the earlier models explaining other categories of risk, the assumption was that greater size was related to lesser degrees of risk by the public, investors, regulators, and so forth. In a model explaining attitudes toward assuming greater credit risk, however, the safety characteristic identified, by the public and others, with size may be used by the larger banks to justify undertaking greater risk in credit extension policies—that is, a large bank will "tradeoff" its size-safety feature by assuming greater willingness to make loans with larger dispersions of expected return. A similar argument is that the larger the bank, the greater is its customer diversification of risk and thus the more risk it can bear. Therefore, TA is expected to be positively related to net loan losses.

The three measures of other categories of risk defined above—equity capital to risk assets, long-term debt to capital, and interest sensitive funds to short-term assets—are again included in the model to hold constant possible tradeoffs in risk (or attitude toward risk taking). Moreover, the nonbank asset ratio, NBA, is employed to account for the effect of holding company diversification on credit risk taking. The final determinant is the bank holding company affiliation variable, which is hypothesized to be positively related to the dependent variable. The affiliation binary variable is used in the previously mentioned intercept-shift form and yields the following functional formulation:

$$NLL/GL = f_6\ [TA, C\&I/GL, SMSA, CV(NI), EC/RA, LTD/GCF, ISF/STA, NBA, BHC], \tag{8.6}$$

where

NLL/GL = ratio of net loan losses to gross loans,
TA = total assets of bank,
C&I/GL = ratio of commercial and industrial loans to gross loans,
SMSA = 1 if bank is headquartered in a standard metropolitan statistical area and 0 if not,
CV(NI) = coefficient of variation of net income,
EC/RA = equity capital to risk assets,
LTD/GCF = long-term debt to gross capital funds,
ISF/STA = interest sensitive funds to short-term assets,
NBA = total nonbank assets of the holding company as a percentage of total holding company assets (zero value for independent banks),
BHC = 1 if bank is affiliated with a holding company and 0 if bank is independent.

The above equations (8.1) through (8.6) represent functional models of four different types of risk that can be identified and measured in banks. These equations are summarized in Table 8-1. (Definitions of the variables are found in Table 8-2.)

The Data and Sample Design

The data for this study are drawn primarily from the following reports submitted to the Federal Reserve System: Consolidated Report of Condition (Form F.R. 105), Consolidated Report of Income (Form F.R. 107), and the Annual Report of the bank holding company to the Federal Reserve System (Form F.R. Y-6). The last document includes the S.E.C. 10-K Report.

The cross-section models developed above are estimated by ordinary least squares (OLS) regression for Federal Reserve System member banks operating in New York State. The tests are replicated on a sample of New Jersey member banks to analyze the consistency (or lack thereof) of the models' results. The equations are estimated for year-end 1973 and year-end 1974; the statistical findings are reported below.

The samples for each state were developed as follows: The universe of banks was restricted to those institutions operating in the Second Federal Reserve

Table 8-1
Summary of Equations

Specific Risk Mechanisms

Capital adequacy:

EC/RA = f_1 [NI/TA, %GD, %INS, TA, NBA, BHC, LTD/GCF, ISF/STA, NLL/GL] (8.1)

GCF/RA = f_2 [NI/TA, %GD, %INS, TA, NBA, BHC, LTD/GCF, ISF/STA, NLL/GL] (8.2)

Debt leveraging:

LTD/GCF = f_3 [%GTA, CV(NI), NIBT/GI, TA, NBA, BHC, EC/RA, ISF/STA, NLL/GL] (8.3)

TotD/GCF = f_4 [%GTA, CV(NI), NIBT/GI, TA, NBA, BHC, EC/RA, ISF/STA, NLL/GL] (8.4)

Liquidity risks:

ISF/STA = f_5 [CV(TD), DD/TD, TA, NBA, BHC, EC/RA, LTD/GCF, NLL/GL] (8.5)

Credit risks:

NLL/GL = f_6 [TA, C&I/GL, SMSA, CV(NI), EC/RA, LTD/GCF, ISF/STA, NBA, BHC] (8.6)

Note: All variables are bank observations for current period *t* unless otherwise noted.

District. The Second District encompasses all of New York, the twelve northern counties of New Jersey, and Fairfield County in Connecticut. Although the New Jersey universe only includes part of that state geographically, the Second District part of that state accounts for over 75 percent of the total number of banks and a greater percentage of total assets and deposits.[m] Furthermore, only member banks are examined so that we may hold constant differences in bank behavior due to differing influences of member and nonmember bank status.

After accounting for name changes, location changes and mergers, we found that 289 member banks in the Second District operated continuously during the period 1969-1974. This time frame was used so that various time trend variables (e.g., growth in assets and deposits) might be calculated for five-year periods. Of these 289 banks, 237 were used to construct the final samples for the two states.

The 52 deletions resulted from various causes. First, in each state several holding companies were formed after 1971, and these firms and their banks were omitted because we felt that at least two years of operations were required for representation as a "typical" bank holding company. For similar reasons, any holding company bank that joined a bank holding company after 1971 was excluded even though it may have existed over the entire period.[n] Second, any foreign-controlled bank holding company (or bank) was excluded because either precise data could not be obtained on the nonbank components (including the parent companies) of the holding company or the accounting practices were

---

[m]For a description of the banking structure, banking statutes and regulations, and the expansion of banks and bank holding companies in New York and New Jersey, the reader is referred to the following articles: K. Kidder, "Bank Expansion in New York State: The 1971 Statewide Branching Law," *Monthly Review* (Federal Reserve Bank of New York), 1971, pp. 266-74, and J. Kunreuther and K. Kidder, "Competition and the Changing Banking Structure in New Jersey," *Monthly Review* (Federal Reserve Bank of New York), August 1973, pp. 203-10. We should note that in both states bank holding companies have been permitting statewide expansion during the period under study. Moreover, statewide branching has been permitted in New Jersey since 1973 and in New York since the beginning of 1976. In the latter state, several of the large New York City bank holding companies have consolidated all or some of their banks to form statewide branching systems subsequent to the commencement of statewide branching in New York State.

[n]We should note that previous research has found that the length of postacquisition intervals does have a significant effect on differences in the performance of banks acquired by bank holding companies. Johnson and Meinster found that at least two years of lag following affiliation were required before significant differences in performance could be detected statistically. (See R. Johnson and D. Meinster, "The Performance of Bank Holding Company Acquisitions: A Multivariate Analysis," *The Journal of Business* 48 (April 1975): pp. 204-12.) Moreover, requiring this interval of affiliation avoids the problems associated with the behavior of new banks and newly affiliated banks. In this regard we might hypothesize that holding companies make newly acquired banks (whether de novo or going concerns) relatively more risky in the early years of affiliation—in order to gain a competitive foothold in their markets—but such risk-taking behavior declines as the banks mature. The development of such a theory and tests of its validity, however, are outside the scope of the present study.

Table 8-2
Definitions of Variables in Table 8-1 Equations

Variable	Definition
EC/RA	= equity capital to risk assets (i.e., total assets minus the sum of cash and balances due from banks and U.S. Treasury securities).
GCF/RA	= gross capital funds to risk assets.
LTD/GCF	= long-term debt to gross capital funds.
TotD/GCF	= sum of long-term debt and short-term (nondeposit) debt to gross capital funds.
ISF/STA	= interest sensitive funds to short-term assets.
NLL/GL	= net loan losses to gross loans.
%GD	= percentage change in deposits over preceding five-year period.
%INS	= passbook savings deposits divided by total deposits.
NI/TA	= net income to total assets.
NBA	= total nonbank assets of the holding company as a percent of total holding company assets (zero value for independent banks).
%GTA	= percentage change in total assets over preceding five-year period.
CV(NI)	= coefficient of variation of net income.
NIBT/GI	= net income before taxes and securities gains and losses divided by gross income.
TA	= total assets.
CV(TD)	= coefficient of variation of total deposits.
DD/TD	= total demand deposits divided by total deposits.
C&I/GL	= ratio of commercial and industrial loans to gross loans.
SMSA	= 1 if bank is headquartered in a standard metropolitan statistical area and 0 if not.
BHC	= 1 if bank is affiliated with a holding company and 0 if bank is independent.

inconsistent with the practices of domestic firms to the extent that serious distortions might arise. Third, also omitted was any bank affiliated with a bank holding company (as defined by the Bank Holding Company Act) not actively exercising control over the bank. Fourth, Connecticut banks were eliminated as was any holding company bank in New Jersey whose parent company is not registered in the Second District.

For the above reasons, 17 out of the 32 bank holding companies existing in New York at the end of 1974 and 10 out of the 17 bank holding companies in New Jersey for the same date are represented in this study's data samples. In New York these 17 firms control 50 banks that satisfy the requirements of our sample design and therefore are included in the New York sample consisting of 171 observations (i.e., 121 independent banks and 50 holding company banks). In New Jersey, the ten holding companies control 20 banks. The resulting New Jersey sample consists of these 20 plus 46 independent banks, for a total 66 observations.

Statistical Findings

Tables 8-3 to 8-9 present the results of statistical tests of the bank models. Results of univariate differences-between-means tests on the risk variables are given in Table 8-3, and the regression estimates of equations (8.1) through (8.6) are displayed in Tables 8-4 to 8-9, respectively. Each of the latter tables presents its respective equation estimated for three cross-section data samples: the New York sample of banks for 1974, the New Jersey sample for 1974, and

Table 8-3
Univariate Analysis of Bank Risk Variables (Observations as of Year-end 1974)

	t-values	
Variables	*New York*	*New Jersey*
Dependent variables of bank models:		
Equity capital/risk assets	–3.769[c]	–1.710[a]
Gross capital funds/risk assets	–3.895[c]	–1.271
Long-term debt/gross capital funds	0.018	2.262[b]
Total debt/gross capital funds	5.030[c]	3.219[c]
Interest sensitive funds/short-term assets	4.220[c]	3.064[c]
Net loan losses/gross loans	–0.408	0.601
Other risk-related variables:		
Size (total assets)	11.260[c]	3.252[c]
Coefficient of variation of net income	0.563	0.409
Growth (5-year) in total assets	0.032	1.064
Net income/total assets	–1.197	–0.800
Total debt plus deposits/gross capital funds	3.602[c]	1.054

Note: Difference-between-means tests (holding company versus independent banks) using two-tailed *t*-test. There are 171 observations for the New York sample and 66 observations for the New Jersey sample.

[a]Significant at the 90% level.

[b]Significant at the 95% level.

[c]Significant at the 99% level.

the combined sample of New York and New Jersey banks for 1974. (The results for the 1973 regressions are not tabulated here to conserve space but are discussed in the text.) In each of the six models estimated on the combined New York-New Jersey sample (n = 237 observations), there is included a dummy variable—equal to one for the New Jersey banks and zero for New York banks—to hold constant differences in bank behavior arising from differences between the banking environments of the two states.[o]

Capital Adequacy Models

Equations (8.1) and (8.2) represent the models designed to test for differences in capital levels between holding company and independent banks. Estimations of these two models—equation (8.1) explaining the ratio of equity capital to risk assets, EC/RA, and equation (8.2) explaining the ratio of equity capital plus long-term debt to risk assets, GCF/RA—are given in Tables 8-4 and 8-5, respectively. Table 8-3 shows that univariate t tests on both of these variables indicate a significant difference exists between affiliated banks and independent banks in New York. The t tests on the New Jersey sample show a significant difference only in terms of EC/RA.

The regression results yield far more information than such univariate tests. Looking first at equation (8.1), Table 8-4, we see the most striking result is that in 1974 (and 1973 as well) for New York banks and the combined sample of New York and New Jersey banks, the coefficient on the bank holding company affiliation variable, BHC, is significant and negative. This result confirms our hypothesis that affiliated banks have less capital coverage of their risk asset portfolios than independently owned banks. However, the estimation of this equation on the New Jersey sample did not yield a significant coefficient on BHC, thereby indicating that no statistically significant difference exists between the two groups in that state.

The estimation of equation (8.2) showed basically the same results as equation (8.1). When long-term debt is included in capital, the coefficient on BHC is negative and significant for the New York and the combined sample but not significant for the New Jersey sample. Such a result implies—at least for New York banks—that even when capital adequacy standards are weakened to include long-term debt as a part of capital, holding company banks maintain less capital coverage of risk assets. This result is indeed surprising when we consider that

[o]A warning regarding the combined sample estimates is necessary. Although the New Jersey dummy variable (NJDUM) detects whether or not a significant difference exists between the two samples for a particular dependent variable in terms of the intercept, the estimation of the models on the combined sample assumes that each component sample (i.e., New York banks and New Jersey banks) takes on the same average value for the slopes (or the coefficients) of respective independent variables. This assumption is not necessarily valid.

Table 8-4
Regression Estimates of Bank Model: EC/RA (1974)

Dependent Variable: EC/RA

Independent Variables	*Regression Coefficients of Equation (8.1)*		
	New York Sample	*New Jersey Sample*	*Combined Sample*
BHC	–0.0195 (–2.96)[c]	0.0008 (0.12)	–0.0140 (–2.82)[c]
NI/TA	2.8550 (5.16)[c]	1.2232 (2.10)[b]	2.4983 (5.92)[c]
%GD	–0.0226 (–3.24)[c]	–0.0117 (–2.27)[b]	–0.0166 (–3.47)[c]
%INS	0.0163 (0.78)	0.0582 (1.87)[a]	0.0290 (1.72)[a]
NBA	–0.0169 (–0.31)	–0.0105 (–0.35)	0.0005 (0.02)
LTD/GCF	–0.1526 (–3.28)[b]	–0.1263 (–2.87)[c]	–0.1570 (–4.69)[c]
ISF/STA	0.0169 (2.07)[b]	0.0013 (0.12)	0.0148 (2.20)[b]
NLL/GL	1.2377 (3.05)[c]	0.2993 (0.62)	1.1030 (3.50)[c]
Total Assets	–1.43 E-10 (–0.20)	–1.76 E-9 (–0.15)	–1.79 E-10 (–0.28)
NJDUM			–0.0077 (–1.76)[a]
Constant	0.1039 (8.86)[c]	0.0823 (5.35)[c]	0.0984 (11.00)[c]
Number of Observations	171	66	237
$\bar{R}^2$	.363	.334	.356
Standard Error of Estimate	.032	.020	.029
F	11.756	4.618	14.033

Note: The equations are in linear form; *t*-values are in parentheses; the overall *F* statistic is significant at the 99% level for all equations.

[a]Significant at 90% level.

[b]Significant at 95% level.

[c]Significant at 99% level.

Table 8-5
Regression Estimates of Bank Model: GCF/RA (1974)

Dependent Variable: GCF/RA

	Regression Coefficients of Equation (8.2)		
Independent Variables	*New York Sample*	*New Jersey Sample*	*Combined Sample*
BHC	–0.0195 (–2.95)[c]	0.0004 (0.06)	–0.0141 (–2.82)[c]
NI/TA	2.9093 (5.24)[c]	1.2288 (2.09)[b]	2.5511 (6.02)[c]
%GD	–0.0223 (–3.18)[c]	–0.0117 (–2.25)[b]	–0.0163 (–3.41)[c]
%INS	0.0164 (0.79)	0.0597 (1.90)[a]	0.0294 (1.73)[a]
NBA	–0.0158 (–0.29)	–0.0095 (–0.31)˙	0.0005 (0.02)
LTD/GCF	–0.0615 (–1.32)	–0.0246 (–0.55)	–0.0631 (–1.89)[a]
ISF/STA	0.0175 (2.12)[b]	0.0020 (0.18)	0.0152 (2.26)[b]
NLL/GL	1.2357 (3.03)[c]	0.3091 (0.63)	1.1082 (3.50)[c]
Total Assets	–1.31 E-10 (–0.18)	–3.17 E-9 (–0.27)	–1.65 E-10 (–0.25)
NJDUM			–0.0007 (–1.74)[a]
Constant	0.1035 (8.79)[c]	0.0820 (5.29)[c]	–0.0076 (–1.74)[a]
Number of Observations	171	66	237
$\overline{R}^2$	.311	.204	.294
Standard Error of Estimate	.032	.020	.029
F	9.536	2.850	10.849

Note: The equations are in linear form; *t*-values are in parentheses; the overall *F* statistic is significant at the 99% level for all equations.

[a]Significant at 90% level.

[b]Significant at 95% level.

[c]Significant at 99% level.

bank holding companies and their subsidiaries are reputed to be the most frequent users of debt sources of funds. (But, as is described below, this result may not be so surprising in light of the results obtained for equations [8.3] and [8.4].)

We should note that in both equations (8.1) and (8.2), when estimated on the combined sample, the variable NJDUM was significant in 1974 (and 1973). This result indicates that the two states' samples are statistically different in terms of dependent variables (i.e., New Jersey banks have lower capital-to-asset ratios than New York banks) and that individual equations on the separate state samples should be examined. Moreover, the holding company diversification variable, NBA, did not enter significantly in either of the two equations, for any year or any sample.

For each sample, the results are consistent between the two periods examined, thereby implying a general constancy of the estimates over time. Moreover, both equations are statistically significant across all samples, as measured by the overall F statistic. The estimates of both equations (8.1) and (8.2) for the New Jersey sample have lower explanatory power than the estimates on the New York sample, primarily because holding company affiliation does not account for as much of the variance of capital levels in New Jersey banks as in New York.

Also apparent is that in all estimates of the two models the independent variables do not explain more than 36 percent of the variation of the dependent variables. This result is not unexpected in cross-section regressions; nevertheless, it may be due to the obvious (but unavoidable in the present study) omission of certain factors. First, no attempt was made to hold constant either local market economic conditions or local market competitive conditions—both of which may partially explain a bank's level of risk taking.[p] Second, all of this study's models seek to explain managerial behavior—a factor that is, at best, a complex composite of many operational and exogenous elements (some of which are not measurable).

Debt Leveraging Models

Equations (8.3) and (8.4) are the models explaining differences in debt leveraging policies between the two groups of banks, and their regression estimates are

[p]As mentioned earlier, data are not available to account for these two factors for specific, well-defined banking markets. Mingo has attempted to account for banking market competition in a model explaining differences in capital to asset ratios among affiliated and independent banks. (See Mingo, "Managerial Motives.") His measure of competition was the Herfindahl index computed for counties and SMSAs in which his sample banks operate. Obviously, such boundaries do not generally define actual banking markets and certainly are not appropriate to banks that branch outside those boundaries (Mingo only examined unit banking states). In any case, Mingo's model was able to explain only 17 percent of the variance in the capital-to-asset ratio, even with his measure of competition included.

reported in Tables 8-6 and 8-7. Univariate tests on the dependent variables are shown in Table 8-3 and indicate that significant differences exist between affiliated and independent banks in New Jersey in terms of the two leverage measures (i.e., the ratio of long-term debt to gross capital funds, LTD/GCF, and the ratio of total short-term and long-term debt to gross capital funds, TotD/GCF). A significant difference is indicated between the two bank groups in New York in terms of TotD/GCF but not for LTD/GCF.

Examination of equation (8.3) reveals that bank holding company affiliation had a significant, negative impact on debt leveraging in New York banks. In 1974 (and 1973) the estimated coefficient of BHC is negative (and statistically significant), thereby indicating that affiliated banks employ less long-term debt in their capital structure than independent banks, ceteris paribus. In terms of this study's theory, this result implies that holding company banks are assuming less financial risk, although no such relationship was found for the New Jersey bank sample nor the combined sample (i.e., BHC was not significant in these equations).

Interestingly, the results for equation (8.4) offer a striking contrast with those for equation (8.3) in terms of the relationship between debt leveraging and affiliation. When short-term debt is included in the numerator of the leveraging variable, TotD/GCF, the estimated coefficient on BHC becomes significant and positive. This result occurred in both years for the New York sample and the combined sample; BHC is not significant in the estimate of equation (8.4) for the New Jersey banks. Such a result implies that affiliated banks are incurring greater financial risk when the leverage variable is defined more broadly to include all maturities of debt.

The contrasting results for equations (8.3) and (8.4) are not too surprising when analyzed in comparison with the results for equations (8.1) and (8.2). We have seen in equations (8.1) and (8.2) that holding company banks are maintaining lower capital levels than independent banks, even when long-term debt is included in the capital account. This latter result (equation [8.2]) is confirmed by the estimation of equation (8.3): Affiliated banks use less long-term debt. One explanation may be that parent holding companies are issuing long-term debt and channeling the funds down to the subsidiary banks in forms other than long-term debt. The findings for equation (8.4) would appear to indicate that these funds enter the banks under the category of short-term debt.[q]

Finally, regarding equation (8.3), the variable NJDUM is not statistically significant in 1974 (nor in 1973) when the equation is estimated for the com-

---

[q]Examination of the balance sheets and other reports on parent company investments in subsidiaries indicate that this practice frequently occurs. In many cases, bank holding companies issue debt and channel the funds down to the subsidiaries as short-term debt. However, the short-term loans frequently are, in effect, a source of long-term capital to the banks because the loans are "rolled over" as often as considered necessary by the banks.

Table 8-6
Regression Estimates of Bank Model: LTD/GCF (1974)

Dependent Variable: LTD/GCF

	Regression Coefficients of Equation (8.3)		
Independent Variables	*New York Sample*	*New Jersey Sample*	*Combined Sample*
BHC	–0.0289 (–2.73)[c]	0.0094 (0.51)	–0.0102 (–1.08)
NBA	0.1119 (1.26)	–0.0364 (–0.45)	0.0160 (0.26)
CV(NI)	0.0002 (0.94)	0.0049 (1.97)[a]	0.0003 (1.05)
%GTA	0.0097 (0.82)	–0.0154 (–1.02)	0.0031 (0.33)
NIBT/GI	–0.1325 (–2.24)[b]	0.0915 (0.97)	–0.0043 (–0.08)
EC/RA	–0.3543 (–2.63)[c]	–1.0915 (–3.31)[c]	–0.5897 (–4.67)[c]
ISF/STA	0.0128 (0.95)	0.0326 (1.13)	0.0252 (2.01)[b]
NLL/GL	–0.5319 (–0.84)	4.2452 (3.44)[c]	0.8616 (1.50)
Total Assets	2.19 E-9 (1.90)[a]	4.50 E-8 (1.72)[a]	1.12 E-9 (0.94)
NJDUM			0.0025 (0.30)
Constant	0.0886 (5.00)[c]	0.1228 (3.00)[c]	0.0925 (5.60)[c]
Number of Observations	171	66	237
$\overline{R}^2$	.170	.355	.140
Standard Error of Estimate	.052	.054	.055
F	4.878	4.975	4.849

Note: The equations are in linear form; *t*-values are in parentheses; the overall F statistic is significant at the 99% level for all equations.

[a]Significant at 90% level.

[b]Significant at 95% level.

[c]Significant at 99% level.

Table 8-7
Regression Estimates of Bank Model: TotD/GCF (1974)

Dependent Variable: TotD/GCF

Independent Variables	*Regression Coefficients of Equation (8.4)*		
	New York Sample	*New Jersey Sample*	*Combined Sample*
BHC	0.0989 (1.67)[a]	0.1288 (1.44)	0.0968 (1.96[b]
NBA	–0.0035 (–0.07)	0.2988 (0.77)	0.0999 (0.31)
CV (NI)	0.0005 (0.40)	–0.0141 (–1.16)	0.0020 (0.15)
%GTA	0.0142 (0.22)	–0.1424 (–1.95)[a]	–0.0677 (–1.37)
NIBT/GI	–0.4976 (–1.50)	–0.4913 (–1.08)	–0.4897 (–1.83)[a]
EC/RA	1.0702 (1.42)	–1.3536 (–0.85)	0.6544 (0.99)
ISF/STA	1.7312 (23.14)[c]	2.1363 (15.22)[c]	1.8370 (28.00)[b]
NLL/GL	–4.7485 (–1.34)	–20.9951 (–3.51)[c]	–8.0650 (–2.69)[c]
Total Assets	1.75 E-8 (2.71)[c]	–7.81 E-8 (–0.62)	1.53 E-8 (2.44)[b]
NJDUM			–0.0531 (–1.23)
Constant	–0.0730 (–0.74)	0.3305 (1.67)	0.0382 (0.44)
Number of Observations	171	66	237
$\overline{R}^2$	.823	.864	.826
Standard Error of Estimate	.290	.262	.291
F	88.597	47.030	113.249

Note: The equations are in linear form; *t*-values are in parentheses; the overall *F* statistic is significant at the 99% level for all equations.

[a]Significant at 90% level.

[b]Significant at 95% level.

[c]Significant at 99% level.

bined sample. This result implies that the two state samples (New York versus New Jersey) did not differ statistically in terms of their debt-to-equity structures (although the individual sample estimates weaken such a conclusion, at least in regard to the impact of affiliation on LTD/GCF). All sample estimates of equation (8.3) were statistically significant, although at best only 36 percent of the variation of the dependent variable is explained. The results in Table 8-7 indicate equation (8.4) explains a very high percentage of the variation of TotD/GCF. All estimates of this model are highly significant.

Liquidity Model

Equation (8.5) offers, perhaps, the strongest and clearest indication that affiliated banks are assuming greater risks than independent banks, at least as regards banks' liquidity positions. Table 8-8 shows that BHC is significant and positive for every sample estimate of this equation. These results are consistent with the univariate tests performed on the liquidity risk variable, ISF/STA, between the two groups of banks (Table 8-3). Therefore, both the univariate *t* tests and the regression estimates indicate consistently across all samples that holding company banks operate with a more illiquid asset and liability structure than independent institutions.

The results for both years in each sample are generally consistent, and the replication of the model on the New Jersey sample implies robustness on the part of the New York results. As we would expect, the coefficient on NJDUM in the combined sample estimate is not significant, given the consistency of the model's individual estimates for two states. The model is able to explain no more than 24 percent of the variation of the liquidity variable.

Credit Risk Model

The final model tested is designed to analyze differences between the two bank groups in terms of their willingness to make riskier loans. To capture such behavior, the ex post measure, net loan losses to gross loans, is used. Univariate *t* tests on this variable indicate no significant difference exists between the two groups in either New York or New Jersey. This result is confirmed by the regression estimates on equation (8.6) given in Table 8-9. In no sample estimate is BHC statistically significant.

We should note that the size variable, TA, is negative in the New Jersey estimates of equation (8.6). We expected a priori that larger banks would trade on the public's identification of size with safety in order to assume greater credit risk. However, apparently a true diversification effect is present—that is, larger banks have more diversified portfolios, and this spreading of risk has resulted in less loss in relation to the total portfolio than that experienced in smaller institutions.

Table 8-8
Regression Estimates of Bank Model: ISF/STA (1974)

Dependent Variable: ISF/STA

Independent Variables	*Regression Coefficients of Equation (8.5)*		
	New York Sample	*New Jersey Sample*	*Combined Sample*
BHC	0.1997 (3.19)[c]	0.2024 (2.61)[b]	0.2030 (4.18)[c]
NBA	−0.0134 (−0.03)	−0.4276 (−1.21)	−0.1958 (−0.61)
CV(TD)	−0.3660 (−1.05)	−0.4687 (−1.46)	−0.4915 (−2.02)[b]
DD/TD	0.0916 (0.39)	0.2391 (0.63)	0.1015 (0.53)
EC/RA	0.8402 (1.08)	−0.0007 (−0.0004)	0.7248 (1.09)
LTD/GCF	0.7300 (1.55)	0.6622 (1.16)	0.7034 (1.95)[a]
NLL/GL	2.1880 (0.81)	−12.8177 (−2.37)[b]	−0.3077 (−0.13)
Total Assets	1.65 E-8 (2.38)[b]	9.56 E-8 (0.72)	1.71 E-8 (2.70)[c]
NJDUM			−0.0236 (−0.54)
Constant	−0.2814 (−2.13)[b]	−0.2107 (−0.99)	−0.2408 (−2.25)[b]
Number of Observations	171	66	237
$\bar{R}^2$	.123	.240	.145
Standard Error of Estimate	.314	.245	.297
F	3.967	3.567	5.460

Note: The equations are in linear form; t-values are in parentheses; the overall F statistic is significant at the 99% level for all equations.

[a]Significant at 90% level.

[b]Significant at 95% level.

[c]Significant at 99% level.

Table 8-9
Regression Estimates of Bank Model: NLL/GL (1974)

Dependent Variable: NLL/GL

	Regression Coefficients of Equation (8.6)		
Independent Variables	*New York Sample*	*New Jersey Sample*	*Combined Sample*
BHC	–0.0027 (–1.51)	0.0025 (1.50)	–0.0015 (–1.12)
NBA	0.0036 (0.24)	–0.0040 (–0.52)	–0.0007 (–0.08)
C&I/GL	0.0157 (3.23)[c]	0.0251 (3.88)[c]	0.0183 (4.68)[c]
SMSA	0.0020 (1.35)	0.0011 (0.43)	0.0016 (1.23)
CV (NI)	–0.0001 (–2.37)[b]	–0.0005 (–2.21)[b]	–0.0001 (–2.87)[c]
EC/RA	–0.0042 (–0.21)	–0.0312 (–0.99)	–0.0045 (–0.28)
LTD/GCF	0.0061 (0.46)	0.0209 (1.65)	0.0114 (1.17)
ISF/STA	0.0010 (0.47)	–0.0057 (–2.13)[b]	–0.0010 (–0.57)
Total Assets	–1.98 E-10 (–1.01)	–7.69 E-9 (–2.90)[c]	–2.42 E-10 (–1.37)
NJDUM			–0.0012 (–0.88)
Constant	0.0009 (0.30)	–0.0001 (–0.02)	–0.0001 (–0.03)
Number of Observations	171	66	237
$\overline{R}^2$	.080	.468	.122
Standard Error of Estimate	.128	.005	.008
F	2.633	7.355	4.284

Note: The equations are in linear form; *t*-values are in parentheses; the overall *F* statistic is significant at the 99% level for all equations.

[a]Significant at 90% level.

[b]Significant at 95% level.

[c]Significant at 99% level.

This model has the lowest explanatory power of all the models examined. The estimates for the New York sample and the combined sample have rather low coefficients of multiple determination. (All F values are significant except in the case of the 1973 New York estimate.) The New Jersey sample estimates, however, are much better in terms of the percent of variation of NLL/GL explained.

General Observations Regarding the Empirical Results

Some interesting, general inferences can be drawn from the above results. Foremost, the relationship between the risk variables except in NLL/GL and holding company affiliation, all else being equal, is significant for the New York sample but not for the New Jersey sample, except in the case of the liquidity model where this relationship is significant for both states' samples. Generally, each sample's estimates of the models are consistent over time. (Table 8-10 gives a summary of these results.) This experience implies that the behavior of affiliates (and independent banks) in the two states may be different and that we should examine bank behavior within individual states as well as in larger samples aggregating across states.[r]

The regression results based on the New York sample data might be questioned as to their general applicability because of the inclusion of the New York City banks, especially the major money markets banks. These particular institutions are involved extensively in money market and foreign transactions, which by their very nature may be considered overly risky vis-à-vis the traditional commercial banking functions performed by the majority of the nation's banks. To detect whether or not a bias is introduced by the inclusion of New York City banks, the six models were reestimated for the New York sample excluding New York City institutions. The regression, based on 153 observations (38 affiliated and 115 independent banks), yielded results very similar to those based on the larger sample of all New York banks. In equations (8.1), (8.2), (8.3), and (8.5), the coefficients on BHC were statistically significant with the same signs as determined in the larger sample equations reported above. However, in equation (8.4) BHC was not significant.[s] Thus, the results based on data without New York City banks appear to indicate that no significant bias is introduced by the New York City institutions. Moreover, including these large banks is desirable

---

[r]This result supports a similar conclusion by Boczar (G. Boczar, "The Determinants of Multibank Holding Company Formations," *Southern Economic Journal* 42 (July 1975): 120–29). Of course, this is not to say that political boundaries matter in a pure economic sense. Bank behavior would be the same across such boundaries if the rule, ceteris paribus, were applicable. But the diversity of economic environments—state law and regulation, for example—makes this assumption invalid.

[s]All equations had F values that were statistically significant and the coefficient of multiple determination for each equation was nearly the same as that of its comparable equation based on the larger New York sample.

since they are probably the most interesting institutions in terms of risk-taking behavior.

Another area of interest arising from the regression analysis of the models involves the degree to which bank holding company product diversification has affected subsidiary bank behavior. In none of the regression estimates of the six models was the nonbank activity diversification variable, NBA, statistically significant (see Tables 8-4 to 8-9). This result implies that holding company diversification into nonbanking fields has not been sufficient to yield a risk reduction benefit that would permit holding company management to make a tradeoff between greater risk taking and diversification gains. The question arises as to what impact holding company diversification has actually had on all the operational and behavioral aspects of the firm, especially regarding reduction of the firm's risk class.

To pursue this question somewhat more directly, this study examined differences in the effect of diversification on the volatility of earnings flows between consolidated bank holding companies and independent banks. We normally think of a stabilized earnings path when we consider the benefits from product diversification. Thus, consolidated holding companies should have more stable earnings patterns than individual independent banks if diversification into nonbanking areas has been of significant benefit. A model was developed to explain the variability of net earnings (measured by the coefficient of variation of net income over the period 1970-1974), and the explanatory variables consisted of the following: size (TA); the proportion of holding company resources in nonbank assets (NBA); growth in assets (%GTA); the ratio of loans to assets (GL/TA); the ratio of deposits to total liabilities plus net worth (TD/TL); demand deposits to total deposits (DD/TD); the return on assets (NI/TA); a dummy variable equal to one for New Jersey institutions and zero otherwise (NJDUM); and a dummy variable equal to one for holding companies and zero for independent banks (BHC).

Using as observations the 27 bank holding companies and the 167 independent banks of the New York-New Jersey study above, the model was estimated by OLS regression. Unfortunately, the estimated relation was not statistically significant, and nothing meaningful can be said about the coefficients on the independent variables.[t] We can recognize, however, that the simple correlations between BHC and CV(NI) and between NBA and CV(NI) were extremely low (.031 and .11, respectively) and also that univariate *t* tests on CV(NI) showed no significant difference between consolidated holding companies and independent banks (*t* value = 0.425).

The fact that nonbank diversification by bank holding companies has not had a statistically noticeable impact on reducing the volatility of earnings flows

[t]The estimated equation is CV (NI) = 19.903 – 0.727 (TA) – 23.906 NBA + 2.262 %GTA + 11.625 GL/TA – 32.406 TD/TL + 4.000 DD/TD + 186.699 NI/TA + 1.454 NJDUM + 0.050 BHC (n = 194; F = 0.577; R^2 = 0.027; and no *t* values are significant).

Table 8-10
Summary of Regression Results for Bank Models: Relationship between BHC Affiliation and Risk

	Sign on BHC[a]					
	New York Sample		*New Jersey Sample*		*Combined Sample*	
Risk Variable	*1974*	*1973*	*1974*	*1973*	*1974*	*1973*
EC/RA	–	–	ns	ns	–	–
GCF/RA	–	–	ns	ns	–	–
LTD/GCF	–	–	ns	ns	ns	ns
TotD/GCF	+	ns	ns	ns	+	+
ISF/STA	+	+	+	+	+	+
NLL/GL	ns	ns	ns	ns	ns	ns

[a] + = significant positive relationship.
– = significant negative relationship.
ns = relationship is not statistically significant.

nor on various types of risk-taking behavior in affiliated banks is not surprising in light of the fact that only a small percentage of holding company resources comprise nonbank assets and that Congress has constrained bank holding companies to nonbanking activities that are "closely related to banking." In this study's sample of 27 holding companies, the mean value of NBA is 7.91 percent. Perhaps it is too early to make a judgment about the benefits accruing from nonbank diversification. Bank holding companies have aggressively pursued expansion into the permissible nonbank areas only since the latter 1960s, and many firms did not enter these areas until a year or two after the 1970 Amendments to the Bank Holding Company Act. Holding companies may eventually expand more extensively into the nonbank-related fields as their banks have done in the foreign area. To the extent the theory of Chapter 7 is valid, we would certainly expect such expansion to occur in the absence of regulatory constraints (e.g., the Federal Reserve Board's "go-slow" policy).

Summary and Conclusions: Impact on Soundness

We have offered in Chapters 7 and 8 a theoretical framework in which to view the behavior of bank holding companies and have shown that in theory there are reasons to expect a greater level of risk taking by the bank and nonbank susidiaries of these firms vis-à-vis comparable independent institutions. Emphasis has been placed upon a dependency relationship among the individual components of the bank holding company, with the implication that the behavior of the whole is more important than that of its parts as far as the public welfare is concerned. There is little economic validity to viewing the individual subsidiary separate from its affiliates and parent organization; public policy efforts should be directed at evaluating the totality of the holding company organization and its subsidiaries in terms of their interrelationships as well as their individual behavior.

We have presented empirical evidence that banks affiliated with bank holding companies are pursuing riskier operating practices than independently owned institutions, although there apparently are differences in bank risk-taking behavior among states.[u] In the areas of capital adequacy, debt leveraging, and liquidity, holding company banks have exhibited a desire to assume greater levels of risk. In our tests, the evidence is strongest in the case of New York banks. On the other hand, there is some evidence that affiliated banks have been extending no more risky loans and employing lesser amounts of long-term debt in their capital structure than independent banks. As regards the latter practice, however, affiliated banks also have lower levels of equity capital, which implies a very low level of gross capital funds protection vis-a-vis that of independent banks.

Generalizing these results to a larger regional or national sample is difficult. The replication of the bank models on New Jersey banks showed a lack of constancy, with the exception of the liquidity model. There is strong evidence that affiliated banks in both states pursue less liquid asset and liability policies. Over time the models' results appear to be consistent within the states. However, the inconsistency in the models' estimates across the two states of this study suggests that future research should examine a larger assortment of regions and states, perhaps nationwide, but careful attention should be paid to aggregation problems.

The theory and empirical research of this study lead us to suspect less aversion toward risk in bank holding company subsidiaries, but we should temper this conclusion by emphasizing that risk taking by our financial institutions may be of considerable benefit to the public interest. If banks are not

---

[u]A few studies have examined the risk-taking behavior of nonbank subsidiaries of bank holding companies. For example, see M. Jessee, "An Analysis of Risk-Taking Behavior in Bank Holding Companies," unpublished Ph.D. dissertation, University of Pennsylvania, Philadelphia, 1976, for tests of models similar to the equations (8.1) through (8.6) that were applied to a sample of holding company consumer finance subsidiaries and independent consumer finance companies. This research found evidence of lower capital coverage of risk assets and greater use of leverage in the affiliated consumer finance firms. A second study found that holding company consumer finance and mortgage banking affiliates were less profitable than their respective industries while, at the same time, were much more highly leveraged than those industries. (See S. Talley, "Bank Holding Company Performance in Consumer Finance and Mortgage Banking," *The Magazine of Bank Administration,* July 1976.)

assuming average risks or even above-average risks, they may not be supplying sufficient credit to finance the optimal real growth rate of their community, region, or nation. Moreover, we may go further and state that in many cases greater risk taking by financial institutions will improve the allocational efficiency of our financial system, where allocational efficiency is broadly defined as equating social marginal costs and social marginal revenues.

However, when risk taking becomes excessive to the point that bank failure occurs—and possible nationwide bank failures erupt because of loss of confidence in banks by the public—greater risk exposure becomes costly to society. The goal of bank regulation, of course, is to prevent bank failure—not to protect inefficient banks but to avert instability in our financial system and to maintain public confidence. Gilbert addresses this goal of regulation in the following statement:

> A primary objective of bank regulation in this country is prevention of bank failures. In addition, relaxation of some banking regulations has been recognized as another desirable policy goal. In recent years some regulations have been relaxed to give banks greater freedom to respond to changing market conditions. As regulations are relaxed, however, banks have a tendency to assume greater risks and, hence, increase their vulnerability to failure. The goal of maintaining a low rate of bank failure, in turn, is placed in jeopardy.[22]

Suffice it to say that although risk taking may be of benefit to the public's welfare, it is important to assess its extent within our banking institutions, and this applies to bank holding companies as well. The public would appear to agree that risk levels in banks are important. A study made by the Gallup Poll for the United States Savings and Loan League in 1972 found that the most important reason for choosing a bank or thrift institution in which to maintain a deposit account was bank safety.[23]

In addition to noting that risk-taking behavior can be beneficial to the public interest, we should reemphasize that conglomerate organizations in banking may offer advantages in terms of synergism, diversification, and the reduction of the probability of bankruptcy, for example. Theory and empirical evidence in this study indicate that these benefits, if they do exist, are not particularly significant. However, difficulties in measuring their existence and impact on firm behavior and risk class are apparent. Future research is needed in this area so that we can assess the desirability of the holding company organizational form in banking over other forms.

Part III
Public Policy Implications

Significant Public Policy Issues of the Bank Holding Company Movement

The bank holding company movement has enabled the nation's banking organizations to expand their products and markets and to obtain financial resources in ways that are largely foreclosed to them as banks. In effect, the movement has been responsible to some degree for transforming the role of commercial banking from that of a traditionally conservative intermediary acting as a fiduciary in handling the public's funds and a provider of prime commercial credit to one of a financial department store pervading nearly all financial product lines and geographic markets. An important issue raised by this movement, and one that is the main concern of this book, is the extent to which bank holding company growth has produced changes that are in the public interest.

This issue was only indirectly addressed in Part II wherein the authors considered the individual case rulings of the Federal Reserve Board on bank holding companies' applications to expand in determining those factors deemed critical by the Board in directing the early development of the industry. Likewise, the analysis of the movement's impact on soundness was based on a theoretical model of bank behavior under a holding company framework. In this chapter, the authors take a more pragmatic approach to assessing the public interest impact of bank holding company expansion. We consider that impact in the following key areas: (1) the impact on competition in financial markets, (2) the impact on the aggregate concentration of financial resources, (3) the impact on financial flexibility and soundness in banking, and (4) the impact on the regulation of financial institutions in the United States.

Impact on Competition in Financial Markets

The Bank Holding Company Act of 1956, as amended, states that bank holding company expansion in both banking and related nonbanking markets should be in the public interest. One of the important ways in which holding company entry into a new market potentially benefits the public is through increased competition. The far-flung nature of bank holding company activity in the United States has made a systematic record on competition that is suitable for testing difficult to assemble. The wide diversity of product lines and markets in which the nation's large bank holding companies operate have added to the complexity of the problem.[a] Nonetheless, there are certain well-founded assumptions and scattered evidence that the bank holding company movement has enhanced competition in the nation's banking and financial markets.

Geographical Expansion and Allocational Efficiency

The bank holding company movement has enabled banks to expand their operations nationally through permissible nonbank affiliates, which are not constrained by law to operate within home state boundaries. Also, in those states that limit statewide branching but permit bank holding companies to operate statewide, banks have been able to reach all points within their respective home states to provide full-service commercial banking.

Bank holding companies have served to further statewide bank expansion, especially in states that restrict branching. Table 9-1 and Figure 9-1 classify the states by types of branching law and note those states whose statutes restrict branching but effectively permit statewide expansion via merger or holding company acquisition. Furthermore, as Table 9-1 shows, multibank holding company activity has been most substantial in those states that have restrictive branching laws. Table 9-2 lists the states in which multibank holding companies have been most active, both in terms of share of deposits and number of offices gained during the period 1965-1973. Significantly, 14 of the 15 states in which holding companies have the highest share of deposits were those that restricted branching during that period.[b]

Several states (e.g., Florida, New York, and New Jersey) in recent years have permitted more liberal branching following a period of transition in which they had experimented with statewide banking via bank holding companies. Such

---

[a]Holland notes that while entry of an out-of-market bank holding company subsidiary into an existing market apparently has resulted in increased competition, there may still arise oligopolistic practices when firms face one another in multiple markets, with the tendency to engage in such practices heightened when the markets are closely adjacent. As expressed in the "linked oligopoly" hypothesis, competitive actions in one market are not independent of other markets, and rivals may be aware of their multimarket interdependence and in turn seek to avoid a competitive struggle in all the markets in which they face each other. On the other hand, the existence of adjacent markets may yield pro-competitive benefits due to threat of entry, as expressed in the theories of potential competition and probable future competition or threat of customer exit. The existence of multiple markets for banking firms has greatly complicated competitive theory and the issues have yet to be resolved. (See R. Holland, "Bank Holding Companies and Financial Stability," paper presented at the Conference of the Western Economic Association, San Diego, June 26, 1975.)

[b]Table 9-2 is based on a study by G. Boczar, *The Growth of Multi-bank Holding Companies: 1956-1973*, Staff Economic Study No. 85, (Washington, D.C.: Board of Governors of the Federal Reserve System, 1975), p. 11, in which he found that of the 38 states that had multibank groups in 1973, 13 saw the companies' share of offices rise by over 20 percentage points, and these same 13 plus 2 other states experienced deposit share increases in excess of 20 percentage points. Most of this growth occurred during the period 1970-1973.

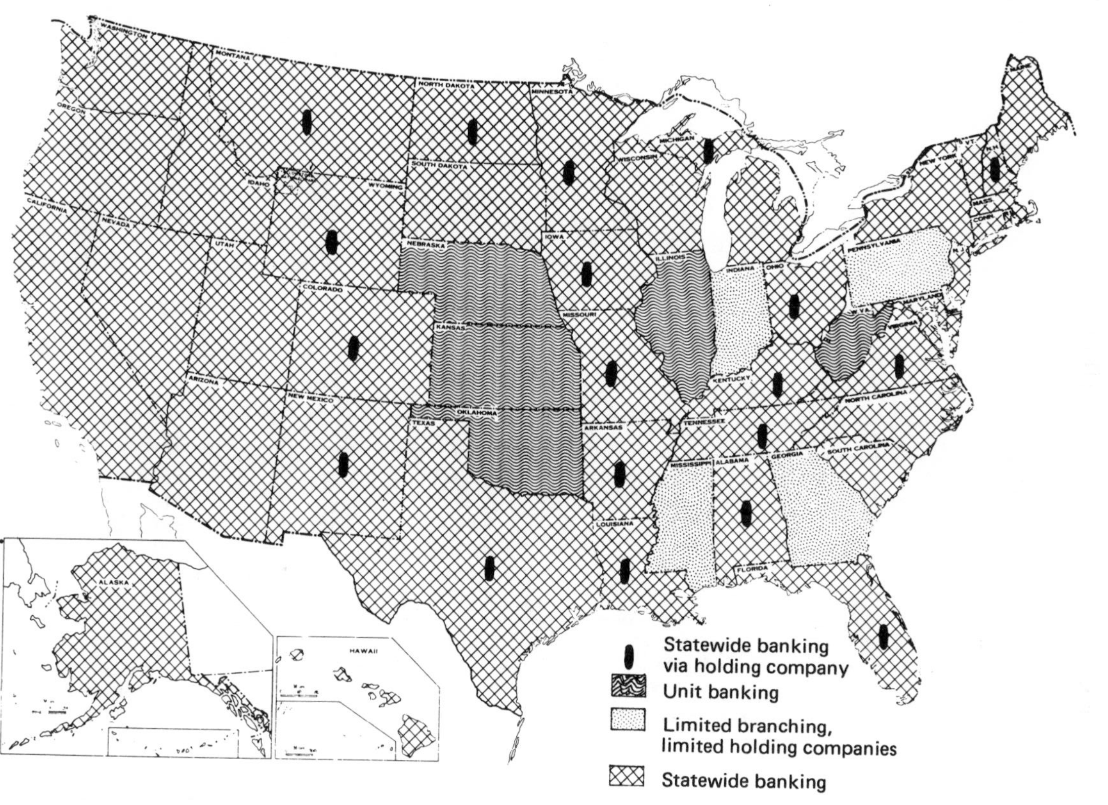

Source: Association of Bank Holding Companies, *Compilation of State Laws Affecting Bank Holding Companies,* Washington, D.C., January 1976.

Note: Effective December 31, 1975, states are classified as statewide banking if holding companies are permitted to hold 25% or more of the stock of two or more banks.

Figure 9-1. State Holding Company Laws

Table 9-1
Characteristics of Bank Holding Companies by States (As of end of year 1974)

Unit Banking States	*Number of Bank Holding Companies*	*Number of Branches*	*Percent of All State Commercial Bank Deposits*	*In-State Nonbank Firms of BHCs Headquartered in State*	*In-State Nonbank Firms of Those 100 Largest BHCs Headquartered Outside State*[a]	*Restraints*[b]	
						One-BHC	*Multi-BHC*
Colorado[c]	75	32	79.3	76	9	NR	NR
Florida[c]	62	74	80.0	136	27	NR	NR
Illinois	161	42	60.9	191	5	NR	R
Kansas	136	49	34.3	73	0	NR	R
Minnesota[c]	111	26	68.7	123	1	NR	NR
Missouri[c]	98	144	67.7	130	8	NR	NR
Montana[c]	32	8	67.9	9	2	NR	NR
Nebraska	140	50	55.8	63	1	NR	R
North Dakota[c]	20	29	42.2	2	1	NR	NR
Oklahoma	63	25	47.6	89	3	NR	R
Texas[c]	93	30	56.3	270	8	NR	NR
West Virginia	9	2	4.6	7	0	NR	NR
Wyoming[c]	22	0	56.7	16	2	NR	NR
Limited Branching States							
Alabama[d]	15	270	56.4	28	5	NR	NR
Arkansas	21	259	20.3	33	2	NR	NR
Georgia[d]	30	343	55.1	91	9	NR	R
Indiana	32	261	34.3	93	3	NR	R
Iowa[d]	147	150	40.9	89	0	NR	R

Kentucky	8	97	18.4	5	6	NR	NR
Louisiana	16	118	34.5	38	13	NR	NR
Maine	7	202	71.4	3	1	NR	NR
Massachusetts[d]	33	702	88.4	72	7	NR	R
Michigan[d]	45	876	71.5	32	7	NR	NR
Mississippi	4	70	25.6	38	3	R	R
New Hampshire	6	30	37.1	5	0	NR	R
New Mexico	10	114	67.7	8	2	NR	R
New York	46	2,485	89.8	186	43	NR	NR
Ohio	37	850	61.2	127	8	NR	NR
Pennsylvania	26	916	54.9	76	6	NR	R
Tennessee	17	390	62.3	43	5	NR	NR
Virginia	21	893	78.4	98	1	NR	NR
Wisconsin	62	112	51.2	87	2	NR	NR
Statewide Branching States							
Alaska	2	4	10.0	3	0	NR	NR
Arizona	5	259	54.7	23	16	NR	NR
California	43	3,079	93.4	148	18	NR	NR
Connecticut	9	349	71.6	20	2	NR	NR
Delaware	4	32	18.2	28	16	NR	NR
Hawaii	2	108	68.6	5	0	NR	NR
Idaho	5	111	52.9	3	2	NR	NR
Maryland	14	496	73.2	30	6	NR	NR
New Jersey	21	671	54.1	53	10	NR	NR
Nevada	3	74	65.7	0	2	NR	NR
North Carolina	10	978	71.0	110	5	NR	NR
Oregon	5	310	80.0	13	4	NR	NR
Rhode Island	10	198	96.2	16	1	NR	NR
South Carolina	7	304	52.6	25	9	NR	NR

Table 9-1 *cont.*

Unit Banking States	*Number of Bank Holding Companies*	*Number of Branches*	*Percent of All State Commercial Bank Deposits*	*In-State Nonbank Firms of BHCs Headquartered in State*	*In-State Nonbank Firms of Those 100 Largest BHCs Headquartered Outside State*[a]	*Restraints*[b]	
						One-BHC	*Multi-BHC*
South Dakota	29	82	60.5	14	4	NR	NR
Utah	9	163	80.9	6	2	NR	NR
Vermont	3	30	26.8	2	1	NR	NR
Washington	6	398	70.8	10	5	NR	R
District of Columbia	5	41	23.7	1	0	NR	NR

Sources: *FRB;* Association of Registered Bank Holding Companies, *Washington Financial Report,* Washington, D.C., 1975; and Conference of State Bank Supervisors, "A Profile of State-Chartered Banking," Washington, D.C., December, 1975.

Note: New York and Maine instituted statewide banking after 1974. Florida allowed limited branching beginning January 1, 1977. Georgia permitted statewide holding company expansion on July 1, 1976.

[a]The number of nonbank firms of the 100 largest bank holding companies does not reflect the total number of offices of these firms but rather only the firms of these holding companies at year-end 1974.

[b]NR = No restrictions; R = restricts ownership of more than 25 percent of the stock of more than one bank or specifically prohibits multiunit or one-bank holding companies.

[c]Unit banking state that allows statewide banking by holding companies.

[d]Limited branching state that allows statewide banking by holding companies.

Table 9-2
Most Active Bank Holding Company States, 1965-1973

State	*Rank in Terms of Percentage Increase in BHC Share of State Offices*	*Rank in Terms of Percentage Increase in BHC Share of State Deposits*
Maine	1	3
New York	2	1
Florida	3	2
Virginia	4	6
Alabama	5	5
Massachusetts	6	4
Tennessee	7	8
New Jersey	8	12
New Mexico	9	10
Ohio	10	13
Colorado	11	11
Maryland	12	15
Missouri	13	7
Texas		9
Connecticut		14

Source: Based on study by G.E. Boczar, *The Growth of Multibank Holding Companies: 1956-1973,* Staff Economic Studies (Washington, D.C.: Board of Governors of the Federal Reserve System, 1975).

Note: Maryland is the only state of the above that permits "pure" statewide branching with no home office or de novo restrictions during this period. Several of the other states (e.g., New York and New Jersey) have since permitted statewide branching.

experimentation with organizational forms in banking permits the states to determine which forms meet their particular financial needs. We should note, moreover, that as states liberalize their branching laws, multibank holding companies most likely will have less impact on bank expansion. Indeed, if the recent experience in New York is any indication, branching may be more desirable to bankers than expanding through multibank companies. Holding companies may consolidate their banking subsidiaries and convert to branch systems in those states that move to statewide branching.

The Bank Holding Company Act respects the intention of the McFadden Act of 1927 (Section 5155 of the Revised Statutes) to maintain state law as the prevailing authority over bank expansion. Section 3(d) of the Bank Holding Company Act states in part that no application shall be approved that would permit a bank holding company to acquire a bank located outside the company's state of primary activity, ". . . unless the acquisition . . . of a State bank by an out-of-state bank holding company is specifically authorized by statute laws of the State in which such bank is located. . . ." The term *bank* is precisely defined by the act to include only those institutions that both accept demand deposits and engage in the business of making commercial loans. With only a few exceptions of interstate bank operations by bank holding companies grandfathered under provisions of the 1956 act, interstate bank acquisitions presently are not premissible under state laws.[c] Several states (e.g., Maine, Connecticut, and New York), however, have legislation in force or proposed that would permit such acquisition by out-of-state firms if reciprocity could be established.[d]

The McFadden Act does not apply to nonbank expansion by bank holding companies. However, Section 7 of the Bank Holding Company Act recognizes the right of each state to forbid the entry of outside bank holding companies into nonbanking activities located within its jurisdiction.[e] The vast majority of states do permit such entry. Accordingly, the most limiting restriction on nonbank expansion arises from the act's requirements that any proposed nonbank endeavor be closely related to banking and yield benefits to the public that outweigh possible adverse effects.

Since 1970, bank holding companies have established many out-of-state facilities that apparently meet these requirements. The most recent data available show that by year-end 1975 bank holding companies of all types controlled more than 6,000 nonbank subsidiaries, up from 3,632 such subsidiaries in 1971. Between 1971 and 1975, moreover, 69 percent of the 2,406 nonbank subsidiaries formed were de novo, as shown in Table 4-5. There are no data compiled that pinpoint how many of these acquired or de novo subsidiaries were out-of-state, although Table 8-1 gives an indication of such out-of-state expansion for the 100 largest bank holding companies. Evidence gathered for New York State, for example, indicates that at year-end 1975, 32 out-of-state bank holding companies, representing 13 states, owned some 20 nonbank subsidiaries and their banks or parent companies owned 22 Edge Act corporations in New York. Moreover, the major New York bank holding companies had entered markets in about 40 states in the nation as of that date.

The above information supports the view that the bank holding company movement has had a major impact on the ability of the nation's banks to expand geographically. It also provides indirect evidence to suggest that the allocation of financial resources probably has been improved by the wider geographic scope of competition in credit services. Generally, there is an assumption that such expansion made possible by bank holding companies has increased the efficiency of the allocation of financial resources. A statewide or national network of

---

[c]Furthermore, one state (Mississippi) outlaws all types of bank holding companies and six states (Louisiana, Pennsylvania, South Carolina, Oklahoma, Kansas, and Illinois) permit only one-bank holding companies.

[d]Some states, such as Virginia, are proposing reciprocal interstate branching without addressing bank holding company expansion.

[e]For example, Kansas prohibits entry by outside bank holding companies into nonbank operations within its borders, and Florida does not allow out-of-state bank holding companies to engage directly or indirectly in certain trust-type activities.

offices helps to contribute to an efficient transfer of funds from areas in surplus to areas in deficit. The principal beneficiaries probably have been consumers and small businesses since the nation's major banks have for some time operated in national and international markets for large deposits and large business loans.

The Effect of Holding Company Entry on Market Structure

The most pro-competitive forms of bank holding company expansion are generally believed to be through de novo and foothold (i.e., the acquisition of a firm with a small market share) market entry. De novo entry adds a new decisionmaker to the market, whereas the acquisition of a small market participant by a larger bank holding company is frequently regarded as potentially strengthening the competitive position of the acquired firm.

Regarding bank holding company expansion through acquisition of banks, de novo entry has been a frequently used form of expansion, in part because of the regulatory encouragement given to this mode of expansion over acquisitions of going concerns. As of year-end 1974, bank holding companies accounted for 19.4 percent of the 1,418 de novo banks that were formed since 1970 (see Table 9-3). Although approximately two-thirds of these were established in markets in which the holding company was already represented and thus did not effectively add a new decisionmaker to the market, these new banks did add to the flow of banking services available to the public at convenient locations.[1]

Because of the high cost of de novo entry into banking markets, holding companies have made frequent use of foothold acquisitions to gain entry into

Table 9-3
Number of De Novo Banks Approved by Banking Authorities, by Year, 1971-1974

	Number of De Novo Banks Approved		
Year	*Bank Holding Companies*	*Independent Banks*	*Percent of All De Novo Banks Accounted for by Bank Holding Companies*
1971	22	248	8.1
1972	54	202	21.1
1973	80	337	19.2
1974	74	401	15.6
Total	230	1,188	19.4

Source: Federal Deposit Insurance Corporation, *Annual Report,* Washington, D.C., various years as shown; Federal Reserve System Board of Governors, *Annual Reports,* Washington, D.C., various years as shown.

new areas. This approach, too, reflects regulatory pressures that strongly discourage acquisition of large competitors or potential competitors. Studies of the structural effects of foothold entry have been suggestive of a favorable competitive impact from the point of view of the public interest. Shull, for example, studying multiunit expansion in New York and Virginia metropolitan areas, found that new entry by large outside organizations generally retarded the amount of increase in concentration in local banking markets over the period studied (1960-1970).[2] Shull also found that where bank holding companies acquired relatively small banks in local markets, the market share of the acquired banks subsequently increased, whereas the market share declined where the acquired bank was relatively large. Berkowicz[3] found similar evidence in his study of 227 banks in 9 unit-banking states during the period 1962-1970.[f]

Holding company acquisitions do tend to increase deposit concentration at the state level. In addition to the potentially adverse effect of this phenomenon on aggregate concentration (see discussion below), increasing statewide concentration may reduce competition in local markets by reducing the number of potential entrants into those markets, by increasing barriers to entry, or by encouraging anticompetitive behavior on the part of banks facing each other in many separate local markets (linked oligopoly). Shull's study found that although statewide concentration did increase, the number of potential entrants into selected metropolitan New York and Virginia banking markets was far from exhausted during at least a two-year period following bank holding company entry into local markets. In fact, Shull concludes that the number of large potential entrants was reasonably well maintained.

Talley's examination of trends in state concentration also found minimal adverse impact of the bank holding company movement.[4] Talley found that the percentage of statewide deposits held by the largest five banking organizations increased between 1968 and 1973 in 27 states and the District of Columbia, declined in 22, and remained constant in one. The mean and median changes in statewide concentration for the 50 states amounted to less than 1 percentage point, and acquisitions by holding companies directly caused concentration to increase in 24 states. Talley concluded that on a statewide basis, holding company acquisitions have increased concentration significantly (more than 10 per-

---

[f]We should note that demographic factors may have played an important role in determining the market share effects found by Shull and Berkowicz. Specifically, small banks tend to be located in suburban areas, while larger banks often are headquartered in urban centers. Deposit growth in suburban parts of the nation generally has outstripped that in cities. Thus, holding company acquisitions of small suburban banks were consistent with the public interest but may not have contributed any more to the de-concentration of banking markets than that which would otherwise have occurred in many local or regional areas. (See comment of R. Lawrence in B. Shull, "Multiple-Office Banking and the Structure of Banking Markets: The New York and Virginia Experience," *Proceedings of a Conference on Bank Structure and Competition* [Chicago: Federal Reserve Bank of Chicago, 1972], pp. 30-40.)

centage points) in only 6 states, and these states are ones where concentration is not regarded as being high.

The evidence on bank holding company expansion into nonbanking areas also suggests a beneficial effect on market structure. De novo entry by bank holding companies into nonbank ventures has been substantial. About 1,650 new firms were established by bank holding companies in all nonbank product lines during the period 1971-1975. (See Table 4-5.) This figure compares with 756 acquisitions of going concerns.[g] The popularity of de novo entry into nonbanking ventures has resulted primarily because the such entry has been made administratively easier by the Federal Reserve Board and reflects its view, with respect to the net public benefits requirements of Section 4(c)(8), that de novo expansion is more likely to be considered in the public interest than the acquisition of a going concern. Most of the going concern acquisitions approved have been of the foothold type precisely because of the Board's strict enforcement of the net public benefits test in such a way as to preclude the acquisition of large market participants.

Pricing Effects

The conditions under which Federal Reserve Board approvals of holding company applications to expand have been granted are suggestive of a pro-competitive effect on pricing of bank holding company services. Rate reductions on banking and nonbanking services are regarded as an important direct benefit to the public and conducive to improved competition in the markets involved. In numerous proposed bank acquisitions, the applicants have promised to reduce interest charges on loans below those charged by other participants in the market (e.g., First National City Corporation, 71 *FRB* 944), or to eliminate service charges on demand deposits (e.g., First Holding Company, 71 *FRB* 139), or to pay higher rates on time deposits (e.g., Chemical New York Corporation, 38 *FR* 31472).

Likewise, in nonbank cases rate reductions have been crucial to obtaining the approval of the Board (see, for example, the Board order involving BankAmerica Corporation's acquisition of GAC Finance, Inc., 73 *FRB* 687). Indeed, in the case of entry into the credit life insurance field, Regulation Y explicitly requires an applicant to demonstrate

> . . . that approval will benefit the consumer or result in other public benefits. Normally such a showing would be made by a projected reduction in rates or increases in policy benefits due to bank holding company performance of this service.

---

[g]This figure is inflated by the practice of recording individual offices of some firms (primarily consumer finance) as separate purchases.

In this regard, the Board has approved applications that have provided for rate reductions of 2 to 20 percent below existing average levels for each state in which consumer credit is extended by the bank holding company and for other improved terms. A review of more than fifty applications to acquire or form underwriting firms approved during the period 1973–1975 found that the average rate reduction promised was 13.1 percent overall (credit life and credit accident and health insurance combined), which resulted in estimated premium savings of slightly more than $7 million for the first year following approval.

Statistical evidence on the price effects of bank holding company expansion is very limited, especially with respect to the pricing of specific products in nonbank lines of activity. Lawrence found no statistically significant difference between holding company banks and independent banks in the average rates charged on loans or in interest paid on time deposits, although affiliated banks' service charges on demand deposits were significantly higher.[h] These findings were confirmed in subsequent studies by other investigators, with the exception that no significant differences were found in the charges on demand deposits.[5] Also, these early studies generally found no difference in profitability between independent and affiliated banks. While these results seem to indicate no significant competitive impact on pricing from holding company expansion, the conclusion that bank holding companies have not influenced price competition may be unwarranted. A possibility is that bank holding company pricing policies have influenced those of independent banks. Thus, empirical evidence on pricing by bank holding companies and independent banks in the same market might show no difference. What is needed is a before-and-after analysis of the behavior of market participants in a market that has been penetrated by a bank holding company affiliate. A step in this direction is suggested by studies of the impact of bank holding companies on convenience and needs of the public, as discussed below.

More recent investigations have found mixed evidence of competitive effects. Jackson, for example, in his study of 1,644 banks located throughout 44 states for the period 1969–1971, found that bank affiliates of multibank holding companies charge higher rates on loans, after adjustment for risk than do comparable independent banks (although this finding could be the result of a different loan mix not adequately compensated for by the risk adjustment).[6] On

---

[h]Lawrence examined 43 holding company banks of all sizes that were acquired between 1954 and 1963 and located throughout the United States. These banks were paired with 55 independent banks of similar size and location, and such pairing yielded tests of significant differences between the two groups of banks. Lawrence also examined these paired differences over time (i.e., before and after acquisition of the affiliated banks) and found with respect to pricing effects that only in the case of deposit service charges did acquisition result in a significant change in pricing behavior—that is, affiliated banks charged higher service charges on deposits after acquisition than before. (See R. Lawrence, *The Performance of Bank Holding Companies* (Washington, D.C.: Board of Governors of the Federal Reserve System, 1974).

the other hand, affiliated banks were found to pay higher interest rates on time and savings deposits. To determine the net effect of these apparently conflicting competitive implications, Jackson examined the "spread" between the risk-adjusted loan rate charged and the interest rate paid on deposits and found that holding company affiliation had no significant effect on this variable. This evidence, therefore, suggests that holding company bank expansion appears to have had no substantial impact on pricing of bank services, but such studies have been handicapped by insufficient data to perform many tests that might shed light on this question. Also, one interpretation of Jackson's results is that there has been a restructuring of the pricing of bank services, which in itself could be beneficial if the effect is to achieve more efficient pricing.

The only systematic empirical evidence on pricing in the nonbank activities of bank holding companies involves the profitability of these subsidiaries. A recent study by Talley indicated that mortgage banking and consumer finance subsidiaries of bank holding companies have a much lower return on invested capital than the average return for the respective industries.[i] One inference from this data could be that such firms are pricing their products lower than competitors in order to increase their share of the market. (Conceptually, these lower rates of return might also be due to higher capital levels in nonbanking affiliates, but there is evidence that indicates that this is not the case.)[7] There is no direct evidence, however, on pricing policies of individual nonbank subsidiaries and also no indication that these firms are engaging in predatory pricing.

Product Differentiation and Innovation

Product differentiation is generally recognized as a useful strategy for market entry. A new firm may often gain a significant market share by offering a product that is in some way distinct from that of its established competitors. In the present context we might consider "banking" as a broadly defined product. A bank may differentiate its product from that of others by offering a wide array of financial services or improving common services. To the extent that differentiation results in availability of a better "product" it may be in the public interest.

Traditionally, product differentiation in banking has been addressed in terms of the effects of bank entry on the convenience and needs of the commu-

---

[i]For example, Talley found that in 1973 and 1974, respectively, a sample of 42 holding company mortgage banking firms earned on average 3.0 percent and –10.9 percent on equity versus 11.0 percent and –6.0 percent for the industry. Similarly, a sample of 14 consumer finance affiliates earned 4.9 percent on equity in 1973 and –3.4 percent in 1974 versus 9.3 percent and 8.8 percent, respectively, for the industry. (See S. Talley, "Bank Holding Company Performance in Consumer Finance and Mortgage Banking," *The Magazine of Bank Administration*, July 1976, pp. 41–43.)

nity to be served. As noted in Chapters 5 and 6, improvements affecting the convenience and needs of the community are the most significant public benefits accepted by the Federal Reserve Board in its approvals of bank acquisitions and holding company formations. Such improvements take the form of new services or the expansion of existing services or facilities, and the Board has especially favored the introduction of new services not yet offered in a market. Moreover, the Board has recognized benefits in the provision of an alternative source of services that are already offered in a market since such an alternative source may stimulate competition (see, for example, Missouri Bancshares, 71 *FRB* 143).

Similarly, in nonbank cases the introduction of new, or the extension of existing, services to a market, particularly the provisions of specialized credit services, is regarded as a benefit leading to increased competition. Such improvements are often offered by bank holding companies in support of proposed nonbank acquisitions. This has been notably apparent in the acquisition of consumer finance firms where bank holding companies have converted acquired firms from institutions offering a narrow range of financial services to full service firms.[j]

The degree to which new services promised in bank holding company applications have improved competition depends, of course, on the extent to which these promises have been fulfilled. Unfortunately, there is dearth of evidence on this experience.[8] The Federal Reserve has not yet formally compiled its observations on the fulfillment of proposed benefits. As Lawrence and Talley note, these observations have been mixed:

> . . . some Reserve Bank investigations have concluded that certain BHC's have made few changes whereas others have fostered significant improvements in the facilities and the services of acquired banks.[9]

Some limited questionnaire surveys undertaken outside the Federal Reserve System have contributed information in this regard. Lee and Reichert[10] and Fischer[11] found evidence that nonprice competition has been increased in rural areas by aggressive holding company affiliate behavior upon entry and the defensive reaction of existing independent banks. The question also arises whether new services introduced by bank holding companies met real needs or were token offerings that served as window dressing for the application. Although

---

[j]For example, Citicorp offered in 1976 a new type of full service consumer finance service in numerous markets in its Person-to-Person Financial Centers—a convenient bundling of services not typically offered in most markets. In terms of holding company entry into commercial banking markets, Fidelity Union Bancorporation's acquisition of Colonial First National Bank in Red Bank, New Jersey, is an example of an acquisition that resulted in the provision of new services (i.e., no-charge checking and bank credit card service) that were not formerly offered in that banking market.

there is no systematic evidence in this regard, the Board and Reserve Bank staffs generally review these promised new services for their reasonableness and the extent to which there is a demand for such services.[k]

There is, nevertheless, some statistical evidence that indicates that bank holding companies have in fact improved the convenience and needs of the markets entered, and these improvements have had pro-competitive effects. Lawrence[12] and Talley,[13] among others, have shown that holding company banks make more credit available to their local markets than do comparable independent banks holding more loans and local government securities and less correspondent balances. Moreover, if holding companies do improve the quality and range of services offered, their subsidiaries should outperform market competitors over time in terms of gaining market share. The previously mentioned studies by Shull and Berkowicz show that bank subsidiaries that were foothold acquisitions have performed in this manner.

Apart from the product differentiation question, there is the related issue of product innovation or the impact of holding companies on the creation of new products. Most of the types of financing that bank holding companies have been permitted to perform through subsidiaries have also been permitted to individual commercial banks, either through corporate divisions or subsidiaries. Examples of such similarities include factoring, consumer and sales financing, commercial financing, leasing, mortgage financing and servicing, credit cards, and data processing. Many independent nonbank firms also supply these services. Thus, not surprisingly, the impact of the holding company form of organization in banking appears to be slight regarding credit product innovation, except insofar as the resources of bank holding companies have enabled them to refine or enlarge the availability of the service (e.g., the extension of large tanker and aircraft leases).

The pooling of managerial and financial resources of smaller firms into a larger organization is believed to be conducive to improvement in the production of banking services. Such combinations are thought to yield managerial economies of scale and lead to the provision of more resources for research and development than would be feasible in a smaller firm. Of course, these benefits often are available through the consolidation of one or more banking units not affiliated with a bank holding company.

---

[k] For example, in the Board order approving State Street Boston Financial Corporation's acquisition of Union National Bank, Lowell, Massachusetts (73 *FRB* 526), the Board recognized that there was "... no evidence on the record that any major needs of the market are presently going unserved. However, Bank is presently not competitive in providing many services." Similarly, in an order approving First National Boston Corporation's (73 *FRB* 759) acquisition of the First Bank and Trust Company of Wellesley, the Board found "... no evidence that any major banking needs of the areas served by Wellesley Bank ... are currently going unserved. However, Applicant proposes to offer ... new services not currently provided in the area," which would have pro-competitive results.

Summary of Competitive Effects

The available evidence mildly suggests that the bank holding company entry into banking and nonbanking markets has resulted in added price competition, but the effects are not easy to isolate through statistical means. Competition among market participants has likely been heightened in those cases where bank holding companies have fulfilled their application promises of price reductions and new services, but little postacquisition information is available. The most substantive evidence involves the effect of holding company expansion on market structure. There is a reasonably clear indication that foothold entry into new banking markets has resulted in decreased market concentration, particularly in states that limit branching. While encouraging, this finding is based on circumstantial evidence rather than direct information on the competitive behavior of the market participants. Bank holding company entry in nonbanking markets also appears to have resulted in added competition on more or less the same grounds.

Impact on Aggregate Concentration of Resources

An important issue in appraising the overall significance of the bank holding company movement is its impact on concentration in the banking industry and in the broader financial aggregates. Aggregate concentration of resources refers to the development of economic power whereby the largest firms in an industry or a sector of the economy can control a large percentage of the resources of that industry on a nationwide—or statewide—basis. This concentration of resources is distinguished from market concentration, which is relevant in appraising local competitive conditions. The problems associated with aggregate concentration are twofold: (1) a high concentration of financial resources could give a relatively small number of firms inordinate economic power that, in turn, could translate into inordinate political power; and (2) the development of very large firms in an industry, especially one such as banking, raises the social costs of a firm's inefficiency and failure.

Aggregate concentration is an issue that has long concerned the Congress and the public. A large resource base potentially gives a firm a degree of economic power that arises without regard to its position in specific markets. The significance of size is clearly seen in diversified firms in which power due to size is not necessarily reinforced by power due to monopoly.[14] Thus, the diversification that is occurring in commercial banking as a result of bank and nonbank acquisitions by bank holding companies under the authority of the 1970 Amendments to the Bank Holding Company Act raises a legitimate concern over aggregate concentration of financial resources. As noted in Part II, the Federal Reserve Board, charged by the act to determine whether public benefits of a proposed acquisition outweigh such adverse effects as "undue concentration of resources," has expressed its concern in this regard in several denials of proposed nonbank acquisitions on the grounds of undue aggregate concentration (e.g., First National City Corporation, 74 *FRB* 50, and the Chase Manhattan Corporation, 74 *FRB* 142).

Although the bank holding company movement has the potential for increasing aggregate concentration, the evidence to date does not indicate that bank holding company acquisitions have pushed concentration levels in banking or banking and nonbanking activities combined to threshold levels that could be considered dangerous. Talley studied the trend in the percentage of total domestic deposits held by the nation's 100 largest banking organizations between 1968 and 1973 and found that this concentration ratio actually fell from 49.0 to 47.0 percent during the period.[15] Talley noted, nevertheless, that if bank holding company acquisitions during this period—resulting in an addition of $17 billion in deposits—were eliminated, nationwide concentration would have declined by another 2.3 percentage points.

Additional data show that since 1973 the percentage of deposits held by the 100 largest banking organizations rose to 48.1 percent as of the end of 1975, thus reversing the downward trend begun in the late 1960s, but remained below the 1968 level. (See Table 9-4.) Much of the earlier decline in concentration re-

Table 9-4
Aggregate Concentration in Banking, Selected Years, 1961-1975

Percent of Domestic Deposits Held	*1961*	*1966*	*1968*	*1973*	*1974*	*1975*
Largest banking organization	4.6	4.2	4.0	3.8	3.9	4.2
5 largest banking organizations	14.3	14.3	14.3	12.1	13.5	13.5
100 largest banking organizations	49.4	49.3	49.0	47.0	n.a.	48.1
300 largest banking organizations	63.0	62.9	62.8	n.a.	n.a.	63.4
Percent of Financial Sector Assets Held						
50 largest banking organizations[a]	n.a.	10.8	n.a.	24.6	26.7	n.a.
100 largest banking organizations[a]	n.a.	16.0	n.a.	29.2	31.4	n.a.

Sources: S.H. Talley, *The Impact of Holding Company Acquisitions on Aggregate Concentration in Banking,* (Washington, D.C.: Board of Governors of the Federal Reserve System, 1974); *FRB,* various years; *Consolidated Reports of Condition,* various years; Paine, Webber, Jackson and Curtis, Inc. *A Comparative Analysis of the 100 Largest Banks and other Representative Banking Institutions,* New York, 1967; and Federal Reserve System Board of Governors, *Flow of Funds Accounts 1965-73, Annual Total Flows and Year-End Assets and Liabilities,* Washington, D.C., 1975.

Note: All deposit data as of June 30; asset concentration figures as of end of year.

[a]The assets of the 100 and 50 largest banking organizations include assets of foreign branches. If foreign branch asset data are eliminated from the numerator of these ratios for the 100 largest organizations, the shares for 1966, 1973, and 1974 are, respectively, 14.8, 23.8, and 25.9 percent.

flected the relatively strong performance of small- and medium-sized banks. There is no clear indication whether such institutions were hurt more by the inflation and recession of 1974 and 1975 than were the nation's larger organizations. More time is clearly needed to appraise nationwide trends in concentration in banking.

The evidence accumulated thus far suggests that holding company expansion has retarded somewhat the downward trend in nationwide concentration, which is due primarily to the slower-than-average internal domestic growth of the nation's largest banks. Yet this conclusion may be misleading. Talley's analysis was based on deposit data, whereas the crucial question of aggregate concentration must also be addressed in terms of total financial resources, as suggested by Seelig.[16] Deposit figures do not indicate the growth of the nonbank assets controlled by holding companies or the growth in bank assets financed from nondeposit sources of funds. Banking organizations' substantial use of nondeposit sources of funds to finance expansion has resulted in sizable increases in their share of total domestic financial resources of the private financial sector. Table 9-4 shows that the share of the total domestic assets of the private financial sector accounted for by the 100 largest banking organizations, after foreign branch assets are eliminated, increased from 15 percent in 1966 to 26 percent in 1974 (see footnote a to Table 9-4).

This growing trend toward increased asset concentration in the aggregate, however, can be attributed only in part to the bank holding company movement. Although the nonbank assets of bank holding companies have grown absolutely, they are estimated to be only a small proportion of total consolidated holding company assets—only about 3 percent of the assets of the 50 largest bank holding companies in 1973 were held by nonbanking subsidiaries. This small percentage is due to the Federal Reserve Board's reluctance to approve large nonbank acquisitions and to the generally small size of nonbanking industries that bank holding companies can enter. Thus, bank holding companies' nonbank acquisitions have not contributed importantly to increased concentration of financial assets in the economy.

The increased share of the nation's largest banking organizations in the domestic private financial sector reflects several factors, including: (1) increased use by large banks of nondeposit sources of funds (i.e., federal funds purchased, Eurodollar borrowings, other short-term borrowings, and long-term debt and equity), (2) a larger share of bank credit in total financial sector credit, and (3) the bank acquisition and merger activity of the large banking organizations during this period. With respect to the bank financing patterns, the ratio of total deposits to total sources of funds for all banks declined from 87 percent in 1966 to 81 percent in 1974, thereby implying a greater reliance on nondeposit sources of funds to finance asset growth. There was also a slight shift to banks from nonbank firms over this period in the economy's reliance on private financial intermediaries to finance credit needs. The proportion of bank assets in the private financial sector rose from about 37 percent in 1966 to a little over 41 percent in 1974. Finally, the consolidation of banks smaller than the largest 100 into the 100 largest banking organizations accounted for some of the upward shift in asset concentration between 1966 and 1974, although sufficient data to pinpoint precisely this phenomenon are not readily available. We should also note that credit extended abroad by the 100 largest banks' domestic offices is included in the asset share data and, since these organizations probably have been the most active suppliers of foreign credit, may impart an upward bias in the share of domestic private financial sector assets accounted for by large banks.

In sum, the increasing trend toward aggregate concentration when measured by bank asset holdings within the total private financial sector appears, therefore, to be attributable only in part to the growth of bank holding companies. Some of the influx of nondeposit funds probably can be attributed to the financing innovations introduced by bank holding companies (see below), which involve the channeling of added funds from the parents to both bank and nonbank subsidiaries. Bank holding company acquisitions also have contributed somewhat to greater concentration.

Impact on Financial Flexibility and Soundness

The bank holding company form of organization has undoubtedly introduced greater financing flexibility to banking operations. At the same time, greater financial risk has been introduced. Banks operating under a holding company umbrella are frequently able to tap credit markets more easily and, in some cases, new sources of capital not available to independent banks. This flexibility has been manifested by increased use of nondeposit debt in bank holding companies and their affiliates. The holding company form also permits greater flexibility in the internal allocation of funds. Depending on the degree of control and centralization exercised by the parent company, intercompany transactions that channel funds to activities yielding the highest return can be facilitated, to the extent permitted by Section 23A of the Federal Reserve Act. Both the flexibility in financing bank and holding company expansion and in allocation of funds within the firm have potential beneficial and adverse implications for bank soundness.

The Financing Decision

Improved Access to Capital Markets. Proponents of bank holding companies argue that banks affiliated with holding companies have greater access to debt and equity capital markets than do independent banks. This advantage is claimed to arise from greater market receptiveness in view of the size and ostensible strength of the combined organization and the benefits of affiliation with a large regional bank and from the supposed benefits from product diversification accruing to a conglomerate firm.

In the past, bank holding companies have acquired numerous banks and nonbanking firms that were small and undercapitalized typically because of their limited access to capital markets. The parent companies have frequently injected additional equity into these new firms. For example, Schotland notes that in the first half of the 1970s the Federal Reserve Board had conditioned 397 approvals of bank acquisitions on the injection of new capital, which in the aggregate amounted to nearly $788 million.[17] However, statistical investigations into bank holding companies' capital positions have found that on average their equity capital ratios are below those of independent banks while, at the same time, they make more use of debt—primarily short-term debt as noted in Chapter 8.

Increased Use of Debt. There is evidence indicating that affiliated banks are more highly leveraged (i.e., debt as a percentage of equity or of debt plus equity) than independent banks of comparable size.[1] Nonbanking affiliates of bank holding companies also show higher debt-to-equity ratios than comparable independent firms.[18] At the same time, the capital market does not appear to be charging bank holding companies and their affiliates a higher risk premium (i.e., effective yield at issue minus a risk-free rate) on their increased debt obligations. Pettway, for example, found that holding company affiliation did not affect significantly the risk premiums charged on long-term bonds.[19] Humphrey and Talley observed that the degree of leverage in a bank holding company had no effect on the firm's cost of debt or its stock price-earnings ratio.[20] Jacobs, Beighley, and Boyd, on the other hand, found that holding company consolidated leverage had a negative effect on the price per share, although no significant relationship was detected between leverage and the P/E ratio.[21]

The parent companies of bank holding companies also have placed an emphasis on debt sources of funds. At the end of 1973, the 50 largest parent companies had slightly more than $8 billion of debt outstanding (all maturities). The debt-to-equity ratio (with only equity capital in the denominator) for these

---

[1]For example, in our study of the impact of affiliation on bank soundness reported in Chapter 7, the sample of 70 affiliated banks and 167 independent banks in the Second Federal Reserve District had an average ratio of long-term debt to debt plus equity capital in 1974 of 3.5 percent for affiliated banks compared to 2.3 percent for independent banks. When nondeposit, short-term debt is included in the numerator, the average debt-to-capital ratio was 17.7 percent for the holding company banks versus −37.7 percent for the independent group (the negative number being due to the fact that federal funds sold, which was netted out of the numerator, exceeded the sum of short- and long-term debt). Jacobs, Beighly, and Boyd also found affiliated banks to be more highly leveraged. In 1973, for example, the ratio of all debt plus deposits to equity was 15.9 compared to 14.2 for all insured banks. (See D. Jacobs, H. Beighly and J. Boyd, *The Financial Structure of Bank Holding Companies* [Chicago: Association of Reserve City Bankers, 1975], p. 9.)

firms averaged about 0.45. There was significant variation in this ratio among individual firms, however, ranging from zero for several parent companies to almost 2.4 for a large regional company.

Thus, the capital markets appear to be permitting bank holding companies and their affiliates to be more highly leveraged without incurring a higher cost of funds than independent banks. While this finding is consistent with the proposition that bank holding companies are more diversified and therefore less risky than independent firms,[m] more likely the market is not effectively regulating bank holding company leverage because of the market's identification of regulatory protection of banks with the remainder of the holding company (i.e., Hypothesis I of Chapter 7). Under this interpretation the markets do not charge an appropriate—at least from a regulatory point of view—risk premium on the debt and equity obligations of bank holding companies or their affiliates. This view tends to cast doubt on the value of market discipline to help limit undue risk taking by bank holding companies and diminishes the force of the argument that suggests that the bank holding company form of organization can insulate affiliated banks from problems that affect the parent or its nonbank subsidiaries.

The most pressing problem with high use of leverage is not necessarily the total amount of debt issued, but rather the maturity structure of that debt.[n] In several cases, the parent companies have issued a substantial amount of unsecured short-term debt (usually commercial paper) while at the same time having a relatively illiquid asset structure.[o] These funds are highly sensitive to word of possible adverse developments affecting the seller. Without a sufficient amount of liquid assets or back-up lines of credit to repay maturing obligations, the company may be unable to roll over its short-term debt and a liquidity crisis could result, as in the case of Beverly Hills Bancorporation in 1974.

Another aspect of leveraging at the holding company level involves double leveraging—that is, the issuance of long-term debt by the parent company to be

---

[m] That is, this finding is consistent with the view that diversification reduces firm risk for any given level of leverage. Yet, the degree of leverage and diversification are expected to be positively related. And, as discussed in Chapter 7, we have no clear answer to whether product diversification in bank holding companies has resulted in significant gains in stability or whether such stability necessarily implies decreased bank risk vis-à-vis depositors.

[n] This is not to say that the Board has not been concerned in specific cases where excessive leverage was evident. In 1976, for example, the Board denied the merger of two Minneapolis bank holding companies primarily because one of them—Bank Shares, Inc.—had so much debt outstanding that interest expense consumed 50 percent of its operating revenue in 1975.

[o] As of December 3, 1975, bank-related commercial paper consisting almost exclusively of the nonreservable portion of paper issued by bank holding companies, totaled $8.7 billion, or approximately 1.3 percent of total assets of all bank holding companies. This compares with $8.3 billion in 1974, $4.9 billion in 1973 and $2.6 billion in 1972. The ratio of commercial paper to total holding company assets was up about 50 percent in 1974 over the preceding two years, although part of this increase was due to an increase in the number of commercial paper issuers reporting after August 1974.

channeled as equity or debt to a subsidiary.[p] This innovation introduced into the banking industry by bank holding companies may have adverse implications for the risk exposure of the financial system. Double leveraging shifts risk from the subsidiary to the creditors of the parent. While the capital support for asset growth and protection of the subsidiary is increased, the risk exposure of the consolidated firm also is expanded. The potential for difficulties at the holding company level is thus widened, and these difficulties could adversely affect the affiliated banks, particularly if the servicing of holding company debt depends primarily on dividends from bank subsidiaries.

Thus, we can see that no additional risk per se is created by double leveraging; risk is merely transferred from one group to another. Indeed, under the dependence assumption espoused in Chapter 7, where debt is located makes little difference in a bank holding company—that is, whether in the bank subsidiaries, the nonbank firms, or the parent company.[q] The risk exposure for the holding company entity is the same. The real danger lies, however, in the extent to which double leveraging encourages the holding company to issue excessive amounts of debt, say, to meet regulatory demands for increases in subsidiary bank capital or as a possible way to evade market discipline in tapping the debt markets directly by the subsidiaries (whose equity positions have been increased by double leveraging) to finance their expansion.

Presumably, policies that shift funds among bank holding company subsidiaries are designed to maximize the earnings of the consolidated firm.[22] To the extent that these policies improve the financial position and profitability of the entire holding company, even at the cost of slightly weakening a bank subsidiary, there is a net gain. (Of course, for a net gain to occur in the face of a limited weakening of bank soundness, it must be assumed that the holding company stands ready to aid a subsidiary bank that incurs financial difficulties.)

However, there have been instances of abuse where intersubsidiary transactions have led to significant financial problems in affiliated banks. One ex-

---

[p]The Federal Reserve Board has endorsed this practice in a number of cases. See, for example, Aplington Insurance, Inc., 74 *FRB* 778. Holland cites data indicating the extent of double leveraging by bank holding companies. The 25 largest companies combined invested $417 million and $371 million in new equity of their subsidiary banks in 1972 and 1973, respectively—exclusive of acquisitions of banks and of existing shares in partially-owned banks. These equity investments in subsidiary banks exceeded the net new equity issued by the parent companies—$140 million and $116 in 1972 and 1973, respectively. (See Holland, "Bank Holding Companies and Financial Stability.")

[q]For an opposing view, see E. Lerner, "Three Financial Problems Facing Bank Holding Companies, A Comment," *Journal of Money, Credit, and Banking* 4(May 1972), pp. 445–55. He argues that although the holding company may enjoy greater flexibility in the employment of debt-generated funds if debt obligations are issued by the parent, greater risk is created for the investor since the only assets available on liquidation in case of default by the holding company are the equity investments in the subsidiaries. On the other hand, debt issued by the subsidiaries could be backed by the more tangible assets of those firms. The flaw in such an argument is that it abstracts from the prevalence of dependence among subsidiaries within bank holding companies.

ample is the sale of poor quality mortgage paper to Hamilton National Bank by its mortgage banking affiliate and subsequent deterioration of the former institution.[r] Other examples include the purchase by bank subsidiaries of Palmer Bank Corporation in Sarasota, Florida, of participations in poor quality loans originated by the mortgage banking affiliate, Coastal Mortgage Company, and subsidiary bank loans to and purchases of assets from bank holding company advised real estate investment trusts. The advised REIT experience of bank holding companies is perhaps the best known problem area of bank holding company nonbank activity (although we must recognize that advised REITs cannot be subsidiaries of bank holding companies or banks). Chase Manhattan, First Wisconsin, First Pennsylvania, and Citizens and Southern, to name a few, are some major bank holding companies that advise REITs that have experienced severe financial problems and have committed sizable resources to salvaging such advised firms.

Overall Financial Impact

In sum, the evidence accumulated to date leads us to conclude that the bank holding company movement has contributed to a deterioration in the financial condition of some of the nation's banking organizations, although these effects are probably not irreversible. These adverse financial effects seem largely to be attributable to the behavioral characteristics of the firm itself and only in part were due to the economic downturn of the early 1970s. When comparisons are made between comparable affiliated banks and independent banks at a point in time, typically the holding company banks are operating with a greater risk exposure. One explanation may be that the lead banks of holding companies are the most venturesome institutions of the banking industry—and would be whether or not they had formed holding companies—and they tend to instill their riskier operating policies in acquired banks and nonbank affiliates. Such theories were examined in more detail in Chapter 7.

The bank holding company movement appears to have permitted banks to expand and experiment in new means of financing operations and in bank-related areas in ways that probably would not be feasible for individual banks, because of financial or regulatory obstacles that would not be easy to remove. At the same time, there has emerged from our experience with the bank holding

---

[r]Relationships among REITs and bank holding companies and other examples of abusive intracompany shifts of funds are documented in R. Nader and J. Brown, "Disclosure and Bank Soundness: Non-Bank Activities of Bank Holding Companies," *Public Interest Research Group, Washington, D.C.*, June 30, 1976. Nader and Brown also point out that over half of the nonbank subsidiaries of the 23 bank holding companies analyzed in their study experienced losses in 1974, equal to 19.6 percent of the income of their affiliated banks, although these nonbank subsidiaries represented only 3.25 percent of total holding company assets.

company movement to date a clear need for closer supervision of the nonbanking and parent operations of these organizations than heretofore in order to ensure that the further evolution of the bank holding company will be in the public interest. From a regulatory point of view, the distinction between banks and bank holding companies may now be far less significant than might have been anticipated when the Bank Holding Company Act and its amendments were enacted into law. As noted in Chapters 7 and 8, supervising and monitoring the activities and soundness of individual banks separately from their respective holding companies makes little sense.

Impact on the Regulation of Financial Institutions

At present, banks and other financial institutions in the United States may come under the jurisdiction of a variety of federal and state regulatory agencies. Under our dual banking system, banks may choose a federal charter and be supervised to varying degrees by the Comptroller of the Currency, the Federal Reserve System, and the Federal Deposit Insurance Corporation. State-chartered banks are regulated by the banking department of their respective states and by the FDIC if insured and by the Federal Reserve System if they choose to be members. For the most part, the nonbanking industries permissible for bank holding company entry are regulated by states. Thus, our system of financial institution regulation and supervision is quite fragmented.

One little recognized, but significant, effect of the bank holding company movement has increasingly been to bring the supervision of a large number of banks, regardless of their form of charter, as well as many nonbank financial activities under the control of the Federal Reserve System. The Federal Reserve Board is required by the Bank Holding Company Act of 1956 to consider in its processing of holding company applications to acquire or form banks ". . . the financial and managerial resources and future prospects of the [holding] company or companies and the banks concerned," as stated in Section 3(c), in addition to any "unsound banking practices" that might result from a proposed nonbanking activity, as noted in Section 4(c)(8). (The Board has implemented these responsibilities primarily on a case-by-case basis.) Also, Section 5(b) authorizes the Board ". . . to issue such regulations and orders as may be necessary to enable it to administer and carry out the purposes of this Act and prevent evasions thereof," while Section 5(c) permits the Board to require reports and to make examinations of each company and each subsidiary to ascertain compliance with those regulations and orders. Thus the Federal Reserve Board is empowered to supervise any component and activity of a holding company that impacts on the safety of a subsidiary bank.

The Board of Governors appears to have interpreted its authority under the act broadly to include monitoring the operations of any firm affiliated with a bank holding company and taking supervisory action (e.g., cease and desist orders)[s] when indications are that a particular action of a nonbank or bank subsidiary might affect a sister bank affiliate adversely. As a part of its bank holding company supervision, the Board has instituted on-site examination procedures for nonbank subsidiaries and parent companies of bank holding companies and has the authority to inspect any bank subsidiary as well. The Board and the Reserve Banks also have developed comprehensive programs to monitor bank and bank holding company performance over time and have been conducting research on sophisticated, statistical "early warning" models that classify institutions as to their vulnerability to economic downturns. In effect, therefore, the Federal Reserve Board's authority is pervasive and to some extent permits it to circumvent the jurisdictional rights of the chartering authorities or other financial regulatory authorities.

The pros and cons of our complex, multijurisdictional financial regulatory system have been debated extensively. Critics of the current fragmentary structure argue that it does not provide equality of treatment of federally and state-chartered institutions, inhibits prompt and effective regulatory action to curb unsound practices, generates pressure on regulatory agencies to establish lowered standards, and is burdened by duplication of effort by the various agencies with attendant inefficiencies and higher levels of cost. On the other hand, proponents contend that such fragmentation precludes concentration of power into any one agency, provides for flexible and innovative regulation, and serves as a safeguard against oppressive or capricious regulation. Moreover, the proponents have argued that the present structure has worked well to preserve the safety and stability of our banking system.

To the extent that diversity and dispersion of bank regulatory authority is beneficial to the public, the buildup of supervisory and regulatory power within the Federal Reserve Board arising from its role in supervising the bank holding company movement may eventually reach a point that is not desirable. Significant power is being concentrated within this agency such that the Board is gaining supervisory control over nonmember as well as member banks and nonbank financial and service institutions in the consulting, leasing, consumer, mortgage and commercial financing, and data processing industries. This trend represents encroachment on the power of states and a gradual move to federal regulation of nonbank, financially related firms. Consequently, we feel that a review of this trend in bank regulation should be undertaken.

[s]Each bank regulator has cease-and-desist authority to protect the soundness of banks within its jurisdiction, and the Federal Reserve Board has similar authority with respect to "unsafe and unsound" bank holding company practices under Public Law 93–495 (October 28, 1974), which amended 12 U.S.C. Section 1818(b)(1970). The latter cease-and-desist powers have been rarely used, however. Rather, the Board has chosen to correct or prevent abuses through its actions on applications to expand, either by denials or conditions on approval.

In addition, the authors conclude that the Federal Reserve System has administered the Bank Holding Company Act in a reasonably efficient and equitable manner, with the result that the public has benefited. Moreover, the Federal Reserve System appears well equipped to handle in a like manner its broad authority over bank and nonbank institutions in the future. We are not concerned about the System's ability to supervise effectively and fairly. However, two problems appear to have arisen since 1970 that diminish the effectiveness of Board bank holding company supervision. First, we wish to point out that the rapid turnover of governors during the past few years increases the likelihood that regulatory consistency will suffer. Second, we also question whether the Board's primary emphasis on the applications process and its case-by-case approach as a means of regulating bank holding company expansion can adequately deal with the potentially serious problems of increased aggregate concentration of financial resources and reduced financial soundness of banking organizations.

10 Conclusions

The bank holding company movement as it has developed during the 1970s has enabled banking organizations to expand their product and geographic markets in ways that are largely foreclosed to them as commercial banks. This change has had significant implications for public policy. This study has focused on those aspects of bank holding company growth that impact on the public interest and has indirectly evaluated the performance of the Board of Governors of the Federal Reserve System in carrying out the mandate of Congress that bank holding company expansion be in the public interest. In particular, we addressed the individual case rulings of the Federal Reserve Board on applications by bank holding companies to expand, analyzed the implications of the holding company movement for bank soundness, and examined certain significant policy issues.

Analysis of Public Benefits Test

We conclude from our examination of the Board's orders in bank and nonbank cases, presented in Chapters 5 and 6, that the willingness of the Board to attach significance to the public benefits cited by an applicant was heavily dependent on the severity, or lack thereof, of any adverse competitive, financial, or managerial factors the Board perceived to be inherent in the application. We should note that with the economic downturn that began in 1974 the Board introduced its "go-slow" policy and became much more concerned with the potential financial implications of holding company expansion. Nevertheless, in those instances where the Board determined a proposal involved no seriously adverse competitive or other effects, it generally accepted the applicant's claim of probable benefits to the public and approved the acquisition. We believe it is particularly significant, however, that the Board appears never to have found, so far as we can tell, proposed public benefits sufficient to outweigh the adverse effects of a substantial reduction of competition, unsound banking practices, or what it considered an undue concentration of resources.

In view of the often unique circumstances of each case, we are unable to generalize on the exact situation in which the Board would conclude that public benefits would outweigh or be outweighed by adverse effects. The overall results of our analysis suggest, however, that public benefits provide the strongest support for an application when the benefits are concrete, when they result in the alleviation of a specific problem, or when they result in lower prices or increased services to the public. Applicants must recognize that such benefits are essential in cases where even a small amount of competition would be eliminated. Yet the value of substantive benefits is increasingly uncertain the more severe are the anticompetitive or other adverse factors perceived by the Board. In addition, applicants should be sensitive to the economic climate and its implications for the public interest factors relevant to a bank holding company's expansion plans.

Bank Soundness

In Chapters 7 and 8 we examined the characteristics of the bank holding company form of organization that lead to increased risk for subsidiary banks as well as those factors that might lead to risk reduction in bank holding companies. Basically, both the ability of bank holding companies to exploit the desire of the public to protect banks from failure and the wider latitude for riskier investment by holding companies than individual banks, lead us, in theory, to expect a greater proclivity for risk taking in bank holding company subsidiaries than in similar independently owned firms.

The empirical evidence presented in Chapter 8 indicates that indeed banks affiliated with bank holding companies are pursuing riskier operating policies than independently owned banks, although there are apparently differences in bank risk taking among states. In the areas of capital adequacy, debt leveraging, and liquidity, banks affiliated with holding companies have exhibited a desire to assume greater levels of risk. We should note that the evidence presented is strongest in the case of institutions located in New York State.

While the evidence regarding New York banks indicated a greater assumption of risk by bank subsidiaries of bank holding companies, it also indicated that affiliated banks have been extending no more risky loans than independent banks. In addition, holding company banks appear to be employing lesser amounts of long-term debt in their capital structure than independent banks. However, our conclusion is that much of the debt in affiliated banks accounted for as short term is in fact debt of a longer-term nature that is generated by double leveraging (i.e., the parent issuing debt or equity and allocating it to the subsidiaries as short-term debt that is frequently extended).

Our findings of inconsistencies when the models were replicated for New Jersey banks suggests that future research should examine a larger assortment of regions and states, but careful attention should be paid to the problems of aggregation discussed in Chapter 8.

Public Policy Issues

Our analysis of the data on holding company expansion leads us to conclude that the bank holding company movement has had a major impact on the ability of the nation's banks to expand geographically. It also indicates that the wider geographic scope of competition in financial services may have improved the allocation of financial resources. Moreover, we believe that the principal beneficiaries of this expansion probably have been consumers and small businesses since the nation's major banks have traditionally operated in national and international markets for large deposits and large business loans.

The available evidence (discussed in Chapter 9) mildly suggests that bank holding company entry into banking and nonbanking markets has resulted in added price competition. Competition among market participants has most likely been increased in those instances where bank holding companies have fulfilled their promises of price reductions and new services. The most substantive evidence involves the effect of holding company expansion on market structure. There is a reasonably clear indication that foothold entry into new banking markets has resulted in decreased market concentration, particularly in states that limit branching. In addition, in all likelihood bank holding company foothold or de novo entry into nonbanking markets has had a similar effect. However, we should note that this circumstantial evidence does not provide direct information on the competitive behavior of market participants.

Aggregate Concentration

We consider the impact of the bank holding company movement on concentration within the banking industry and the financial sector of the economy to be a significant issue. Aggregate concentration is an issue that has long concerned Congress and the public. A large resource base potentially gives a firm a degree of economic power that arises independently of its position in specific markets. This concern of Congress was manifested in the public benefits test discussed in Part II of the book, and as we noted there, the Federal Reserve Board has addressed itself in certain cases to this issue. However, our analysis of the relevant data relating to share of financial sector assets indicates that there has been a striking increase in the share of domestic assets of the private financial sector accounted for by the 100 largest banking organizations from 15 percent in 1966 to 26 percent in 1974.

Based on our analysis of available data we conclude that bank holding companies' nonbank acquisitions have not contributed significantly to the increase in aggregate concentration. Nevertheless, in our view, the increasing trend toward aggregate concentration as we have measured it appears to be attributable in part to the growth of bank holding companies. We believe that the increased share of the nation's largest banking organizations in the private financial sector results from a variety of factors including: (1) the bank acquisition and merger activity of the largest banking organizations, most of which are bank holding companies; (2) increased use by large banks of nondeposit sources of funds, some of which is due to holding company financing flexibility; and (3) increasing share of bank credit in total financial sector credit.

Financial Soundness

The evidence that we have accumulated and presented in Chapters 8 and 9 leads us to conclude that the bank holding company movement has contributed to a deterioration in the financial condition of some of the nation's banking organizations. These adverse financial effects appear largely to be attributable to the behavioral characteristics of the firm itself, as theorized in Chapter 7, and only in part to the economic downturn of the early 1970s. We also believe that this deterioration is reversible with appropriate supervision of the holding company as a whole rather than just supervision of individual subsidiary banks.

Implication for the Structure of Regulation

One significant effect of the bank holding company movement has been to bring the supervision of a large number of banks, regardless of charter or primary regulator, under the control of the Federal Reserve System. In addition, the Federal Reserve Board is gaining increasing influence over numerous nonbank financial activities. As a result of the amended Bank Holding Company Act of 1956, the Federal Reserve Board's authority is pervasive and to some extent permits it to circumvent the jurisdictional rights of the chartering authorities or other financial regulatory authorities. Inasmuch as the Board is gaining supervisory control over nonmember and national banks as well as nonbank financial and service institutions, we feel that a review of the implications of this trend in bank regulation should be undertaken.

Concluding Comments

Our analyses indicate to us that the bank holding company movement has permitted banks to expand in bank-related areas and experiment in new means of financing operations in ways that probably would not be feasible to banks, because of financial or regulatory obstacles. We believe that on balance this expansion has benefited the public and therefore has been in the public interest. At the same time our experience in studying the bank holding company movement has indicated a need for closer supervision of the nonbanking and parent operations of these organizations than heretofore has existed in order to ensure that the further evolution of bank holding companies will be in the public interest.

In addition, we conclude that the Federal Reserve System has administered the Bank Holding Compnay Act in a reasonably efficient and equitable manner, with the result that the public has benefited. While we are not concerned with the Board's ability to supervise effectively and fairly, we note a present lack of evidence on postacquisition performance regarding commitments made by holding companies seeking to acquire banks and nonbank firms. Moreover, we question whether the Board's primary emphasis on the applications process and its case-by-case approach can adequately deal with the potentially serious problems of aggregate concentration of financial resources and reduced financial soundness of banking organizations.

Notes

Notes

Chapter 1
Introduction

1. See dissenting statement in the Board order regarding the application of Chemical New York Corporation to acquire Eastern National Bank of Long Island (72 *FRB* 167). (Throughout this volume *FRB* is used to refer to *Federal Reserve Bulletin;* the number preceding *FRB* represents the year of issue; and the number following *FRB* is the initial page on which the order appears.)

Chapter 2
Early Development of the Bank Holding Company Movement

1. G. Eccles, "Registered Bank Holding Companies," in H.V. Prochnow, ed., *The One-Bank Holding Company,* (Chicago: Rand McNally, 1969), pp. 83-84.

2. R.J. Lawrence, *The Performance of Bank Holding Companies–Part I* (Washington, D.C.: Board of Governors of the Federal Reserve System, 1967), pp. 1-2.

3. G.C. Fischer, *Bank Holding Companies* (New York: Columbia University Press, 1961), p. 95.

4. Federal Reserve System Board of Governors, *Annual Report for the Year 1927,* Washington, D.C., p. 31.

5. 68 *FRB* 100-01.

6. U.S. Congress, House, Committee on Banking and Currency, *Control and Regulation of Bank Holding Companies: Hearings on H.R. 2674,* 84th Cong., 1st sess., July 1955, pp. 380-82.

7. U.S. Congress, Banking Act of 1933 (48 Stat. 162).

8. C. Arlt, "Background and History," in H.V. Prochnow, ed., *The One-Bank Holding Company,* pp. 17-19.

9. U.S. Congress, Bank Holding Company Act of 1956 (70 Stat. 133), May 9, 1956.

10. J. Bunting, Jr., "One-Bank Holding Companies: A Banker's View," *Harvard Business Review* 47 (May-June 1969): 99-106.

11. See K. Randall, "An Evolutionary Process in Banking," pp. 48-55, and H. Keefe, Jr., "The One-Bank Holding Company–A Result, Not a Revolution," pp. 116-41, both in H.V. Prochnow, ed., *The One-Bank Holding Company.*

12. Keefe, ibid., pp. 118-23.

13. Ibid., p. 123.

14. Bunting, "One-Bank Holding Companies," p. 43.

15. Keefe, "The One-Bank Holding Companies," p. 125.

16. See, for example, P. Jessup, "Portfolio Strategies for Bank Holding Companies," *Bankers Magazine* 152 (Spring 1969): 78-85, and W. Whitesell, "Economics of the One-Bank Holding Company," *Bankers Magazine* 152 (Winter 1969): 28-34.

17. The reader is referred to 72 *FRB* A99, for a table describing the extent of one-bank holding company participation in nonbank fields during the 1960s.

Chapter 3
The 1970 Amendments to the Bank Holding Company Act

1. U.S. Congress, House, Committee on Banking and Currency, *Bank Holding Company Act Amendments: Hearings on H.R. 6778,* 91st Cong., 1st sess., April 15-18, 21-25, 1969.

2. U.S. Congress, House, Committee on Banking and Currency, *Report No. 91-387, Bank Holding Companies,* 91st Cong., 1st sess., July 23, 1969.

3. Ibid., p. 15.

4. Ibid., p. 3.

5. Ibid., pp. 19-27.

6. U.S. Congress, *Congressional Record–House,* 91st Cong., 1st sess., November 5, 1969, pp. 33125-53.

7. Ibid., p. 33139.

8. U.S. Congress, Senate, Committee on Banking and Currency, *Report No. 91-1084, Bank Holding Company Act Amendments of 1970,* 91st Congress, 2nd sess., August 10, 1970.

9. Ibid., pp. 4–5.

10. Ibid., p. 8

11. Ibid., p. 10.

12. Ibid., pp. 30–33.

13. Ibid., pp. 34–38.

14. U.S. Congress, *Congressional Record–Senate,* 91st Cong., 2nd sess., September 16, 1970, p. 32136.

15. Ibid., pp. 32118-23.

16. Ibid., pp. 32104–16.

17. Ibid., pp. 32133–35.

18. Ibid., p. 32124.

19. Ibid., pp. 32124-33.

20. U.S. Congress, House of Representatives, *Report No. 91-1747, Bank Holding Company Act Amendments, Conference Report,* 91st Cong., 2nd sess., December 15, 1970.

21. Ibid., p. 23.

22. Ibid., pp. 13-14.

23. Ibid., p. 21.

24. U.S. Congress, *Congressional Record–Senate,* 91st Cong., 2nd sess., December 18, 1970, p. 42422.

25. U.S. Congress, Senate, *Report No. 91-1084,* p. 14.

26. U.S. Congress, House, *Report No. 91-1747,* pp. 16-19.

27. Ibid., p. 17.

28. Ibid.

29. Ibid., pp. 18-19.

30. Ibid., p. 19.

Chapter 4
The Bank Holding Company Movement Since 1970

1. Data are reported in P. Coldwell, "Bank Holding Company Regulation," address before the Bank Holding Company Administration Conference, New Orleans, May 5, 1975.

2. For a list and discussion of these original proposed activities, see B. Leavitt, "The Fed Discusses the Bank Holding Company Act," *Banking* 63 (March 1971): 51 and 82.

3. R. Janssen and E. Foldessy, "Holding-Firm Law Designed to Limit Banks Instead Opens New Finance-Service Vistas," *The Wall Street Journal,* January 7, 1972, p. 24.

4. Ibid.

5. See, for example, case decisions regarding State Street Boston Financial Corporation (73 *FRB* 526), Continental Bancor, Inc. (71 *FRB* 676), Manufacturers Hanover Corporation (37 *Federal Register* [hereafter *FR*] 27659), and Chemical New York Corporation (73 *FRB* 698). In the last order, the Board reemphasized a position it has taken in several cases that ". . . one of the primary purposes of a holding company is to serve as a source of financial strength for its subsidiary banks."

6. See 74 *FRB* 517-23.

7. 74 *FRB* 517.

8. See American Fletcher Corporation-Southwest Savings and Loan Association, 74 *FRB* 868, for denial of S&L acquisition and 74 *FRB* 727 for state-

ment of denial of underwriting mortgage guaranty insurance as a permissible nonbank activity.

9. 74 *FRB* 868.

10. R. Holland, Testimony before the Subcommittee on Bank Supervision and Insurance of the Committee on Banking and Currency, U.S. House of Representatives, December 12, 1974. (See 74 *FRB* 838.)

11. P. Coldwell, "Multibank Holding Companies–Dictator or Servant to the Public Interest," address before the 14th Annual Convention of the Independent Bankers of Minnesota, Minneapolis, August 14, 1975.

12. 76 *FRB* 794.

Chapter 5
Analysis of Public Benefits: Bank Expansion

1. See First Union National Bancorporation (72 *FRB* 72) and First Chicago Corporation (72 *FRB* 175).

2. See 74 *FRB* 595.

3. See, for example, Atlantic Bancorporation (71 *FRB* 689), Imperial Bancorporation (72 *FRB* 503), U.N. Bancshares, Inc. (73 *FRB* 204), and First New Mexico Bankshare Corporation (76 *FRB* 373).

4. See 75 *FRB* 174.

5. See First Alabama Bankshares (71 *FRB* 404) and First Florida Bancorporation (71 *FRB* 256).

6. Barclays Bank DCO (71 *FRB* 44).

7. See, for example, Barnett Banks of Florida, Inc. (71 *FRB* 529), United Missouri Bankshares, Inc. (72 *FRB* 655), and Missouri Bankshares (71 *FRB* 542).

8. First National Bancorporation (71 *FRB* 345).

9. See 71 *FRB* 345.

10. See, for example, First American Bancshares (72 *FRB* 730).

11. See 76 *FRB* 541.

12. For example, Great Lakes Holding Company (71 *FRB* 545), Wyoming Bancorporation (75 *FRB* 37), and Northeast United Bancorp, Inc. of Texas (76 *FRB* 155).

13. For additional examples see, State Street Boston Financial Corporation (73 *FRB* 526) and the First National Bancorporation (71 *FRB* 613).

14. See, for example, Depositors Corporation (71 *FRB* 36).

15. See First Banc Group of Ohio (71 *FRB* 418).

16. Bank Securities, Inc. (72 *FRB* 280).

17. Newport Savings and Loan Association (72 *FRB* 313) and Old Colony Co-Operative Bank (72 *FRB* 417). As a result of various legal and regulatory re-

strictions, savings and loan associations in Rhode Island have been at a competitive disadvantage with respect to other thrift institutions in providing checking account services. Mutual savings banks have been able to issue demand deposits through commercial bank subsidiaries acquired prior to 1971. Since 1971, credit unions with shares of more than $1 million have been permitted to accept demand deposits. Noting this competitive disadvantage, the Board has allowed each of the above savings and loan associations to become a bank holding company and acquire a commercial bank in Rhode Island.

18. The Board subsequently approved the acquisition after Cegrove offered to raise additional equity capital (39 *FR* 8387).

19. See 74 *FRB* 290.

20. See Security Financial Services, Inc. (70 *FRB* 834).

21. First at Orlando Corporation (73 *FRB* 302).

Chapter 6
Analysis of Public Benefits:
Nonbank Expansion

1. See, for example, First Union National Bancorporation (72 *FRB* 72) and First Chicago Corporation (72 *FRB* 175).

2. See, as examples of cases involving acquisitions of consumer finance companies: First Bank System (72 *FRB* 172), American Fletcher Corporation (72 *FRB* 741), and Manufacturers Hanover Corporation (75 *FRB* 42). Second mortgage lender acquisitions involved Bank of Virginia Company (72 *FRB* 934) and Dominion Bankshares Corporation (72 *FRB* 597).

3. Industrial National Corporation (72 *FRB* 171) and Bank of Virginia Company (72 *FRB* 935).

4. Citizens and Southern Holding Company (71 *FRB* 1037).

5. See Lincoln First Banks (72 *FRB* 169).

6. Marshall and Ilsley Bank Stock Corporation (72 *FRB* 74), Provident National Corporation (72 *FRB* 933), and Midlantic Banks, Inc. (75 *FRB* 329).

7. Western Kansas Investment Corporation, Inc. (72 *FRB* 737).

8. See, for example, First Bank System (72 *FRB* 172) and American Fletcher Corporation (72 *FRB* 741).

9. See First Union National Bancorporation (72 *FRB* 72).

10. See, respectively, Marine Bancorporation (72 *FRB* 504) and Northwest Bancorporation (73 *FRB* 701).

11. See, for example, U.N. Bancshares, Inc. (73 *FRB* 204).

12. Bank of Virginia Company (72 *FRB* 934).

13. United Virginia Bancshares (72 *FRB* 938).

14. See, respectively, American Bancorporation, Inc. (75 *FRB* 177) and The Citizens and Southern Corporation (74 *FRB* 226).

15. See BankAmerica Corporation (73 *FRB* 687) and Manufacturers Hanover Corporation (75 *FRB* 42).

16. See, for example, Fourth Financial Corporation (73 *FRB* 687), Northwest Bancorporation (38 *FR* 14205), Irwin Union Corporation (74 *FRB* 138), and Central Mortgage Bancshares, Inc. (76 *FRB* 342).

17. See 76 *FRB* 537.

18. See Carolina Bancorp (74 *FRB* 385) and South Carolina National Corporation (74 *FRB* 514).

19. See The Citizens and Southern Corporation (74 *FRB* 226).

20. See First Arkansas Bankstock Corporation (73 *FRB* 28), Deposit Guaranty Corporation (73 *FRB* 593), Manufacturers Hanover Corporation (37 *FRB* 27659), and Security Pacific Corporation (74 *FRB* 607).

21. See, for example, BankAmerica Corporation (73 *FRB* 687), Northwest Bancorporation (73 *FRB* 701), Third National Corporation (38 *FR* 9686), and Fidelcorp, Inc. (75 *FRB* 323).

22. See Industrial National Corporation (72 *FRB* 171).

23. See, for example, concurring statement in the BankAmerica-GAC order (73 *FRB* 687).

24. See BankAmerica Corporation (73 *FRB* 687), Zions Utah Bancorporation (72 *FRB* 72), and Citicorp (76 *FRB* 390).

25. See First National City Corporation (38 *FR* 31711).

26. See Mellon National Corporation (75 *FRB* 45).

27. See First Banc Group of Ohio (71 *FRB* 418).

28. See, for example, Northwest Bancorporation (73 *FRB* 701).

29. See Bank of Virginia Company (74 *FRB* 512).

30. See American Fletcher Corporation (38 *FR* 14203).

31. See, for example, U.S. Bancorporation (72 *FRB* 177) and Crocker National Corporation (72 *FRB* 419). In addition, two proposed de novo insurance agency applications were denied without considering public benefits because these agencies were to be located in offices of banks that the applicants wished to acquire and the Board denied (Union Bank and Trust Company, 74 *FRB* 463, and Stuarco Oil Company, Inc., 75 *FRB* 178).

32. Steven Seelig, "Convenience and Advantage Clause as a Barrier to Entry in the Consumer Finance Industry," Working Papers in Financial Economics, No. 7601, Fordham University, New York, February 1976.

33. See BTNB Corporation (72 *FRB* 70). See also Marine Bancorporation (72 *FRB* 504), Philadelphia National Corporation (73 *FRB* 913), and Pittsburgh National Corporation (74 *FRB* 391).

34. See Manufacturers Hanover Corporation (73 *FRB* 532) and First Tulsa Bancorporation (72 *FRB* 317). The Board later reconsidered the former case subsequent to the order of denial and approved this acquisition after the applicant submitted pertinent new information. Moreover, the applicant agreed to

eliminate a covenant not to compete from various employment agreements. Such covenants, if unreasonably restrictive, have beeen cited by the Board as anticompetitive (see Manufacturers Hanover Corporation, 73 *FRB* 908).

35. In addition to those cases mentioned in the text, consumer finance company acquisitions that have been denied on competitive grounds include First National Holding Corporation (73 *FRB* 203), Bankers Trust New York Corporation (73 *FRB* 694), First National Holding Corporation (74 *FRB* 381), and Carolina Bancorp, Inc. (74 *FRB* 385).

36. See American Fletcher Corporation (74 *FRB* 868) and Memphis Trust Company (75 *FRB* 327).

37. Bancshares of Indiana, Inc. (74 *FRB* 872). This case was subsequently approved after applicant made certain commitments to use the assets of the acquired firm to bolster the bank's capital (see 75 *FRB* 40).

38. First National City Corporation changed its name and is now Citicorp.

39. See, for example, Manufacturers Hanover Corporation (73 *FRB* 532) and Citizens and Southern National Bank (74 *FRB* 136).

40. See dissenting statement regarding Chemical New York Corporation (72 *FRB* 165).

41. In a speech before the Bank Counsel Seminar of the California Bankers Association, Santa Barbara, April 26, 1974, Governor Bucher emphasized that ". . . the Board requires measurable indications of gains for the public from bank holding company acquisitions, [and] . . . the Board has moved significantly in the direction of making those gains quite specific."

42. Stephen Rhoades, "The Effect of Bank-Holding Company Acquisitions of Morgage Bankers on Mortgage Lending Activity," *Journal of Business* 48 (July 1975): 344.

43. Ibid., p. 348.

44. See, for example, First Virginia Bankshares Corporation (73 *FRB* 202).

Chapter 7
Impact of Holding Company Affiliation on Bank Soundness: Theory

1. See the Federal Reserve Board's order regarding the proposed acquisition of CNA Nuclear Leasing, Inc., by Chemical New York Corporation (73 *FRB* 698).

2. Such a motivating factor is implicit in the discussion by B. Shull, "Multiple-Office Banking and the Structure of Banking Markets: The New York and Virginia Experience," *Proceedings of a Conference on Bank Structure and Competition* (Chicago: Federal Reserve Bank of Chicago, 1972), pp. 30-40.

3. See, for example, R. Lawrence, *Operating Policies of Bank Holding Companies–Part I* (Washington, D.C.: Board of Governors of the Federal Reserve System, 1974).

4. See J. Bunting, Jr., "One-Bank Holding Companies: A Banker's View," *Harvard Business Review* 47 (May-June 1969): 99-106.

5. See, for example, J. Guttentag, "Reflections on Bank Regulatory Structure and Large Bank Failures," *Proceedings of a Conference on Bank Structure and Competition* (Chicago: Federal Reserve Bank of Chicago, 1975), pp. 136-49.

6. R. Holland, "Bank Holding Companies and Financial Stability," paper presented at the Conference of the Western Economic Association, San Diego, June 26, 1975, p. 10.

7. J. Mingo, "Managerial Motives, Market Structure, and the Performance of Holding Company Banks," *Economic Inquiry* 4 (September 1976): 411-24.

8. Two sources of data submitted to the Federal Reserve System concerning intracorporate transactions are the Annual Report (F.R. Y-6) of the bank holding company and the Report of Intercompany Transactions and Balances (F.R. Y-8).

9. A complete discussion of potential abusive intracorporate practices is contained in M. Jessee, "An Analysis of Risk-Taking Behavior in Bank Holding Companies," unpublished Ph.D. dissertation, University of Pennsylvania, Philadelphia, 1976, pp. 152-67.

10. H. Levy and M. Sarnat, "Diversification, Portfolio Analysis and the Uneasy Case for Conglomerate Mergers," *The Journal of Finance* 25 (September 1970): 795-802, and W. Lewellen, "A Pure Financial Rationale for the Conglomerate Merger," *The Journal of Finance* 26 (May 1971): 521-35.

11. A. Heggestad, "Riskiness of Investments in Nonbank Activities by Bank Holding Companies," *Journal of Economics and Business* 27 (Spring 1975): 219-23.

12. Jessee, "An Analysis of Risk-Taking Behavior."

13. S. Schweitzer, "Economies of Scale and Holding Company Affiliation in Banking," *Southern Economic Journal* 39 (1972): 258-66.

14. R. Dugger, "The Impact of Holding Company Affiliation on the Operating Efficiency of Commercial Banks," unpublished paper, Board of Governors of the Federal Reserve System, Washington, D.C., 1974.

15. F. Kalish, III, and R. Gilbert, "An Analysis of Efficiency of Scale and Organizational Form in Commercial Banking," *Journal of Industrial Economics* 21 (July 1973): 293-307.

16. W. Longbrake and J. Haslem, "Productive Efficiency in Commercial Banking: The Effects of Size and Legal Form in Organization on the Cost of Producing Demand Deposit Services," *Journal of Money, Credit and Banking,* August 1975.

17. D. Mullineaux, "Branch Versus Unit Banking: An Analysis of Relative

Costs," unpublished paper, Department of Research, Federal Reserve Bank of Philadelphia, 1973.

18. R. Johnson, "The Rationale for Acquisition of Finance Companies by Bank Holding Companies," Paper No. 481, Institute for Research in the Behavioral, Economic, and Management Sciences, Purdue University, Lafayette, Ind., September 1974, p. 21.

19. D. Mueller, "A Theory of Conglomerate Mergers," *Quarterly Journal of Economics* 83 (November 1969): 643.

Chapter 8
Tests of the Impact of Affiliation on the Soundness of Bank Subsidiaries

1. A complete discussion of these risk concepts may be found in G. Vojta, *Bank Capital Adequacy* (New York: First National City Bank, 1973), pp. 16–17, and H. Crosse and G. Hempel, *Management Policies for Commercial Banks,* 2nd ed. (Englewood Cliffs, N.J.: Prentice-Hall, 1973), Chapter 8.

2. See, for example, S. Chase, Jr., "Bank Holding Companies, the Profit Motive and the Public Interest," *Proceedings of a Conference on Banking Organizations and Their Regulation* (Minneapolis: Federal Reserve Bank of Minneapolis, 1974), pp. 15-21. A discussion of this and other evidence on dividend withdrawals is found in M. Jessee, "An Analysis of Risk-Taking Behavior in Bank Holding Companies," unpublished Ph.D. dissertation, University of Pennsylvania, Philadelphia, 1976, pp. 156–58.

3. See R. Lawrence, *The Performance of Bank Holding Companies* (Washington, D.C.: Board of Governors of the Federal Reserve System, 1974): S. Talley, *The Effect of Holding Company Acquisitions on Bank Performance,* Staff Economic Study No. 69 (Washington, D.C.: Board of Governors of the Federal Reserve System, 1971); J. McCleary, "Bank Holding Companies: Their Growth and Performance," *Monthly Review* (Federal Reserve Bank of Atlanta), October 1968, pp. 131-38; J. McCleary, "Absentee Ownership—Its Impact on Bank Holding Company Performance," *Monthly Review* (Federal Reserve Bank of Atlanta), August 1969, pp. 99-101; and G. Fischer, *Bank Holding Companies* (New York: Columbia University Press, 1961).

4. Lawrence, *The Performance of Bank Holding Companies,* pp. 19-20.

5. R. Johnson and D. Meinster, "The Performance of Bank Holding Company Acquisitions: A Multivariate Analysis," *The Journal of Business* 48 (April 1975): 204–12.

6. See A. Frass, *The Performance of Individual Bank Holding Companies,* Staff Economic Study No. 84 (Washington, D.C.: Board of Governors of the Federal Reserve System, 1975), and J. Mingo, "Managerial Motives, Market

Structure, and the Performance of Holding Company Banks," *Economic Inquiry* 4 (September 1976): 411-24.

7. In particular, L. Mayne, "Supervisory Influence on Bank Capital," *The Journal of Finance* 27 (June 1972); J. Mingo, "Regulatory Influence on Bank Capital Investment," *The Journal of Finance* 30 (September 1975): 1111-122; S. Peltzman, "Capital Investment in Commercial Banking and Its Relationship to Portfolio Regulation," *Journal of Political Economy* 78 (January-February 1970): 1-26; and R. Robinson and R. Pettway, *Policies for Optimum Bank Capital* (Chicago: Association of Reserve City Bankers, 1966).

8. See A. Throop, "Capital Investment and Entry in Commercial Banking: A Competitive Model," *Journal of Money, Credit, and Banking* 7 (May 1975): 193-214, for a discussion of this relationship and a critique of Peltzman's theory.

9. See Mayne, "Supervisory Influence," Robinson and Pettway, *Policies for Optimum Bank Capital,* and Mingo, "Managerial Motives."

10. See J. Mingo, "Capital Management and Profitability of Prospective Holding Company Banks," *Journal of Financial and Quantitative Analysis* 10 (June 1975): 191-203, and Mayne, "Supervisory Influence."

11. D. Jacobs, H. Beighley, and J. Boyd, *The Financial Structure of Bank Holding Companies* (Chicago: Association of Reserve City Bankers, 1975).

12. F. Weston and E. Brigham, *Managerial Finance,* 3rd ed. (New York: Holt, Rinehart, and Winston, 1969), pp. 294-97.

13. See G. Donaldson, *Corporate Debt Capacity* (Cambridge, Mass.: Harvard University Press, 1961).

14. See W. Fichthorn, "Do Bank Capital Notes Merit Investment Stature," *Financial Analysts Journal,* July/August 1967.

15. For a discussion of liquid asset management, see, for example, J. Pierce, "Commercial Bank Liquidity," 66 *FRB* 1093-01, and Crosse and Hempel, *Management Policies*, Chapters 8 and 9. Specific analysis of liability management may be found in S. Schweitzer, "Bank Liability Management: For Better or For Worse?" *Business Review* (Federal Reserve Bank of Philadelphia), December 1974, pp. 3-12; G. Woodworth, "Theories of Cyclical Liquidity Management of Commercial Banks," *National Banking Review* 4 (June 1967): 377-96; and Crosse and Hempel, *Management Policies* pp. 130-2, 138-9, 155-6.

16. See E. Lerner, "Three Financial Problems Facing Bank Holding Companies, A Comment," *Journal of Money, Credit, and Banking* 4 (May 1972): 445-55.

17. See J. Van Horne, *Financial Management and Policy* (Englewood Cliffs, N.J.: Prentice-Hall, 1968), pp. 145-147, for examples.

18. D. Hodgman, *Commercial Bank Loan and Investment Policy* (Urbana: University of Illinois, 1963).

19. G. Morrison, *Liquidity Preferences of Commercial Banks,* (Chicago: The University of Chicago Press, 1966).

20. Lawrence, *The Performance of Bank Holding Compnaies,* Talley, *The*

Effect of Holding Company, and Johnson and Meinster, "The Performance of Bank Holding Company Acquisitions."

21. R. Lawrence, *Operating Policies of Bank Holding Companies–Part I* (Washington, D.C.: Board of Governors of the Federal Reserve System, 1971).

22. R. Gilbert, "Bank Failures and Public Policy," *Monthly Review* (Federal Reserve Bank of St. Louis), Novermber 1975, pp. 7. Gilbert also notes that these two policy goals can be made more compatible by altering the federal deposit insurance program ". . . such that the premiums on deposit insurance are based upon the risk banks assume." We should note, however, that such a change would not protect banks affiliated with holding companies from greater risk exposure arising from risky practices elsewhere in the holding company.

23. J. Smith, "Some Time, Next Year–A Call for Response to Years of Inaction," remarks before the Carter H. Golembe Associates, Inc., Conference, Washington, D.C., December 8, 1975.

Chapter 9
Significant Public Policy Issues of the Bank Holding Company Movement

1. R. Lawrence and S. Talley, "An Assessment of Bank Holding Companies," 76 *FRB* 15-21.

2. B. Shull, "Multiple-Office Banking and the Structure of Banking Markets: The New York and Virginia Experience," *Proceedings of a Conference on Bank Structure and Competition* (Chicago: Federal Reserve Bank of Chicago, 1972), pp. 30-40.

3. J. Berkowicz, "Bank Holding Company Conduct, Structural Change and Performance of Banks," unpublished Ph.D. dissertation, University of Maryland, College Park, 1973.

4. S. Talley, *The Impact of Holding Company Acquisitions on Aggregate Concentration in Banking,* Staff Economic Study No. 80 (Washington, D.C.: Board of Governors of the Federal Reserve System, 1974).

5. S. Talley, *The Effect of Holding Company Acquisitions on Bank Performance,* Staff Economic Study No. 69 (Washington, D.C.: Board of Governors of the Federal Reserve System, 1971).

6. W. Jackson, "Multibank Holding Companies and Bank Behavior," Working Paper 71-1, Federal Reserve Bank of Richmond, 1975.

7. See M. Jessee, "An Analysis of Risk-Taking Behavior in Bank Holding Companies," unpublished Ph.D. dissertation, University of Pennsylvania, Philadelphia, 1976, and S. Talley, "Bank Holding Company Performance in Consumer Finance and Mortgage Banking," *The Magazine of Bank Administration,* July 1976, pp. 41-43.

8. See R. Schotland, "Bank Holding Companies and Public Policy Today," *Compendium of Papers Prepared for the Fine Study: Committee on Banking, Currency and Housing,* House of Representatives, 94th Cong., 2nd sess., June 1976, p. 260-61.

9. Lawrence and Talley, "An Assessment of Bank Holding Companies," p. 17.

10. W. Lee and A. Reichert, "Effects of Multibank Holding Company Acquisitions of Rural Community Banks," *Conference on Bank Structure and Competition* (Chicago: Federal Reserve Bank of Chicago, 1975).

11. G. Fischer, *Bank Holding Companies* (New York: Columbia University Press, 1961).

12. R. Lawrence, *The Performance of Bank Holding Companies,* (Washington, D.C.: Board of Governors of the Federal Reserve System, 1974).

13. Talley, *The Effect of Holding Company Acquisitions on Bank Performance.*

14. S. Seelig, "Aggregate Concentration and the Bank Holding Company Movement," Working Paper in Financial Economics, No. 7602, Fordham University, New York, July 1976.

15. Talley, *The Impact of Holding Company Acquisitions on Aggregate Concentration in Banking.*

16. Seelig, "Aggregate Concentration."

17. Schotland, "Bank Holding Companies," p. 252.

18. Jessee, "An Analysis of Risk-Taking Behavior," pp. 230-36.

19. R. Pettway, "Market Tests of Capital Adequacy of Large Commercial Banks," *The Journal of Finance* 31 (June 1976): 865-76.

20. D. Humphrey and S. Talley, "Market Regulation of Bank Leverage," Research Papers in Banking and Finance (Washington, D.C.: Board of Governors of the Federal Reserve System, December 1975).

21. D. Jacobs, H. Beighley, and J. Boyd, *The Financial Structure of Bank Holding Companies* (Chicago: Association of Reserve City Bankers, 1975).

22. See, for a discussion of such policies, Jessee, "An Analysis of Risk-Taking Behavior," pp. 156-67.

Bibliography

Association of Registered Bank Holding Companies. "The Bank Holding Company: Its History and Significance in Modern America." Washington, D.C., July 1973.

———. *Washington Financial Report.* Washington, D.C., 1975.

Bell, F.W., and N.B. Murphy. *Costs in Commercial Banking: A Quantitative Analysis of Bank Behavior and Its Relation to Bank Regulation,* Research Report 41. Boston: Federal Reserve Bank of Boston, 1968.

Benston, G.J. "Economies of Scale and Marginal Costs in Banking Operations." *National Banking Review,* June 1965, pp. 507-49

Berkowicz, J. "Bank Holding Company Conduct, Structural Change and Performance of Banks." Unpublished Ph.D. dissertation, University of Maryland, College Park, 1973.

Boczar, G.E. "The Determinants of Multibank Holding Company Formations." *Southern Economic Journal* 42 (July 1975): 120-29.

Bratter, H. "Legislative History of One-Bank Holding Company Bill." *Banking* 63 (February 1971): 48.

Bunting, John R., Jr. "One-Bank Holding Companies: A Banker's View." *Harvard Business Review* 47 (May-June 1969): 99-106.

Carter H. Golembe Associates, Inc. *The Future of Registered Bank Holding Companies.* Washington, D.C.: The Association of Registered Bank Holding Companies, 1971.

———. *The Nature and Control of One-Bank Holding Companies.* New York, 1968.

Chase, S.B., Jr. "Bank Holding Companies, the Profit Motive and the Public Interest." *Proceedings of a Conference on Banking Organizations and Their Regulation.* Minneapolis: Federal Reserve Bank of Minneapolis, January 1974, pp. 15-21.

———. "The Bank Holding Company as a Device for Sheltering Banks from Risk." *Proceedings of a Conference on Bank Structure and Competition.* Chicago: Federal Reserve Bank of Chicago, 1971, pp. 38-49.

Chase, S., and J. Mingo. "The Regulation of Bank Holding Companies." *The Journal of Finance* 30 (May 1975): 281-92.

Coldwell, P.E. "Bank Holding Company Regulation." Address before the Bank Holding Company Administration Conference, New Orleans, May 5, 1975.

———. "Multibank Holding Companies–Dictator or Servant to the Public Interest." Address before the 14th Annual Convention of the Independent Bankers of Minnesota, Minneapolis, August 14, 1975.

Conference of State Bank Supervisors. "A Profile of State-Chartered Banking," Washington, D.C., December, 1975.

Consolidated Report of Condition. Various years.

Crosse, H.D., and G.H. Hempel. *Management Policies for Commercial Banks,* 2nd ed. Englewood Cliffs, N.J.: Prentice-Hall, 1973.

DeLong, F.G. "Liquidity Requirements and Employment of Funds." In D. Cohen and F. Hammer, *Analytical Methods in Banking.* Ill.: Richard D. Irwin, 1966, pp. 39-44.

Donaldson, G. *Corporate Debt Capacity.* Cambridge, Mass.: Harvard University Press, 1961.

Dugger, R.H. "The Impact of Holding Company Affiliation on the Operating Efficiency of Commercial Banks." Unpublished paper, Board of Governors of the Federal Reserve System, Washington, D.C., 1974.

Eiseman, P.C. "A Test of the Diversification Motive for Congeneric Bank Holding Companies." Unpublished Ph.D. dissertation, University of Michigan, Ann Arbor, 1974.

Fama, E., and M. Miller. *The Theory of Finance.* New York: Holt, Rinehart and Winston, 1972.

Federal Deposit Insurance Corporation. *Annual Report.* Washington, D.C., various years.

Federal Registers (*FR*). Various years.

Federal Reserve System Board of Governors. *Annual Report.* Washington, D.C., various years.

_____. *Bank Holding Company Act.* Report of the Board of Governors of the Federal Reserve System Pursuant to the Bank Holding Company Act of 1956. Washington, D.C.: Government Printing Office, 1958.

_____. *Flow of Funds Accounts 1965-73, Annual Total Flows and Year-End Assets and Liabilities.* Washington, D.C., 1973.

_____. *Regulation Y–Bank Holding Companies* (12 *CFR* 225), as amended effective December 1976.

Federal Reserve Bulletin (*FRB*). Various years.

Fichthorn. W.H. "Do Bank Capital Notes Merit Investment Stature." *Financial Analysts Journal,* July-August 1967.

Fischer, G.C. *Bank Holding Companies.* New York: Columbia University Press, 1961.

_____. *American Banking Structure.* New York: Columbia University Press, 1968.

Frass, A.G. *The Performance of Individual Bank Holding Companies,* Staff Economic Study No. 84. Washington, D.C.: Board of Governors of the Federal Reserve System, 1975.

Gilbert, R.A. "Bank Failures and Public Policy." *Review* (Federal Reserve Bank of St. Louis), November 1975, pp. 7-15.

Gorecki, P.K. "The Measurement of Enterprise Diversification." *The Review of Economics and Statistics* 56 (August 1974): 399-401.

Guttentag, J.M. "Reflections on Bank Regulatory Structure and Large Bank

Failures." *Proceedings of a Conference on Bank Structure and Competition.* Chicago: Federal Reserve Bank of Chicago, 1975, pp. 136-49.

Hall, G.R. "Bank Holding Company Regulation." *The Southern Economic Journal* 31 (April 1965): 342-55.

Heggestad, A. "Riskiness of Investments in Nonbank Activities by Bank Holding Companies." *Journal of Economics and Business* 27 (Spring 1975): 219-23.

_____, and J.J. Mingo. "Capital Management by Holding Company Banks." *The Journal of Business,* October 1975, pp. 500-05.

_____, and J.J. Mingo. "Prices, NonPrices and Concentration in Selected Banking Markets." *Proceedings of a Conference on Bank Structure and Competition.* Chicago: Federal Reserve Bank of Chicago, 1974.

Hodgman, D.R. *Commercial Bank Loan and Investment Policy.* Urbana: University of Illinois, 1963.

Holland, R.C. "Bank Holding Companies and Financial Stability." Paper presented at the Conference of the Western Economic Association, San Diego, June 26, 1975.

_____. Testimony before the Subcommittee on Bank Supervision and Insurance of the Committee on Banking and Currency, U.S. House of Representatives, December 12, 1974 (*FRB* 838).

Humphrey, D., and S. Talley. "Market Regulation of Bank Leverage." Research Papers in Banking and Finance, Board of Governors of the Federal Reserve System, Washington, D.C., December 1975.

Jackson, W. "Multibank Holding Companies and Bank Behavior." Working Paper 75-1, Federal Reserve Bank of Richmond, 1975.

Jacobs, D.P., H. Beighley, and J. Boyd. *The Financial Structure of Bank Holding Companies.* Chicago: Association of Reserve City Bankers, 1975.

Janssen, Richard, and E. Foldessy. "Holding-Firm Law Designed to Limit Banks Instead Opens New Finance-Service Vistas." *The Wall Street Journal,* January 7, 1972, p. 24.

Jessee, M.A. "An Analysis of Risk-Taking Behavior in Bank Holding Companies." Unpublished Ph.D. dissertation, University of Pennsylvania, Philadelphia, 1976.

_____, and S.A. Seelig. "An Analysis of the Public Benefits Test of the Bank Holding Company Act." *Monthly Review* (Federal Reserve Bank of New York), June 1974, pp. 151-62.

Jessup, P.F. "Portfolio Strategies for Bank Holding Companies." *Bankers Magazine* 152 (Spring 1969): 78-85.

Johnson, R.B., ed. *The Bank Holding Company 1973.* Dallas: SMU Press, 1973.

Johnson, R.D., and D.R. Meinster. "An Analysis of Bank Holding Company Acquisitions: Some Methodological Issues." *Journal of Bank Research* 4 (Spring 1973): 58-61.

_____, and D.R. Meinster. "Efficient Bank Holding Company Diversification and the Effects of Regulatory Constraints." *Proceedings of a Conference on Bank Structure and Competition.* Chicago: Federal Reserve Bank of Chicago, 1975.

———, and D.R. Meinster. "The Performance of Bank Holding Company Acquisitions: A Multivariate Analysis." *The Journal of Business* 48 (April 1975): 204-12.

Johnson, R.W. "The Rationale for Acquisition of Finance Companies by Bank Holding Companies." Paper No. 481, Institute for Research in the Behavioral, Economic, and Management Sciences, Purdue University, Lafayette, Ind., September 1974.

Johnston, J. *Econometric Methods,* 2nd ed. New York: McGraw-Hill, 1972.

Kalish, F., III, and R.A. Gilbert. "An Analysis of Efficiency of Scale and Organizational Form in Commercial Banking." *Journal of Industrial Economics* 21 (July 1973): 293-307.

Kidder, K. "Bank Expansion in New York State: The 1971 Statewide Branching Law." *Monthly Review* (Federal Reserve Bank of New York), November 1971, pp. 266-74.

Korobow, L. "Issues in Bank Expansion: The New York-New Jersey Experience." Remarks to the Central Banking Seminar, Federal Reserve Bank of New York, April 9, 1974.

Kunreuther, J.B., and K. Kidder. "Competition and the Changing Banking Structure in New Jersey." *Monthly Review* (Federal Reserve Bank of New York), August 1973, pp. 203-10.

Lawrence, R.J. *Operating Policies of Bank Holding Companies–Part I.* Washington, D.C.: Board of Governors of the Federal Reserve System, 1971.

———. *Operating Policies of Bank Holding Companies–Part II: Nonbanking Subsidiaries.* Washington, D.C.: Board of Governors of the Federal Reserve System, 1974.

———. *The Performance of Bank Holding Companies.* Washington, D.C.: Board of Governors of the Federal Reserve System, 1974.

———, and S.H. Talley. "An Assessment of Bank Holding Companies." 76 *FRB* 15-21.

Leavitt, B.C. "The Fed Discusses the Bank Holding Company Act." *Banking* 63 (March 1971): 51 and 82.

Lee, W.F., and A.K. Reichert. "Effects of Multibank Holding Company Acquisitions of Rural Community Banks." *Proceedings of a Conference on Bank Structure and Competition.* Chicago: Federal Reserve Bank of Chicago, 1975.

Lerner, E.M. "Three Financial Problems Facing Bank Holding Companies, A Comment." *Journal of Money, Credit, and Banking* 4 (May 1972): 445-55.

Levy, H., and M. Sarnat. "Diversification, Portfolio Analysis and the Uneasy Case for Conglomerate Mergers." *The Journal of Finance* 25 (September 1970): 795-802.

Lewellen, W.G. "A Pure Financial Rationale for the Conglomerate Merger." *The Journal of Finance* 26 (May 1971): 521-35.

Longbrake, W., and J.A. Haslem. "Productive Efficiency in Commercial Banking: The Effects of Size and Legal Form in Organization on the Cost of Producing Demand Deposits Services." *Journal of Money, Credit and Banking,* August 1975.

Markowitz, H. *Portfolio Selection: Efficient Diversification of Investments.* New York: John Wiley and Sons, 1959.

Mayne, L.S. "Supervisory Influence on Bank Capital." *The Journal of Finance* 27 (June 1972): 637-52.

McCleary, J. "Bank Holding Companies: Their Growth and Performance." *Monthly Review* (Federal Reserve Bank of Atlanta), October 1968, pp. 131-38.

_____. "Absentee Ownership–Its Impact on Bank Holding Company Performance." *Monthly Review* (Federal Reserve Bank of Atlanta), August 1969, pp. 99-101.

Mingo, J.J. "Capital Management and Profitability of Prospective Holding Company Banks." *Journal of Financial and Quantitative Analysis* 10 (June 1975): 191-203.

_____. "Regulatory Influence on Bank Capital Investment." *The Journal of Finance* 30 (September 1975): 1111-22.

_____. "Managerial Motives, Market Structure, and the Performance of Holding Company Banks." *Economic Inquiry* 4 (September 1976): 411-24.

Mitchell, G.W. "The Federal Reserve and the Bank Holding Company." Address before the Florida Atlantic Executive Program, Boca Raton, Fla., February 13, 1975.

Modigliani, F., and M. Miller. "The Cost of Capital, Corporation Finance and the Theory of Investment." *American Economic Review* 48 (June 1958): 261-97.

Morrison, G.R. *Liquidity Preferences of Commercial Banks.* Chicago: University of Chicago Press, 1966.

Mueller, D.C. "A Theory of Conglomerate Mergers." *Quarterly Journal of Economics* 83 (November 1969): 643-59.

Mullineaux, D.A. "Branch Versus Unit Banking: An Analysis of Relative Costs." Unpublished paper, Department of Research, Federal Reserve Bank of Philadelphia, 1975.

Murphy, N.B. "A Reestimation of Benston-Bell-Murphy Cost Functions for a Larger Sample with Greater Size and Geographical Dispersion." *Journal of Financial and Quantitative Analysis,* December 1972, pp. 97-106.

Nader, R., and J. Brown. "Disclosure and Bank Soundness: Non-Bank Activities of Bank Holding Companies." Public Interest Research Group, Washington, D.C., June 30, 1976.

Nadler, M., and J. Bogen, *The Bank Holding Company.* New York: Graduate

School of Business, New York University, 1959.

Nadler, P.S. "One-Bank Holding Companies: The Public Interest." *Harvard Business Review* 47 (May-June 1969): 107-13.

"New York OBHC's Start Move to Become Multi-Bank." *Burroughs Clearing House* 55 (April 1971).

Paine, Webber, Jackson and Curtis, Inc. *A Comparative Analysis of the 100 Largest Banks and other Representative Banking Institutions.* New York: 1967.

Peltzman, S. "Capital Investment in Commercial Banking and Its Relationship to Portfolio Regulation." *Journal of Political Economy* 78 (January-February 1970): 1-26.

Pettway, R.H. "Market Tests of Capital Adequacy of Large Commercial Banks." *The Journal of Finance,* June 1976, pp. 865-76.

Pierce, J.L. "Commercial Bank Liquidity." 66 *FRB* 1093-101.

Piper, T.R. *The Economics of Bank Acquisitions by Bank Holding Companies.* Boston: Federal Reserve Bank of Boston, 1971.

Prochnow, H.V., ed. *The One-Bank Holding Company.* Chicago: Rand McNally, 1969.

Rhoades, S.A. "Diversification, Competition, and Aggregate Concentration." *Proceedings of a Conference on Bank Structure and Competition.* Chicago: Federal Reserve Bank of Chicago, 1974, pp. 171-86.

____. "The Effect of Bank-Holding Company Acquisitions of Mortgage Bankers on Mortgage Lending Activity." *Journal of Business* 48 (July 1975): 344-48.

Robinson, R.I. *The Management of Bank Funds,* 2nd ed. New York: McGraw-Hill, 1962.

____, and R.H. Pettway. *Policies for Optimum Bank Capital.* Chicago: Association of Reserve City Bankers, 1966.

Rose, P.S., and D.R. Fraser. "Bank Holding Company Diversification into Mortgage Banking and Finance Companies." *Banking Law Journal,* Winter 1974, pp. 976-94.

Schotland, R.A. "Bank Holding Companies and Public Policy Today." *Compendium of Papers Presented for the Fine Study: Committee on Banking, Currency and Housing.* House of Representatives, 94th Cong., 2nd sess., June 1976.

Schweitzer, S.A. "Economies of Scale and Holding Company Affiliation in Banking." *Southern Economic Journal* 39 (1972): 258-66.

____. "Bank Liability Management: For Better or For Worse?" *Business Review* (Federal Reserve Bank of Philadelphia), December 1974, pp. 3-12.

Seelig, S.A. "Aggregate Concentration and the Bank Holding Company Movement." Working Paper in Financial Economics, No. 7602, Fordham University, New York, July 1976.

____. "Convenience and Advantage Clause as a Barrier to Entry in the Consumer Finance Industry." Working Paper in Financial Economics, No. 7601, Fordham University, New York, February 1976.

Shull, B. "Multiple-Office Banking and the Structure of Banking Markets: The New York and Virginia Experience." *Proceedings of a Conference on Bank Structure and Competition.* Chicago: Federal Reserve Bank of Chicago, 1972, pp. 30-40.

Smith, J.E. "Some Time, Next Year—A Call for Response to Years of Inaction." Remarks before the Carter H. Golembe Associates, Inc., Conference, Washington, D.C., December 8, 1975.

Smith, K.V., and J.C. Schreiner. "A Portfolio Analysis of Conglomerate Diversification." *The Journal of Finance* 24 (June 1969): 413-427.

Talley, S.H. "Bank Holding Company Financing." *Proceedings of a Conference on Bank Structure and Competition.* Chicago: Federal Reserve Bank of Chicago, 1975.

———. "Bank Holding Company Performance in Consumer Finance and Mortgage Banking." *The Magazine of Bank Administration,* July 1976.

———. "Developments in the Bank Holding Company Movement." *Proceedings of a Conference on Bank Structure and Competition.* Chicago: Federal Reserve Bank of Chicago, 1972, pp. 1-18.

———. *The Effects of Holding Company Acquisitions on Bank Performance,* Staff Economic Study No. 69. Washington, D.C.: Board of Governors of the Federal Reserve System, 1971.

———. *The Impact of Holding Company Acquisitions on Aggregate Concentration in Banking,* Staff Economic Study No. 80. Washington, D.C.: Board of Governors of the Federal Reserve System, 1974.

Throop, A.W. "Capital Investment and Entry in Commercial Banking: A Competitive Model." *Journal of Money, Credit, and Banking* 7 (May 1975): 193-214.

U.S. Congress. Banking Act of 1933. 48 Stat. 162.

———. Bank Holding Company Act of 1956. 70 Stat. 133, May 9, 1956.

———. Bank Holding Company Act Amendments of 1956. 80 Stat. 236, July 1, 1966.

———. Bank Holding Company Act Amendments of 1970. Public Law 91-607, December 31, 1970.

———. *Congressional Record–House.* 91st Cong., 1st sess., November 5, 1969.

———. *Congressional Record–Senate.* 91st Cong., 2nd sess. September 16, 1970.

———. *Congressional Record–Senate,* 91st Cong., 2nd sess., December 18, 1970.

U.S. Congress, House of Representatives. *The Growth of Unregistered Bank Holding Companies–Problems and Prospects.* Staff Report for the Committee on Banking and Currency. 91st Cong., 1st sess., February 11, 1969.

———. *Report No. 91-1747, Bank Holding Company Act Amendments, Conference Report.* 91st Cong., 2nd sess., December 15, 1970.

U.S. Congress, House, Committee on Banking and Currency. *Bank Holding Company Act Amendments: Hearings on H.R. 6778.* 91st Cong., 1st sess., April 15-25, 1969.

———. *Control and Regulation of Bank Holding Companies: Hearings on H.R. 6504.* 82nd Cong., 2nd sess., 1952.

_____. *Control and Regulation of Bank Holding Companies: Hearings on H.R. 2674.* 84th Cong., 1st sess., 1955.

_____. *Report No. 91-387, Bank Holding Companies.* 91st Cong., 1st sess., July 23, 1969.

U.S. Congress, Senate. *Report No. 91-1084, Bank Holding Company Act Amendments of 1970.*

U.S. Congress, Senate, Committee on Banking and Currency. *Report No. 91-1084, Bank Holding Company Act Amendments of 1970.* 91st Cong., 2nd sess., August 10, 1970.

_____. *Amend the Bank Holding Company Act of 1956: Hearings on S.2353, S.2418, and H.R.7371.* 89th Cong., 2nd sess., 1966.

Van Horne, J.C. *Financial Management and Policy.* Englewood Cliffs, N.J.: Prentice-Hall, 1968.

Varvel, W.A. "The Motivation for Bank Holding Company Acquisitions." Working Paper 76-2, Federal Reserve Bank of Richmond, 1976.

Vojta, G.J. *Bank Capital Adequacy.* New York: First National City Bank, February 1973.

Watson, R.D. "Banking on Debt for Capital Needs." *Business Review* (Federal Reserve Bank of Philadelphia), December 1974, pp. 17-28.

Weiss, S.J. "Bank Holding Companies and Public Policy." *New England Economic Review* (Federal Reserve Bank of Boston), January-February 1973, pp. 3-29.

Weston, F.J., and E. Brigham. *Managerial Finance,* 3rd ed. New York: Holt, Rinehart and Winston, 1969.

Whitesell, W.E. "Economics of the One Bank Holdng Company." *Bankers Magazine* 153 (Winter 1969): 28-34.

Williamson, O.E. "A Model of Rational Managerial Behavior." In R.M. Cyert and J.G. March, eds., *A Behavioral Theory of the Firm.* Englewood Cliffs, N.J.: Prentice Hall, 1963.

_____. *Corporate Control and Business Behavior.* Englewood Cliffs, N.J.: Prentice-Hall, 1970.

Woodworth, G.W. "Theories of Cyclical Liquidity Management of Commercial Banks." *National Banking Review* 4 (June 1967): 377-96.

Index

About the Authors

Michael A. Jessee is Assistant Vice President in charge of economic research at the Federal Home Loan Bank of San Francisco. Previously he was a staff economist in the banking studies department of the Federal Reserve Bank of New York. Dr. Jessee was a Phi Beta Kappa graduate of Randolph-Macon College and received the M.B.A., M.A., and Ph.D. degrees in finance from The Wharton School of the University of Pennsylvania.

Steven A. Seelig is Assistant Professor of Economics at Fordham University. Previously he was a staff economist in the banking studies department of the Federal Reserve Bank of New York. Dr. Seelig has published articles in *The Journal of Finance* and other professional journals. He received the B.A. with Honors from Clark University, the M.A. from Washington University, and the Ph.D. from Clark University.